STRATEGIC MANAGEMENT AND POLICY ISSUES OF NGOS

STRATEGIC MANAGEMENT AND POLICY ISSUES OF NGOS

Editor

O.P.Goel

ISBN : 978-81-8205-119-5

Published, 2018

Published by

Gyan Publishing House
5, Ansari Road
Daryaganj, New Delhi-110002
Phone: 011-47034999, 9811692060
www.gyanbooks.com
E-mail: books@gyanbooks.com

Printed at: G. Print Process, Delhi.

Contents

Preface

Non-governmental organizations (NGOs) have become significant players in development policy over the last two decades. The evolving relationships among NGOs, developing states and donors are a critical aspect of international development assistance and the wider development policy debate. NGOs vary in their missions, internal management, scope of engagement, source of funding, relations with developing states and targeted areas of operations.

NGOs are the vanguard of civil society. They have increasingly been seen as the vehicles of the new policy agenda of economic liberalization and political democratization. Donors have been generous in channelling resources through northern and indigenous NGOs to support grassroots organizations, social change, political empowerment and sustainable development. Developing states have ceded space to NGOs to deliver services, perform contract development work and promote institutional capacity building.

The role of NGOs in the contemporary world is elaborately described in the present book. The management challenges and other issues faced by NGOs are also examined. It will highly useful to NGOs, social activists, policy-makers and all concerned.

Editor

1

Strategic Management of NGOs

Non-governmental organizations have become significant players in development policy over the last two decades. The evolving relationships among NGOs, developing states and donors are a critical aspect of international development assistance and the wider development policy debate. NGOs vary in their missions, internal management, scope of engagement, source of funding, relations with developing states and targeted areas of operations.

Developing states are constrained by the inadequacy of requisite resources, unmet demand for investment and consumption and the inherent weakness of the existing institutions. These constraints and the over-reach of the developing state lead to "state failure." The markets in developing countries are, on the other hand, not functioning in terms of competition, mobility of factors of production and availability of information. State failure is matched by market failure. The twin failures have opened a space for the NGOs which have acted as intermediary organizations for the delivery of relief and welfare services, lobbying and advocacy of special interest areas, and promotion of sustainable development.

NGOs are the vanguard of civil society. Donors have been generous in channeling resources through northern and indigenous NGOs to support grassroots organizations, social change, political empowerment and sustainable development. Developing states have ceded space to NGOs to deliver services, perform contract development work and promote institutional capacity building.Donor support has been essential but such support has impacted the integrity and autonomy of the NGOs.

NGOs have increasingly been seen as the vehicles of the new policy agenda of economic liberalization and political democratization. The call for the contracting out of important government functions is being seen as the replication of the "hollowed" state in some advanced countries.

Management of NGOs

Many management development and training services available to NGOs are derived from experiences in other types of organisations in the context of the industrialised developed nations. NGOs therefore rightly ask the question, "Is what's on offer suitable for who we are, where we are and for what we do?" But NGOs have a problem in answering this question because they don't find it easy to define the critical differences between organisations whose purpose is socio-economic development in the developing countries and others whose purpose is profit or the running of a nation state. NGOs seldom have a clear idea of the necessary distinctions and demands-in management terms-between themselves and these other types of organisation. As a result, NGOs find it difficult to decide what is appropriate management for development and therefore how best to develop their management.

Almost thirty years of development effort provides grounds for identifying the necessary differences between the management of social development and other enterprises. Analysis of contrasts between commercial, governmental and non-profit voluntary organisations can therefore help in :

(a) designing appropriate methods for improving NGO management,

(b) determining the suitability of the management services already available, and

(c) providing NGOs with insight and more self-confidence in arguing about what can or can't be learnt from the commercial and government sectors in the North.

The management of NGOs involved in rural socio-economic development in developing countries must differ from the other two types of organisations if they are to be effective. Four factors are contrasted.

— the relationship between the producers and the clients of what the organisation achieves;

— the organisation's environmental relations;

— the source of an organisations resources;

— differences in regulation of organisational performance through client feedback.

By understanding differences in these areas NGOs will be in a better position to decide how to tackle the development of their management capabilities; to select from the services on offer; and, most importantly, to realise that most of the learning about improving NGO performance will have to come from within the NGO sector itself.

Relations between Producers and Clients

All organisations are created for a purpose, they are all meant to achieve or produce something. However, the relationship between the producers and clients or an organisation's 'product' varies significantly for commercial, governmental and voluntary agencies, creating quite different management demands. In commercial enterprise the producers are normally employees under a manager's direct control.

What the organisation produces is sold as a material item or a service to a client, the buyer, who decides if he or she wants what competing organisations have to offer(monopolies aside). The buyer pays money, takes ownership and usually here the relationship between organisation and client ends. The producer is distinct and separate from the client. Interaction between client and organisation is self-willed, based on a transaction and more often than not momentary. A manager's span of control does not (need to) encompass the client, as the production process is internal to the organisation.

Governments have employees (civil servants) and clients (citizens). For the client, government's 'products' include: regulations, security, (the value of) money, plans, social and welfare services, infrastructures, legal controls and their enforcement. Again, the civil servant and the client are distinct, but in certain circumstances the client may be officially incorporated into what a government organisation produces.

For example, Africa's farmers are often required to reach government targets in their agricultural production and sell only to parastatal marketing boards at fixed prices. So, in certain situations the client is tied into a government organisation's production process without being its employee. The relationship is often permanent and obligatory.

The simultaneity of citizens being a client in one setting and producer in another is made possible through regulation and authority. Here, a civil servant's span of control does encompass the client and, because of the compulsory relationship provided by legal obligation, the production process is both inside and outside the public enterprise.

It is rural people who produce their (self-) development, not NGOs and their staff. Rural people must own induced social development processes and benefits if they are to be sustainable. These facts dic tate that NGOs relate to clients as the actual producers of the organisation's 'product', ie recognise that client and producer are one.

Thus an NGO's influence has to extend beyond its organisational boundaries into communities because the production process is by the people, ie. outside the organisation itself. Unlike commercial business, NGO managers must bring the producer/client and only extend their influence through dialogue and negotiation. Further, involvement of an NGO with clients in their social development is not momentary, but nor should it be permanent if dependency is to be avoided. NGOs intervene temporarily but do not remain.

Relating to the Outside World

The three types of organisation — commercial, governmental and NGOs — tend to adopt distinctive strategies for relating to their external environments.In order to protect themselves against adverse conditions in the outside world commercial businesses use two major devices.

Firstly, they try and isolate themselves from external influences, for higher productivity is obtained when a production system is not disrupted. Building-up buffer stocks, forward contracts with suppliers to ensure inputs, and negotiating overdrafts with banks to protect cash flow, are all ways by which commercial organisations try to insulate production processes.

Secondly, businesses try to condition the external world to their advantage - normally through advertising - but also by buying out the competition or market manipulation. They endeavour to create the right market conditions for their products and spend a lot of money doing so.

Governments, on the other hand, have the power to create much of their own (national) environments. Laws, regulations, standards, taxes, quotas, plans, incentives, and instruments for their enforcement are all at the disposal of a government whose primary strategy towards the outside world is usually one of regulation and control. And, while the degree to which governments try to direct aspects of economic, social and cultural life vary, control and regulation underlie the way they view and treat the outside world. Management internally and externally is based on authority, hopefully derived from some legitimate, popular democratic process.

Value-driven development agencies rarely possess legal instruments of control and, because it is the client who actually produces development, NGOs must seek to integrate themselves with external environment, normally through dialogue and negotiation with the community. The nature of induced socio-economic development by the nongovernment sector means that NGOs must therefore do the opposite, they must listen, respond to, embrace and be absorbed by their operational environments. Their special challenge is to organise for and manage this necessity.

The contrast between the three type of organisations in their environmental relations are therefore ones of isolation or manipulation, authority or control, and negotiation or integration.

Organisational Resources

The third important distinction between businesses, governments and NGOs is source of the financial resources that they need to function and survive.

Commercial businesses derive their resources from clients who pay for their goods and services, ie. client and resource are coupled. Governments obtain their resources from the populace through taxes and from payments for some of the services they provide, again client and resources are coupled. For NGOs, the financial resources needed to function are derived, in a variety of ways, from donors and very seldom from the client, ie. the client and organisational resources are divorced. The fact that the client to be served is not the source of the funds needed for an NGO to perform and survive is one important reason for differences in management between the three types of organisations. This separation - not to mention the project basis for financing - can be the source of many difficulties because resources play such a critical role in how an organisation develops and functions.

Example of management and performance issues encountered by NGOs when resources are split from clients are: multiple, conflicting accountabilities; prevalence of inappropriate supply-driven services; maintenance of a selfperpetuating supply, unresponsiveness to changing demand; translation of client reality into the world of the donor; and, an NGO growth dominated by supply instead of need.

Performance Control

The dissimilarities described above impact the way that the performance of organisation can be assessed and regulated clients. Feedback on client satisfaction with commercial enterprise is direct and usually quick. Loss of sales is a pretty good and clear message to a profit oriented organisation that something is wrong.

Citizens' ability to indicate (dis)satisfaction governments can be immediate on specific issues, for example through public protests, more structurally through widespread civil disobedience such as large scale tax evasion. Longer term, people's feelings about government performance can communicated through the electoral process where this is fair and representative. However, usually such performance indicators indirect expressions of performance, take long time to affect bureaucratic change democracies and usually fail to do so autocracies.

The ability of clients to provide feedback and through NGOs to donors is diffic ult at best of times. However, it is severely impeded when the clientele reside in a different world hemisphere. In this circumstance the chance any systematic inputs from those supposed to benefit from an NGO's actions to the actual suppliers of resources the NGO relies on, the donors, is very limited, if not non-existent. Hence NGO performance assessment and regulation via client feedback to the resource provider is seldom achieved. Evaluation cannot adequately fulfil this function, yet it is the tool most used to appraise organisational performance. NGOs must create other mechanisms to provide this function.

All of the foregoing are an expression of the fact that a set of values provide the rationale and foundation for the existence of non-profit organisations. Values are critical because they provide the needed impetus, identity, direction, and staff unity required for effective work and determine which tasks must dominate, the skills required, the balance between trust and control, what decisions can be made by who at what levels, the limits of planning, responsibility and authority are spread who "owns" change processes.

Such contrasts, plus differences in political, economic and social systems in Third World countries, all contribute to the unique challenges for NGOs managing socioeconomic development which is intended benefit the poor and vulnerable. NGOs should therefore look critically at the services being offered to help them become more effective. They should try and find out whose experiences are being used, where they come from and how they have been tested. It seems likely, for example, that using management methods proven by Southern NGOs may be more appropriate than those from the North. Trying to improve NGO management by simply adapting and adopting techniques and designs from other types of organisations in Western settings has reached its limits; the differences involved are too significant.

Time is ripe to accord the status of a sub-socioeconomic development by the third sector in the third world. This requires that NGOs learn more methodically by analysing their actions. To do so systematically calls for a higher priority to be given to the allocation of funds for NGO self-reflection and sharing of experiences than has been the case to date.

NGOs and Social Change

NGOs have a crucial role to play in fostering those transformations in the 21st century. The core of our argument is that personal or inner change, and social or outer change, are inseparably linked. This is as obvious as it is neglected in development thinking, including the praxis of most NGOs. This is difficult and sensitive ground on which to tread, and we realise that our arguments are preliminary. However, we are convinced that any realistic vision of sustainable development must tackle the question of personal power relations head-on.

From the perspective of change, all social systems rest on three bases: a set of principles that form an axiomatic basis of ethics and values; a set of processes - the functioning mechanisms and institutions that undergird the system; and the subjective states that constitute our inner being - our personal feelings and intuitions in the deepest sense.The first of these bases of change describes how we understand and rationalise the workings of the social order, while the third describes how we understand ourselves. Some of this understanding revolves around our own place in the social order, but it also concerns the deeper questions we ask ourselves about the meaning of human existence and the nature of reality.When we explore any episode of historical change, we can identify how these three bases of change have worked together to produce a particular set of power relations. For example, the evolution of capitalism was built on the axiomatic basis that individual self-interest leads - by and large - to collective welfare. Its institutional structures are rooted in private property and marketbased incentives. And the subjective state of being most compatible with capitalism is a commitment to individual advancement and competitive behaviour.

The interaction of these three bases of change determines how different forms of power are exercised in society. Economic power is expressed in the distribution of productive assets and the workings of markets and firms; social power is expressed in the status and position awarded to different social groups; and political power defines each person's voice in decision-making in both the private sphere and public affairs. These systems of power combine to produce a "social order", and transforming this social order is the task of social change.

The social order that is emerging under globalising capitalism is one which excludes or oppresses certain groups of people, especially those already on the margins, women in labour-rich economies, and those with less access to skills and education wherever they live. However, the linkages that develop between these different bases of change are not immutable. Considerable room-to-manoeuvre exists to alter the ways in which they interact, in order to produce a different framework of power relations, a better set of outcomes, and a new social order.

It is this room-tomanoeuvre that NGOs are trying to exploit in their work, though as we shall argue later, they rarely do so consciously. For éxample, people may rebel against the subjective state that is promoted by a particular set of social transformations, as they have always done in relation to capitalism and the selfish values it breeds. Or, working from a different subjective or axiomatic base, they may experiment with new processes and institutions that try to produce the same economic outcomes with fewer social and political costs - much as NGOs are doing today in their work with multi-national corporations and corporate codes of conduct.

The point about these experiments is not that they generate ready-made answers to questions of economic and social life, but that they consolidate a new bottom line of values, principles and/or personal behaviour from which better models may evolve in different ways in different contexts. Any relationship that is truly principled will lead towards a more fulfilling conclusion, even though we can never be sure what it will look like at any level of detail.

Social change requires a recognition - and conscious integration - of all three bases of change, and each of these systems of power. The problem is that few theoretical systems acknowledge this, and even fewer institutions use it as a framework to guide their practice. For example, social theories generally emphasise the axiomatic and institutional aspects of change, assuming that the related subjective states are simply universal descriptions of human nature, or that changes in subjective states follow automatically from changes in institutions and incentives. At the opposite extreme, many of the world's religions focus on the subjective states of persons and their transformation, and attach less importance to the institutional basis of social change. Of course, not all religions are identical in this regard. Some assign more importance to outer behaviour; others to the inner motivations that lie behind it. But the tendency to privilege one category over another remains, condemning both social theories and religious teachings to a partial approach that downgrades the links between social change and personal transformation.

A fresh look at the links between value systems, institutional processes, and subjective states is therefore essential, especially at a time when the processes of globalization are altering each of these things and their relationships with each other. Against this background, it is clear that social change requires us to adopt an integrated approach that looks for positive synergies between different bases of change and different systems of power. When change in one area supports change in another, there is more of a chance that the outcome will be sustainable, as when ethics of co-operation are matched by institutions through which they can be expressed, and the deeper personal commitment required to put those ethics into practice. Such self-reinforcing cycles of cooperation, sharing and stewardship are the key to a social order that enables all people to meet their basic needs for security, voice and equality of rights, with less of a risk that in doing so they will deny others the same opportunities for a fulfilling life.

It is important to recognise that integration is an exercise in re-balancing, not the wholesale replacement of one rationality by another. Not all competition generates overweening selfishness, nor do markets always exploit the poor or powerless. There are many examples that show how well-regulated markets and open trade can benefit the poor, and how economic growth can contribute to poverty-eradication, the improved provision of social goods, and the conservation of natural and social capital. If it is unrealistic to focus on economic systems to the exclusion of personal change, it is equally unacceptable to call for inner transformation unless we can show how material needs will be met in less damaging ways. However, the general point we wish to make remains valid: the emergence of a new social order requires those who gain power to make room for those with less; and all to use the power they gain in more responsible ways - not submerging their own self-interest entirely, but modulating it so that individual advancement is not bought at the cost of the broader conditions required for a secure and prosperous world.

History offers us at least some examples of such an integrated approach to social change, notably the Indian nationalist movement under Mahatma Gandhi. There, a powerful underpinning of personal belief in the power of universal love and non-violence energised and sustained large numbers of ordinary Indians in the movement's tumultuous struggle for political independence. The testimony of those who participated in this movement suggests that ordinary people not only behaved and believed differently, but that they *were* different in a more fundamental sense. The failure of Indian politics and society to sustain these transformations in the post-Independence era suggests that the process of integration was far from complete, but it does not invalidate the basic principles involved. Indeed, there are many more examples of incomplete integration which show why social change is so hard to achieve even when many of its component parts are in place. We have chosen the example of "development-asempowerment" because such strategies are central to current NGO practice. By doing so we are not suggesting that NGOs are worse offenders in this respect than other institutions - merely that even the socially-committed will be unsuccessful if they ignore the inner basis of change.

Democratising the ownership of productive assets, capacities and opportunities continues to be a priority under globalisation, even if the nature of these things is changing. NGOs have been enthusiastic advocates of this form of empowerment for a decade and more, yet rarely do they question how people use the power they gain. The assumption is that greater material security, organisational capacity and political voice will be used to promote the common interest as well as the advancement of those individuals who benefit directly. Is this true?

In industrial societies, we know that rising wealth and democratic strength tend to produce a "culture of contentment", or the ebbing away of the "habits of the heart". In these circumstances, rising incomes may act as a block against more fundamental changes which are necessary for the rest of the population to attain the same level of satisfaction of their basic needs. The same pattern is evident from many Third-World communities, though it is often mediated by cultures which do encourage sharing and co-operation, especially in times of crisis.

All over the world, broader economic participation breeds selfish and competitive behaviour unless it is accompanied by a deeper shift in values, and by new institutions which allow those values to be expressed in collective action. This is especially true in a world of integrated markets where the temptation to cut costs and "race each-other to the bottom" is particularly strong. Even when successful, economic empowerment may leave the structures of social power untouched, or even reinforce them, especially discrimination based on gender and age. Equally, social advancement may be unsustainable unless political power is also re-distributed to the benefit of those who have less voice. Rarely do empowerment strategies make the links that could generate shifts in inner values strong enough to ensure that improvements in one area are not bought at the cost of damage done elsewhere.

Generalising from a theoretical situation like this is clearly dangerous, but the problem it describes is familiar: change at the subjective level is exceptionally difficult to achieve. It is rarely possible to generate sustainable changes in human behaviour simply by altering the rules and institutions that govern our lives. The missing ingredient is personal change, which acts as the wellspring of change in all other areas. A common lesson of experience is that processes of social change can easily lose touch with the values and principles that originally motivated and sustained them in the rough and tumble of the struggle. As a result, attempts to generate a new social order can unwittingly be poisoned by the "thieves of the heart" - the negative feelings of personal ego, jealousy and fear that destroy one's inner tranquillity.

If people are not caring and compassionate in their personal behaviour they are unlikely to work effectively for a caring and compassionate society. Resisting these feelings, and developing the inner security required for a lifetime of co-operative endeavour, requires a disciplined process of self-reflection and contemplation about the values and purposes of our lives, and the desire and willingness to change ourselves. Undertaking this inner journey with courage can reward one with inner peace, greater energy and more effectiveness in one's actions, an expansive compassion in our attitudes towards others, and a tenderness of the heart that, on a mass scale, can have profound social implications.

We are not so naive as to believe that a simple recognition of such things will change people's behaviour. But acknowledging the fact that the absence of personal change can impede the social transformations we are searching for can be salutary in the search for a more integrated approach. Nor are we speaking of social indoctrination under duress, exemplified by the Chinese Cultural Revolution or Maoist self-criticism sessions.

Inner change cannot be forced by the self-righteous; when hearts and minds are brutalised into submission or silence there will be little energy left for social engagement. Our vision is a positive one: the energies unleashed by serious and deeprooted personal transformation can fuel the search for more humane social and economic systems as little else can.

What kind of personal changes could energise the move towards an economic order which re-balances competitive and co-operative rationalities, a politics of dialogue rather than unrepresentative democracy, and a social policy that works against marginalisation and values the care and nurture of all human beings? The first principles for such change lie at the heart of the teachings of all the great religions – "Love thy neighbour as thyself" in the Judaeo-Christian tradition, "See God in each other" in Sanskrit. It is fascinating to recognise that the core of religious teaching concerns our feelings towards each other – a deeply social statement as much as it is profoundly personal. But to love our neighbours as ourselves, we must come to understand our own inner being - to recognise that in our deepest essence we are compassionate, capable of giving love, and worthy of receiving it.

Even when imperfectly established in this positive self-knowledge, we can identify more easily with the same inner being in other people - what the Hindu *Vedanta* calls "unity-consciousness." It then becomes easier to empathise with what it means to be the "other" from whom we usually distance ourselves in subtle or overt ways. That shift is crucial because it provides the foundation for personal behaviour which is more expansive and less damaging to others - for why would we damage the life-chances of someone who is as much a part of ourselves?

The irony of today's globalized world is that, as knowledge about each-other grows, so do the criteria of "otherness" that breed selfishness, greed, anger and hatred – the fault-lines of race, ethnicity, gender, sexual orientation, caste, class, nationality, region, and economic blocs. One question that often comes up in this context is whether more attention to inner transformation will divert one's energy away from social change. A related question is whether greater personal tranquillity will sap the angry energy needed to struggle against injustice. Anger is certainly a powerful form of energy that can be harnessed, particularly in the struggles of the socially oppressed. But over time it can be corrosive of those who use it, becoming a deadly and increasingly-uncontrolled weapon. Inner centredness, on the other hand, can take more controllable but no less powerful forms.

Those who have espoused non-violence, in India, South Africa, the USA and elsewhere, have not been weak. Their courage and energy have often been startling, and their example has sometimes and unexpectedly catalysed a process of transformation in their opponents. Inner-centredness can release enormous energy for the struggle against social injustice without having to draw upon the destructive legacy of anger or hatred.

Throughout the ages, organised religions have often spawned fundamentalist bigotry and a narrowing of the realm of personal beliefs to accord with what is considered by some to be "moral" conduct. Our own age shows us the dangers that religious fundamentalism brings to social institutions when it spills over from the private to the public realm.

Social conservatism is rarely more dangerous than when it cloaks itself in religious garb that cannot adequately be challenged by rationalist arguments for social justice because it assumes an other-worldly authority.

The rising tide of religious bigotry across the world in recent decades is one of the reasons why space for serious discussion of the links between social and personal change has been so narrow. The other is a woolly-headed and self-indulgent "new ageism" that confuses material detachment with a wholesale retreat from social engagement. However, disciplined self-enquiry of the kind we have described provides a way out of this impasse, by constantly exposing attitudes and behaviours that masquerade as compassionate or detached.

Paradoxically, the expansive compassion and tenderness of heart of which we speak calls for all the toughness of mind, courage and flexibility that are also required in the outer struggle for social change. Our conclusion then is clear: personal transformation is essential if we are to see society change in the directions we espouse. Confronting this challenge squarely and with honesty is the need of the hour.

Role of NGOs in Personal Change

NGOs are unlikely vehicles for the direct transformation of the individual, though the best traditions of the sector - like selfless service among volunteers and the courage to undertake the seemingly-impossible - sometimes generate experiences that come close to the spiritual realm.

However, the model of social change we have described makes it clear that there are many indirect ways to encourage the transformation of people's subjective states, so long as our approach to processes and institutions is properly-integrated - in other words, that the goal of personal change is a conscious and explicit element in all that we do. Most of us know that our true Self is loving and compassionate, but feel we must disguise it in the streetfighting of everyday life. However, when we consciously create more institutional spaces for inner transformation, we can begin to exercise our economic, social and political responsibilities in ways which both draw from and encourage the personal changes we are looking for.

It may sound romantic to call for an economics or politics that is loving and compassionate, but this is exactly what we can shape through conscious action. We want to look briefly at three areas in which NGOs have a crucial role to play in fostering these integrated changes: their programme activities; their fund-raising and constituency-building work; and their own organisational praxis - the ways in which values are expressed in structures, systems and management. Constraints of space mean that we can only mention a small number of examples.

Programme activities

The overriding challenge for NGOs in the 21st century will be to help re-balance the competitive and co-operative forces that motivate each one of us, whether in economics, politics or social life. They can do this by regulating - and ultimately re-constructing - all systems of power in ways which achieve three things: a more equal distribution of what they deliver, less costly ways of producing it, and more co-operative values and behaviour among those involved as producers or consumers. When we talk of "costs", we explicitly include damage done to ourselves, the social fabric that sustains us as fully-human beings, and the environment we all depend on for our future. Although NGOs rarely see their work in this way, there are plenty of experiments already underway which show how such integrated transformations might work at a much larger scale:

— In economics for example, new forms of enterprise are competing effectively in open markets but distributing work and profits with a social purpose, backed up by codes of conduct to level up working conditions and supported by a growing movement for "ethical consumption." The links that are developing between peasant production systems in Latin America and supermarket campaigns in industrialised countries provide a good example of this wave of the future. The best NGO credit schemes provide another.

— In politics, Latin American municipalities are inventing new forms of "dialogic democracy" in which representatives from civil society and business share in decision-making with local government. Similar experiments are underway in other parts of the world - like India's "Panchayati Raj" system of decentralised governance - and around Agenda-21 planning, post-conflict re-construction, and the elaboration of national development strategies. These innovations give everyone a voice in decision-making and reduce the dangers of "elected dictatorships" which favour the interests of the rich. At the same time, they build new capacities for dialogue and co-operation across old institutional boundaries.

— In the area of social policy, organisations like SEWA in India and the Grameen Bank in Bangladesh are promoting different ways of sharing the costs and responsibilities of child-care so that women can increase their incomes and assets without sacrificing their own health and welfare to the interests of their children. These innovations achieve a better set of tradeoffs between social and economic outcomes, challenging the structures of social power in the process and building the material security people need to participate in dialogic politics.

Although personal change is rarely an explicit element in these experiments, there is a clear linkage between the processes and institutions they foster, and the subjective states they grow from and reinforce. Ethical production systems are not viable without ethical consumers, for example; equitable social policies are impossible if men and women are unwilling to share the burden of paid and unpaid work. Such experiments can consolidate their gains by making personal change a more explicit part of their agenda, so that new, more co-operative institutions can be backed up by corresponding innovations in values and behaviour.

Mainstreaming these experiences will require pioneers in all walks of life, but government and business are unlikely to spearhead moves for radical changes which involve reduced consumption or the ceding of authority to non-state actors. The major pressure must come from those parts of civil society who are committed to new social and economic models. It is NGOs and other civic groups that are already lobbying corporations to be more responsible, organising collective approaches to welfare, and acting as a counterweight to vested interests in decentralised politics. We believe that these activities will dominate civic action in the next fifty years.

Constituency-building

Although there are many interesting experiments like these to report on, they do not add up to much when compared to the forces that really drive change in the contemporary world. What are missing are scale, depth and sustainability - to make these innovations the norm rather than the exception. Achieving those goals requires a mass base to support radical change, and that in turn requires an inner transformation on a scale not realised in any period in history. Motivating large numbers of people to shift to more co-operative behaviour and persuade those in power to create more inclusive institutions goes against the heart of the current socio-economic order.

Without personal change towards more caring and compassionate ways of being and dealing with each other, it will be very hard to generate the momentum to bring about such a shift. At first sight this might appear to be the job of the churches and other faithbased groups in civil society, not of development NGOs. It is no accident that dissatisfaction with current models of development and foreign aid has coincided with a resurgence of interest in the developmental role of the Faiths, even in such non-spiritual organisations as the World Bank.However, there are a number of reasons for thinking that development NGOs also have a crucial role to play, not least because the established religions so often fail to live up to their theology.

More broadly, it is the secular world of environmental and social activism that forms at least as powerful a connection in most people's lives between the "personal and the political." We no longer reserve our moral expressions for church on Sunday; indeed, the increasing diffusion of moral action through civil society and beyond is one of the most heartening developments of the late-20th century.

Development NGOs have been an important part of this expanding moral space, but they have never fulfilled their potential as constituency-builders on the wider stage. In contrast to environmental NGOs, they rarely use their high levels of public trust and extended fund-raising networks as channels for personal transformation and lifestyle change, and their membership of civil society (both domestic and international) is increasingly called into question.

Consequently, we still lack institutional expression for the exercise of conscience on the scale that would be necessary to resolve world poverty or intervene against fundamental abuses of human rights. Without such massbased institutional pressure, there *will* be another Rwanda, and then another.

Under the guise of bringing people closer together they force them further apart, increasing the psychological distance between donor and recipient, and reinforcing the conviction of separateness that lies at the root of our failure to act. "Caught in the models of the limited self, we end up by diminishing one-another. The more you think of yourself as a philanthropist, the more someone else feels compelled to be a supplicant", and the less inclination they both have to co-operate together as equal partners. Fifty years of foreign aid have left us ill-prepared to face a cooperative future.

Paradoxically therefore, the decline of foreign aid provides a window of opportunity to advance a transformative agenda, by re-focusing attention on international co-operation and the values that make co-operation work. There won't be a constituency for international co-operation unless there is a commitment to co-operative living generally, for why should people cooperate with distant strangers if they do not do so with their neighbours? Global regimes impose clear limitations on personal autonomy, so it won't be the United Nations that will solve global warming, but you and us - by reducing the energy we use in our homes, cars and factories.

Co-operation requires the constant exercise of co-operative values, rather than the peddling of stereotypes about other people who need a "sponsor" to "save" them. This implies relationships among equals, and the acceptance of responsibility to put our own house in order. And at root, that is always a matter of personal change.

Organisational praxis

The claim that development NGOs are explicitly "values-based" organisations is something of an article of faith these days. There is less evidence that NGOs put these values into practice in their organisational structures and behaviour, or even that they are clear what their core values are. This is a major weakness, because it is the link between values and actions that is crucial in generating legitimacy when arguing the case for change.

Institutions must be seen to implement values as the bottom line in their own practice if they are to build a coalition in support of those values on the wider stage. The best way NGOs can help to foster the mass movement that has been missing from the field of international development since the end of the Cold War is for them to be exemplars of the society they want to create - to show that it is possible to be an effective organisation which values its employees as it does its partners, fights discrimination, practices internal democracy, and always uses the organisational power it has in liberating ways.

Unfortunately, few development NGOs have done this. For one thing, high levels of dependence on foreign aid and the limitations of contractual relationships make it very difficult to expand into real values-based action - there are simply too many compromises that have to be made. For another, NGOs are not immune to class, race, and gender problems, nor the oppression and sexual exploitation they breed. Behind the screen of progressive attitudes toward social change in the world outside, the world inside the organisation can be an ethical morass. Such organisations cannot be the basis of far-reaching social change. Fortunately, this point is beginning to be taken to heart in many NGOs. The link between personal change and organisational effectiveness is increasingly being recognised, even though its practical application remains weak. These pioneers stress that is certainly possible to help others effectively, but only if we realise that in doing so they help us to grow to a fuller, more independent knowledge of ourselves - closing the circle once more between personal change and change in the wider world. If our own practice is autocratic, closed, and chauvinist it is unlikely that we will be able to encourage others to be democratic, open and egalitarian. What remains is for NGOs to experiment more seriously with management practices, organisational structures, and personnel policies that create the feedback loops we are looking for between personal change, institutional performance, and wider impact.

2

Involvement of NGOs in Civil Society

During the second half of the twentienth century the world witneesd the emergence of institutions and groups organized outside the state yet making claims on the polity and for the polity. Social movements such as those favoring women, the environment, and peace, or those opposing nuclear power and war become crystallized through the creation of organizations to implement their agendas.

Existence of these non-governmental organizations has been examined by scholars in the developing countries and in Europe; interest on the part of US scholars is relatively recent and does not always grasp the core nature of NGOs. Some NGOs started with religious philosophies and sought to create spaces for ethical reflection; others emerged to mitigate the experience of political authoritarianism; still others are helping shape alternative visions of society and thus fit better as the crystallization of new social movements.

There is variation in the objectives and performance of NGOs but the large majority of them are less concerned with their own selfinterest than with collective gains. They also tend to produce flatter organizational structures and to foster steady participation in internal decision-making. In developing countries, they tend to be concerned with populations facing devalued or oppressed cultural expression and living under extremely poor conditions of living. And it is quite true that they must balance alternative visions while operating in environments that are increasingly driven by market dynamics and profit rationales.

Many NGOs in Eastern and Central Europe engage in corrupt practices. In the aftermath of a pervasive socialist regime, it is quite possible that NGOs there are staffed by old government officials under new clothing. Other instances of manipulation by government officials, in various Sub-Saharan and Asian countries, have occurred when governments set up their own "branches," under the guise of NGOs. These distortions and forms of co-optation are unavoidable, especially in countries where economic crises prevail.

There are different kinds of NGOs with different levels of wealth and national scope. How we see them is a matter of perspective, and depends on whether one holds an equilibrium or conflict model of social action. There are several objective grounds for valuing the contribution of NGOs.

NGOs fulfill at least three major functions:

(1) service delivery (e.g., relief, welfare, basic skills);

(2) educational provision (e.g., basic skills and often critical analysis of social environments; and

(3) public policy advocacy (e.g., lobbying for international assistance for specific purposes and monitoring or promoting pertinent state policies).

These functions are critical in the absence of stable political parties or organized low-income constituencies to carry out such activities.

NGOs acting as implementing agencies is neither bad nor good in itself, but it depends on what they are helping to implement. NGOs tend to enjoy greater access to communities, and to have staff that is more committed, experienced, and sensitive to local needs, thus allowing them to function as better intermediaries than government agencies. This does not occur by magic but is rather a by-product of their need to perform well to survive vis-a-vis both donors and the communities they serve. Such groups, organizations and institutions, at times assuming the form of social movements, and favoring women, the environment, and peace, or those opposing nuclear power and war often become crystallized. These organizations are, of course, NGOs.

Some people have accused NGOs of having no formal representation and thus of having no legitimacy. The counterargument is that they often represent the disempowered who have no possibility of electing their own representatives. In the case of the environment, for instance, whales cannot elect their "representatives." Here, it is not a question of representation but rather of expression that gives NGOs the legitimacy to voice the needs of the oppressed and marginalized.

The NGOs in the feminist movement were not elected by women, for women are only now beginning to articulate their interests; and also, many of them have no other means to raise their voices in the public sphere. Sociopolitical movements as forms of collective action usually start in an institutional vacuum with no other institutional resources available to them than the usually partly contested legal and constitutional rights of citizens to assemble, communicate, protest, petition, and demonstrate.

From the perspective of profound thinkers of our social world such as Alain Touraine and Claus Offe, these movements—and their organizations—push the limits of politics by disrupting the existing order when necessary. These groups are concerned with quality of life issues, with the definition and valorization of personal and collective identities, and with the production of new cultural models. These movements have a mainly negative character, not because they are destructive but because they oppose the manipulation and distortion imposed by large-scale institutions and the compromises and routinization required in conventional forms of interest representation and mediation.

NGOs help neoliberal forces by taking the burden of program development and implementation away from the state. Some NGOs thereby unwittingly weaken and delegitimize the state. The scope of NGOs will never be of such magnitude as to allow them to release government from its responsibilities. Many NGOs work on the premise that governments should fulfill obligations and be held accountable for the actions they take or fail to take.

NGOs have taken a crucial role in monitoring government activities. In the case of Latin America, they are acting through two main networks: One is the South American Platform on Human Rights, Democracy and Development, which is developing economic, social and cultural rights (ESCR) indicators for individual countries and setting up new mechanisms to influence national and international decision-making. The other is Social Watch, which produces information on the efforts by governments throughout the world to achieve ESCR goals, and distributes information to the international community on progress made with respect to commitments assumed at international conferences, particularly the eradication of poverty and equal opportunities for women.

The monitoring work that NGOs conduct is not without risk. As women's clinics in the States are targets of anti-abortion extremists, so NGO leaders, particularly those in feminist and ethnic social movements, are vulnerable to reprisals. Recently a woman lawyer member of the Latin American and Caribbean Committee for the Defense of Women's Rights (CLADEM), who had been investigating human rights violations through forced surgical sterilization in Peru, had her home raided and evidence removed. The incident happened shortly after CLADEM presented a major report to the Ministry of Health and the People's Ombudsman.

It should be accepted that the emergence of delivery systems as alternatives to government is in some cases appropriate, especially when governments are corrupt or fail to act on crucial matters. NGOs often do better than government in certain basic matters such as distribution of emergency aid. The most current example is the mobilization of NGOs in the provision of food, medicines, and clothing in Honduras today after the devastation of Hurricane Mitch.

NGOs' agendas are being driven by donor agencies because the latter are the main source of support. The same argument could be extended to governments that depend to large extent on external sources. To receive external support certainly creates a risk for the development of nationalistic agendas; the successful negotiation of priorities will be a function of the integrity of the recipient party.

Serving mostly low-income populations, it is obvious that NGOs cannot generate sufficient revenues from such groups. Over the past 15 years, NGOs have gained greater support from external assistance. Even so, by 1985, NGOs captured only five percent of net financial flows to developing countries; the proportion reached about 8 percent by 1995.

NGOs today enjoy more diversified funding, as they receive not only bilateral assistance but also funding from multilateral agencies such as UNDP, UNICEF, and the Commission of the European Communities. In cases of extreme national poverty, there is high dependency by NGOs on international NGO and bilateral agency support. Some Sub-Saharan countries reportedly have dependency rates exceeding 90 percent.

If donor agencies are giving more money to NGOs, it is not a consequence of mere predilection for NGOs but of the NGOs' ability to show results. Many social movements and their concrete organizations emerge because of "learning incapacities" and structural lack of "responsiveness" by established institutions. At the same time, NGO reliance on external support forces them to oscillate between actions based on ethical convictions and "a logic of efficacy, which leads them to submit to the influence of political actors".

The international conferences on various social issues and the subsequent governmental declarations that follow them are a tenuous terrain. But they constitute the most public and concrete commitments to action to which people in the progressive movements can refer. Today, NGOs are accepted partners in international conferences. Their participation, most coming from developing countries, has increased from the 700 that participated in the UN Environment and Development Conference (Rio) to more than 5000 in the Fourth World Women's Conference (Beijing).

In both the Conference on Social Development in Copenhagen and the Conference on Women in Beijing many governments included NGO representatives in their official delegations, thus reflecting new forms of articulation between government and civil society. Most NGOs have participated in intergovernmental meetings by organizing parallel NGO conferences. Their activities face criticism from two sides. Government may critique their lack of clear "representation;" when they collaborate with government, they are critiqued by other NGOs for becoming part of the "establishment."

Small NGOs cannot bring out changes for societal problems that require structural transformation. But some change would never be launched were one to wait for optimal conditions to emerge. Several observers, seem to assume that NGOs that have grown significantly in membership and funding reflect internal corruption and co-optation by external funders. Cited by both as a case in point is BRAC in Bangladesh, unquestionably the largest NGO in the world. BRAC is supported by multiple donors and carries out tasks that go from nonformal education programs for girls to micro-enterprises with conscientization for adult women. According to external evaluations, BRAC has succeeded in creating a highly effective and disciplined organization, with tangible benefits for individuals and community members. Its performance, far from threatening that of the government, is serving to demonstrate that large organizations are not incompatible with clarity of purpose and accountability.

Today the state is becoming smaller than in previous decades. It would be a mistake, however, to attribute this to the increasing presence of NGOs. Globalization forces and structural adjustment programs have been the main promoters of state minimalism, not NGOs. In fact, often NGOs argue for the provision of more services by the state, particularly for health and education access for poor people.

Role of NGOs in Global Civil Society

Civil society possesses a discrete and distinct *raison d'être* which marks it out as different as well as autonomous both from the state and from the market. Thus, in contemporary political theory it is often posed as an alternative to both the state and to the market. It simply emerges as the third sphere of collective life.

According to Gordon White it is 'an intermediate associational realm between the family and the state populated by organisations which are separate from the state, enjoy autonomy in relation to the state and are formed voluntarily by members of society to protect or extend their interests or values'. Charles Taylor suggests that civil society is 'those dimensions of social life which cannot be confounded with, or swallowed up in, the state'. Jean Cohen and Andrew Arato in a rather well known definition, refer to a 'third realm' differentiated from the economy and the state as civil society. In the hands of them, civil society as a normative moral order is diametrically opposed to both the state and the economy.

The same kind of thinking is more than visible when it comes to global civil society. Many theorists seem to be of the view that global civil society represents a 'third sector', which can not only be distinguished from but which is an alternative to both the statecentric international order and the networks of global markets. Lipschutz, for instance, employs the concept of 'global civil society' to indicate a plurality of agencies such as social movements, interest groups, and global citizens. If the distinguishing feature of these organisations is that they defy national boundaries, the cornerstone of global civil society is constituted by the 'self-conscious construction of networks of knowledge and action, [and] by decentred local actors, that cross the reified boundaries of space as though they were not there'.

Global civil society actors, in other words, engage in practices that can possibly reshape the 'architecture' of international politics by denying the primacy of states or of their sovereign rights. Other scholars are of the opinion that the anti-state character of global civil society is revealed through its projects, for example, through the promotion of values from below, which exist in tension with dominant statist conceptions of the state system. Or that global civil society moving beyond 'thin anarchical society' is in the business of inaugurating a post-foreign policy world.

Contemporary thinking gives us a picture of a global civil society that seems to be supremely uncontaminated by either the power of states or that of markets. Moreover, many theorists believe that global civil society, consisting of transnational non-governmental organisations, political activists, social movements, religious denominations, and associations of all stripe and hue, from trade unions to business and financial groupings, can neutralise existing networks of power by putting forth a different set of values. Global civil society (GCS), it is said, represents 'a post realist constellation, where transnational associational life (TAL) challenges the conceit of the state system... GCS is touted as the antidote for the anarchical structure, inequality, and exclusions of the state system'.

Global civil society organisations have managed to dramatically expand the agenda of world politics by insistently casting and focusing widespread attention on issues such as human rights, the environment, development, and banning land mines. And all these issues, remember, have traditionally fallen within the province of state sovereignty.

Global civil society actors have simultaneously challenged the new contours of the world economic order as mandated by the World Trade Organisation, the World Bank, and the International Monetary Fund: think of the protests against the global economic dispensation at Seattle in November 1999, at Prague in September 2000, and at Genoa in 2001. But to conclude from this that these actors have drawn up a blueprint for a new or an alternative global order, or indeed to assume that they are autonomous of both states and markets, may prove too hasty a judgement.

The idea of internationalism has been central to working-class politics since the end of the nineteenth century. In a parallel development Henri La Fontaine, who was awarded the Nobel Peace Prize in 1913, created the Central Office of International Associations in 1907 to link up nongovernmental organisations (NGOs) in different countries. The United Nations institutionalised procedures for consulting with these organisations in 1945. It is estimated that whereas in 1948, 41 NGOs enjoyed consultative status with the Economic and Social Council of the UN, by 1968 the number had risen to 500.

By 1992 we were to see the Economic and Social Council consulting 1,000 or more NGOs. If we add to this number NGOs that interact with other bodies of the United Nations, and which often participate directly in the proceedings, the number rises to tens of thousands. It is perhaps not surprising that global civil society has come to be dominated by NGOs, even though other actors, such as political activists networking across borders and anti-globalisation movements, were playing an important role in this sphere.

It is indicative of the power of the non-governmental sector that civil society has come to be identified with NGO activism both in influential tomes on civil society and in policy prescriptions of international institutions today. The discussion that follows therefore shifts between NGOs and other civil society actors, even as it recognises that NGOs play a largerthan-life role in global civil society.

However, at the turn of the 1990s we were to witness a veritable explosion of NGOs, which, networking across national borders, propelled critical issues onto international platfórms. The power of global NGOs was first visible at the Earth Summit in Rio in 1992, when about 2,400 representatives of NGOs came to play a central role in the deliberations. By putting forth radically different alternatives, by highlighting issues of global concern, and by stirring up proceedings in general, these organisations practically hijacked the summit. Subsequently, they were given a central role in the Committee on Sustainable Development created by the Rio Summit. At the 1994 Cairo World Population Conference, increasing numbers of international NGOs took on the responsibility of setting the agenda for discussions. And in 1995 this sector almost overwhelmed the Fourth World Conference on Women in Beijing.

Almost 2,100 national and international NGOs, consisting largely of advocacy groups and social activists, completely dominated the conference. Since then we have seen that international NGOs either participate directly in international conferences or hold parallel conferences, which incidentally attract more media attention than official conferences. And in the process they have won some major victories.

One of these major victories occurred when global NGOs launched a campaign to pressurise governments to draft a treaty to ban the production, the stockpiling, and the export of landmines. Almost 1,000 transnational NGOs coordinated the campaign through the Internet. The pooling and the coordination of energies proved so effective that not only was the treaty to ban landmines signed in 1997, but the International Campaign to Ban Landmines and its representative Jody Williams were awarded the Nobel Peace Prize. The citation at the award-giving ceremony spoke of their unique effort that made 'possible to express and mediate a broad wave of popular commitment in an unprecedented way'. similar pooling of energies can be seen in the crusade that led to the 1998 Rome Statute on an International Criminal Court.

Other triumphs followed in the field of human rights: in the battle that led to the ousting of Soeharto in Indonesia in 1998, for instance. After the Indonesian military had massacred more than 150 participants in a funeral procession in Dili, East Timor, in 1991, transnational human rights organisations mobilised massively against the political abuses of the Soeharto regime.

Under pressure from these organisations, Canada, Denmark, and the Netherlands froze economic aid to

Indonesia, and the US, Japan, and the World Bank threatened similar measures. Soeharto appointed a National Investigation Commission, which issued mildly critical report of the incident; and aid was resumed. But Soeharto lost control of events as human rights groups in Indonesia and East Timor mobilised under global human rights organisations to criticise and publicise the violation of human rights. Opposition mounted even as Soeharto designated a national human rights commission, whose reports added to the general discontent.

In 1996, even as the leaders of civil society in East Timor—Jose Ramos Horta and Bishop Ximenes Belo—were given the Nobel Peace Prize, the *Blitzkrieg* launched by global human rights organisations strengthened the general atmosphere of dissatisfaction, despite the intensified repression launched by the regime. In late 1997 the country was buffeted by an economic crisis and mass protests led to the resignation of Soeharto. Transnational human rights organisations had managed to spectacularly overthrow a regime on the grounds that it was not respecting the basic rights of its people.

In India the power of global civil society organisations was revealed in a different way. Soon after independence, a massive project was inaugurated to dam the gigantic Narmada River, which runs through the three States of Madhya Pradesh, Gujarat, and Maharashtra in western India. The Narmada Valley Development Project consists of 30 major dams, 135 minor dams, and 3,000 small dams. The largest dam is the Sardar Sarovar Project, which ultimately will submerge 92,000 acres of land, displacing and affecting more than 300,000 people, a majority of whom are tribals or forest dwellers.

In the mid-1980s a number of voluntary organisations began to mobilise the tribals for better resettlement and rehabilitation policies, as the existing ones had been found sadly wanting. Even as these organisations linked up with international NGOs to pressure the government of India into granting better resettlement and rehabilitation for the displaced, in 1988 about 20 groups formed the Narmada Bachao Andolan (NBA) or the Save Narmada Movement. The NBA launched a massive struggle against big development projects and for the right of the people *not* to be displaced. At the same time, international NGOs such as the Environment Defense Fund and Oxfam began to lobby the World Bank and the Japanese government to withdraw from their commitments to fund the project.

The World Bank, now under public scrutiny, laid down conditions for better resettlement policies, conditions that the Indian government refused to fulfil. In 1993 the government decided to ask the World Bank to withdraw from the project rather than face the embarrassment of having the Bank draw back on its own. Soon afterwards the Japanese government also retracted its funding commitments. Whereas most of the pressure against the dam was generated by the NBA, the matter would not have come to international attention in quite the same manner without the support of international NGOs, which publicised the issue and pressurised centres of power in the West. That the Indian government has now decided to build the dam on its own, after the Supreme Court authorised it to do so in a judgement delivered on 18 October 2000, may point to the limits of political mobilisation in civil society.

However, the most dramatic manifestation of global civil society so far was to appear in what came to be known as the 'battle for Seattle'. At the end of November

1999, massive protests involving some 700 organisations and about 40,000 students, workers, NGOs, religious groups, and representatives of business and finance who were there for their own reasons brought the third ministerial meeting of the World Trade Organisation (WTO) in Seattle to a halt.

The WTO was to set in motion a new multilateral round of trade negotiations. Collective anger at the relocation of industries to the Third World, at the unsafe and abusive work conditions in the factories and sweatshops found there, at environmental degradation, and at the widespread exploitation of working people, exploded in a series of angry demonstrations.

Though large-scale protests against the WTO, the International Monetary Fund (IMF), and the World Bank were not new, what was new was both the scale of mobilisation and the intensity of protest. Angry demonstrations by student unions, environmentalists or 'tree huggers', economic and xenophobic nationalists, church groups, anarchists, protectionists, consumer groups, NGOs, and even business and financial groups were hailed by some scholars as 'globalisation from below' or as heralding a new internationalism.

There were two aspects of the 'battle for Seattle' that proved significant for the consolidation of global civil society. First, for the first time hitherto single-issue groups coalesced into a broad-based movement to challenge the way the world trade and financial system was being ordered by international institutions. Second, whereas in the late 1960s protest groups in the US and in Western Europe had targeted the state, at Seattle they targeted global corporations and international economic institutions. The protests themselves bore the mark of collective ire and resentment at the way in which globalisation that had been set in motion two decades earlier had exacerbated inequality and injustice. And matters did not stop here. Mass protests have become a regular feature of annual meetings of the World Economic Forum, the IMF and the World Bank, and the WTO.

At the same time we have seen students across university campuses in the US demonstrate against the unethical practices of large corporations such as Nike, Reebok, the Gap, and Disney, which use cheap labour in the Third World. Novel methods and vocabularies of protests captured the attention of the international media and generated considerable excitement at the idea of renewed political activism. And the phrase 'global civil society' became an integral part of political, corporate, and technical vocabularies.

In sum, global civil society organisations have emerged as a powerful and influential force on the world stage, affecting as they do both domestic and international policies, deciding as they do the fate of some authoritarian governments at least, and laying down agendas as they do. They not only have the power of influencing international public opinion and mobilising it against policies that they consider undesirable, they do so in ways that are sensationally visible and therefore effective.

Arguably two factors have strengthened the mandate of these organisations. One, the informational revolution, has increased their capacity to collect, collate, select, and publicise information on a variety of specialised issues ranging from development disasters, to the environment, to the effect of WTO policies such a patenting, to human rights violations. In fact, governments often just do not possess the capacity to gather and assemble specialised information or mobilise public opinion in quite the same way as NGOs organised on a global scale can do.

The unprecedented and phenomenal revolution in information and communications often described as the 'third industrial revolution' has allowed organisations to network across the world through the fax, the email, the Internet, and teleconferencing. Loosely structured movements have used the Internet to set up web sites that inform prospective participants about the timing of the meetings of international institutions, on the organisation of protests, and about transportation and accommodation. In fact we have witnessed a new phenomenon bursting onto the political scene: *cyber-space activism*. Via this form of activism, members of a group who may never see each other come together, through cyberspace, around issues that they consider important. Informational networks have allowed concerned organisations to gather and put together data on, for example, violations of human rights, muster opinion and activism around the issue, publicise information through the international media, and pressurise both national and international organisations to change both their mind and their manners.

The revolution in communications and information has allowed NGOs to form coalitions, as for instance the Conference of Peoples Global Action Against Free Trade, that held its first meeting in Geneva in May 1998, the Third World Network, which as a union of Third World NGOs is based in Malaysia, and the formation of the International Federation of Human Rights, a Paris-based transnational NGO, which consists of 89 human rights groups in 70 countries.

In fact, the revolution has also facilitated a new phenomenon: the development of intermediary NGOs, which act as 'facilitators' to help voluntary organisations to find funds from donor agencies such as Action Aid (India) or Charity Aid Foundation (UK). Intermediate organisations are, in other words, involved in the channelling of money and information from one NGO to another or from donor agencies to NGOs.

Global NGOs have become influential simply because they possess a property that happens to be the peculiar hallmark of *ethical* political intervention: moral authority and legitimacy. And they possess moral authority because they claim to represent the *public* or the *general* interest against official- or power-driven interests of the state or of the economy. Though the idea that they are truly representative can be challenged, this is not to deny that NGOs have raised normative concerns in the domain of global civil society.

As the upholders of an *ethical* canon that applies across nations and cultures, international actors in civil society now define as well as set the moral norms, which should at least in principle govern national and international orders. To put it differently, global civil society actors legislate and mandate a normative and thus a morally authoritative structure for the national and the international community. Because they lend moral depth to the agenda of global concerns and because they articulate a global and ethically informed vision on how states should treat their citizens, global civil society actors command the kind of attention that normally does not accrue to political activism within states. And they command this kind of attention because they have access to the international media, they possess high profiles, and they put forth their ideas in dramatic ways. This as a matter of course has significant implications for our traditional concepts of state sovereignty.

Traditionally states, pleading sovereignty and state security, have resisted any intervention by outside agencies,. Today global civil society actors act as the guardians of a morally informed consensus on the minimum that is due to human beings. As the keepers of a moral conscience that applies across borders, global civil society organisations question the monopoly of the nation state over the lives of its people. But they also challenge the workings of international institutions such as the World Bank, the IMF, and the WTO, as well as opposing the working of giant economic corporations.

If the demonstrations at Seattle questioned the viability of economic arrangements set by international institutions, the charting of norms for, say, the banning of child labour, or exploitation of resources, or environmental protection, has mediated the operations of powerful economic corporations.

The two factors set out above have certainly facilitated as well as legitimised the advent of global civil society actors as influential players on the world stage. However, the causes of this phenomenon have to be sought elsewhere, in the deeper structural changes that have occurred in the international political and economic order in the last two decades.

The major change that has taken place in the world system since the 1980s is of course globalisation. Now globalisation is difficult to characterise as it consists of a number of overlapping and even conflicting projects. However, though it is increasingly difficult to define globalisation, the implications of this process—or, rather, of this series of processes—are increasingly clear.

Globalisation has, for one, enabled the transmission of capital across the world as if national boundaries were non-existent. Correspondingly, through the processes of globalisation natural and national resources have been appropriated in the cause of capital. Local knowledge systems have been harnessed and patented for the same purpose. And flows of information and messages that tell people how they should think and what they should think have legitimised the process itself. Therefore, despite the difficulty in capturing the essence of globalisation, we can accept that its core is constituted by a distinct phenomenon: capital's restless and relentless pursuit of profit across the world and across national borders.

Today we see capital flitting across national borders as if they were just not there. But note that there is nothing natural or given in the processes of capital flows that ensure this much-needed erosion of state boundaries. In other words, globalisation demanded and demands sustained political intervention for one main reason. Recollect in this context that the post-Second World War period was to widely disseminate and institutionalise the idea that the state should intervene in matters relating to the production and to the reproduction of the economy and of society. The interventionist state was to take many forms: the Soviet model of the state that commands the heights of the economy, the welfare state that looks after the basic needs of its people, the Keynesian state that regulates the market, or the developmentalist state in the post-colonial world that commandeers both material and human resources to offset the legacies of colonial underdevelopment. Therefore, if capital more often than not originating in the West had to cross boundaries in order to pursue accumulation on the world scale, the state had to be rolled back from its hitherto legitimate tasks of regulating the market as well as providing social services to the people.

In other words, the legitimisation of the ability of the market to regulate itself, as well as to provide for both growth and well-being, demanded the delegitimisation and the consequent withdrawal of the state from the market. The state had to be rolled back both to encourage the unhindered flow of capital and to enable the market to display its dynamics. It was precisely this understanding that underpinned what came to be known as the neo-liberal agenda, or what John Williams termed the 'Washington consensus', which reined in the centres of power in the Western world in the late 1980s.

The consensus manifested itself in the form of ten policy recom mendations, imposed on particularly debt-ridden Third World countries by international financial and lending institutions. Among these recommendations were the following: trade liberalisation, clearing all hurdles to foreign direct investment, privatisation, deregulation, strengthening property rights, and tax reforms. If we translate these economic imperatives into political terms, we find that the consensus dictated the following: (a) the state, particularly in Third World countries, should withdraw from the social sector; (b) the market should be freed from all constraints; and (c) people in civil society should organise their own social and economic reproduction instead of depending on the state.

Ironically, the idea that people in civil society should organise their own reproduction has emerged at exactly the same moment as globalisation has drastically eroded the capacity of the same people to order their own affairs. And reliance on the market for this purpose is inadequate, since the market, remember, has room for only those people who have something to sell and those who have something to buy.

In other words, the market does not provide for those people who cannot participate in its transactions because they have nothing with which they can buy, or because they cannot find buyers for what they sell: labour, for instance. The unleashing of the market simply meant that massive sections of the people had to now fend for themselves in the sense of providing the conditions for their social reproduction.

It was in this particular historical conjunction that NGOs emerged on the horizon to take over functions hitherto reserved for the state, such as providing health and education, instituting income-generating schemes, creating safety nets, and encouraging people to be self-reliant. The space cleared by the rolling back of the state came to be known as 'civil society', and NGOs were transformed into the guardians of civil society even as they subcontracted for the state. To put it in stark terms, the emergence and the growing power of NGOs whether national or global has been actively facilitated by the Washington consensus.

The role of the non-governmental sector has been further strengthened by what came subsequently to be known as the post-Washington consensus. The mid-1990s were to witness a sharp swing in the mood of international trade and financial institutions. For the rhetoric of these institutions was to move away from an emphasis on a free and untrammelled market to the idea that both the market and the generic processes of globalisation had to be governed. The shift had largely to do with one main factor. Doctrines of free trade and unregulated markets had run into trouble ever since 1994, when Mexico was hit by financial devastation.

The second financial crisis, which began when the government of Thailand devalued the bhat, and which then spread to the rest of East Asia, Japan, Brazil, and Russia in 1997 and 1998, impoverished millions, and generated rage and discontent. We saw an inkling of this dissatisfaction when Korean workers rose to defy the IMF. Many scholars saw these economic and financial crises as a consequence of unfettered globalisation, as a result of the working of the free and unregulated market. The neo-liberal agenda had after all failed to deliver the muchpromised benefits of greater growth, stabilisation of financial markets, and political order. Income disparities had increased, the number of the poor had grown drastically, and people had been deprived of their livelihoods and security of life.

A global economic order had been forged through globalisation without any prospect of justice, or democracy, or redistribution. And this posed problems for the defenders of globalisation. For if a system is widely perceived as unjust, it will necessarily engender resistance. Therefore, whereas in the 1980s and the early 1990s free market liberalism had been left to private corporations, this strategy had to be rethought since it had proved counter-productive. In fact, as early as in 1995 the economist Paul Krugman had suggested that the Mexican crisis marked the beginning of the deflation of the Washington consensus.

The very idea that globalisation had rationalised capitalism came to be questioned because what we witnessed was the globalisation of a crisis. Consequently, the managers of international financial and economic institutions were to realise, somewhat late, what Marx had argued in the late nineteenth century: that there is nothing natural or selfregulating about markets and that they unleash their own oppressions. If markets were to endure they had to be controlled or, in the new parlance of international financial institutions, 'governed'

Alternatively, the dominant approach to development needed to be rethought, since neo-liberal policy prescriptions had not only failed, they had intensified dissatisfaction and hostility particularly in the countries of the Third World. This realisation led to a radical shift in the rhetoric of globalisation: the replacement of the language of the market by that of governance, accountability, transparency, and democracy.

The World Bank, under the influence of the economist Joseph Stiglitz, known for his critique of the unfettered market, moved from a narrow economistic focus on development to what came to be known as the Comprehensive Development Framework. Even as policies of structural adjustment were replaced by notions of partnership between the Bank and borrowing governments, the language of the Bank shifted from macroeconomic theory that focused on economic growth to the recognition of the centrality of governance, albeit a notion of governance that was stripped of politics. The shift was not radical inasmuch as the dominant themes of neoliberalism continued to dominate the political imagination of most, if not all, of the international financial institutions.

But now international financial institutions were to cushion neo-liberalism in a vocabulary that spoke of the regulation and the moderation of the processes of globalisation. In effect, these institutions opted for strategies of conflict management. Perhaps the Bank had no choice. For global civil society actors in various demonstrations insisted that 'Fifty Years is Enough', a slogan that overshadowed the golden jubilee of the Wolrd Bank. Even as James Wolfensohn was appointed President in June 1995, he was faced with the need to restructure the policy of the World Bank in the face of sustained criticism by global civil society. In an attempt to legitimise the Bank, the President engaged global NGOs in dialogue and entered into collaborative ventures to reshape the policy prescriptions of the world body.

The result was the adoption of a new language of sustainable development, preservation of natural resources, equitable development, and democratic development. It is of some significance that some global civil society actors, who had earlier emerged on the political scene in and through the politics of protest, now became partners in decision-making activities.

NGOs now attend the annual meetings of the World Bank and the IMF as special guests. In 1982 the World Bank had created a discussion forum in the shape of an NGO-World Bank Committee, which ensured the active involvement of the non-governmental sector in implementing projects.

Now NGOs came to be involved in policy formulation. In 1996 the WTO General Council adopted guidelines that provided for increased contacts between the Secretariat and the NGOs. This of course raises an important methodological question: can we continue to call agencies that become a part of global decision-making structures 'civil society organisations' that supposedly challenge the workings of the global order? But more of that later.

In marked contrast to the earlier two decades that focused on the opening up of national borders to the free flow of global capital and the doctrines of free trade, the post-Washington consensus concentrates on the governance of these activities. For decision-makers recognised that the deep tensions that had been engendered by the processes of globalisation had to be managed if they were not to spiral out of control. To put it bluntly, international trade and financial institutions realised that the processes of globalisation could not be legitimised if they were left to private agencies such as corporate houses or to some 'invisible hand' of the market.

The post-Washington consensus was therefore to focus on three issues.

First, globalisation was too important to be left to the unrestricted corporate world and should be mediated through 'governance' that ensured transparency, accountability, capacity building, and safety networks.

Second, the state needed to be replaced not so much by the market as by civil society organisations that represented the aspirations of the people and that strengthened democracy. This of course meant that the fields of the market and of non-market transactions were, in policy prescriptions, separated.

Third, the new consensus opined that only a strong civil society under the guidance of NGOs can further democracy. However, this avatar of civil society is not marked by democratic contestation but by the building of 'social capital' and 'trust' among the inhabitants. In effect, the earlier move away from the state to the market has now been replaced by a move away from the state to civil society based on networks of trust. However, despite some changes in rhetoric, the post-Washington consensus continues to retain significant elements of the earlier neo-liberal consensus. For neither was the idea that a free market encourages democracy put aside, nor was the role of the state in institutionalising and realising democracy reconsidered.

In the current dispensation, both a minimal state and a free market continue to provide the conditions of a strong and democratic civil society. More importantly, the international policy community now concentrates on the management of discontent, which has erupted in reaction to the liberalisation and the deregulation process that lies at the heart of globalisation. In other words, the post-Washington consensus, views protest and struggle, which happen to be an integral part of civil society, as problems that have to be resolved through managerial techniques. It still does not recognise that a democratic civil society is about struggling for a better world, that it is about politics and not only governance, that it is about visions and aspirations and not only about neutralisation of tensions. Nor does the present consensus address issues such as unequal power relations either in the world or within states. And civil society continues to be identified, as in the earlier version, with NGOs. To put it differently, if earlier versions of neo-liberalism cleared the space for global civil society actors, the present consensus legitimises their activities. Conversely, the activities of most if not all NGOs legitimise the post- Washington consensus, for instance by linking civil society to an apolitical notion of governance.

Now civil society has been subjected to considerable over-theorisation in the post-1989 era. The concept, never too clear at the best of times, has turned into the proverbial will-o'-thewisp that eludes understanding. It has come to mean many things to many people: as the space of solidarity, as a project of projects, as the area of associational life, as a site of contestation, and as a third sector. This may not necessarily be a problem.

Multiple meanings of civil society can provide a space for dialogue. On the other hand, when people come to this overlapping space armed with their own meanings of what civil society is about, we may find that such a dialogue becomes impossible. For any dialogue needs at the least a common referral as a starting point for an exchange of ideas. And such a referral can best be provided by classical political theory.

If we were to reach back into the annals of political theory to investigate the idea of civil society, it would look something like this. The concept of civil society signifies both a space and a set of values. As a space it is metaphorically located somewhere between the state, the market, and the family. Here people come together in projects of all kinds to make their collective histories.

Histories are in turn made through the politics of affirmation as well as conflict-ridden encounters, the politics of solidarity as well as that of struggle. Civil society possesses no one characteristic, no one core, no one essential nature. Civil society is what its inhabitants make of it. It is a site where projects overlap, where they reinforce each other, and where they challenge each other. This is possible, for civil society, unlike pre-modern communities, allows its inhabitants to make their own lives and their own destinies perhaps independently, perhaps in concert with others, in some degree of freedom.

For the values of civil society are those of freedom, accessibility, and publicness. On this ground alone no one is in theory barred from civil society, everyone is allowed entry into the sphere, and everyone—again in theory—is free to link with others to make their own histories even though these histories are not made, as Marx told us long ago, in conditions of their own choice. Thus is associational life born and thus is an activity called politics born. For arguably, it is only when people in and through social associations translate their everyday experiences into expressed vocabularies, and it is only when people interpret the experiential through the prism provided by the expressive, that we see the birth of politics. Politics in the first sense is about translating the experiential into the expressive.

As individuals bring their own world-views into social associations, they transcend individual beliefs into socially responsive and responsible political projects through dialogue as well as through contention. Conversely, politics is about interpreting the experiential in terms provided by the expressive. Consider, for instance, the women's movement. The movement was to gain shape and clarity only when some women—and some men—were to express their discontent with patriarchal structures of oppression in terms of feminism. In turn, feminist insights gave other women the tools with which they could interpret the injustice that was inflicted on them by patriarchy.

Politics is, in short, a two-way activity. It moves from what is experienced to the interpretation of these experiences in terms of specifically political categories such as feminism. In turn, political formulations allow other people to make sense of their experiences. What is important is that the activity is empowering inasmuch as, when ordinary men and women engage in political activity, they acquire agency, they recover selfhood, and they earn self-confidence. This is politics in the best Aristotelian tradition: politics as self-realisation. Therefore, for most theorists of civil society, social associations are vital to collective life simply because they allow people to realise their selfhood through collective action. But note that social associations are significant only because membership in these groupings is voluntary as well as revocable. It is the individual who is the primary actor in civil society; social associations merely enable him or her to realise their own potential and their own projects. Social associations, in other words, are nothing but aggregates of individuals, which in turn reflect the wishes and the desires of their members. It is this interpretation of civil society that finds it difficult to accommodate NGOs, for two reasons.

First, though it is possible that individuals who come together in associations transform their association into an NGO, a number of important and influential NGOs are not created through this process. Global NGOs come in from the outside armed very often with their own ideas of what is wrong and what should be done to remedy the situation. At precisely this point the issue of representativeness arises to bedevil thinking on civil society.

Second, the arrival of global NGOs onto the scene may carry important and not so positive implications for notions of political agency. For if they have their own ideas of what should be done and how should it be done, ordinary human beings who have experienced, say, injustice in their daily lives are denied the opportunity to frame their responses in their own terms. NGOs more often than not have their own programmes, they more often than not speak a highly specialised language that may well be incomprehensible for the inhabitants of the regions in which they operate, and they may well have their own ideas of what is politically permissible and what is not.

Ordinary individuals, it is evident, possess little opportunity to influence agendas that are formulated in far-off places. Associational activity at the global level tends therefore to acquire a life of its own, a life that is quite distinct from the everyday lives of the people who do not speak but who are spoken for. Bluntly put, people are disempowered rather than empowered when highly specialised, professional, and more often than not bureaucratised civil society actors tell them what is wrong with their daily existence and how they should go about resolving the problems of their collective lives. In the process civil society may undergo both depoliticisation and disempowerment. Admittedly, some global civil society actors have initiated novel ways of bringing the problems of everyday existence of poor and impoverished people of the Third World to international platforms and propelling them into the glare of the media spotlight.

When individuals who are otherwise far too preoccupied in eking out a bare and minimum subsistence in adverse conditions come together and think through how to resolve their situation, they are empowered because they are politicised. And to be politicised is to acquire consciousness that collective endeavours offer possibilities of self-realisation. To be politicised is to be made aware that certain rights accrue to every human being by virtue of being human. It means that people who have been constituted as subjects and not as citizens by the policies of the state can rise to demand justice, equality, and freedom; to demand that the state delivers what it has promised in theory.

Political activity simply makes for aware and self-confident human beings because these human beings acquire agency in and through politics. And thereby ordinary men and women make the transition from subject to citizen. It is precisely this notion of politics that is devalued when global civil actors commandeer political initiatives and once again constitute human beings as subjects of political ideas arrived at elsewhere, or, worse, when they constitute individuals as consumers of agendas finalised elsewhere.

It is unclear whether international NGOs strengthen or weaken the role of the community. First, NGO activism, which straddles national boundaries to create global coalitions, is no substitute for self-determining and empowering political action born out of specific experiences. Second, whereas the Third World State has proved notoriously non-responsive to the demands of civil society, it is also a fact that, at moments of crisis, this very civil society has mobilised to hold the state accountable. In December 2001, for instance, the streets of Buenos Aires were filled with agitating and agitated Argentinians who demanded the resignation of President Fernando de la Rua. Even as the country descended into financial chaos and anarchy, even as people banged pots and pans on their balconies, even as the streets of the city overflowed with crowds, and even as deadly riots took the lives of 30 people, the President had to resign. At some point he was held accountable.

For much of the leadership of global civil society organisations appears to be self-appointed and non-accountable to their members, many of whom are passive and confine their activism to signatures to petitions circulated via e-mail. Also note that, whereas we see huge crowds during demonstrations against the WTO or in alternative forums such as the World Social Forum, between such episodes activity is carried on by a core group of NGOs.

It is possible that participants in demonstrations are handed a political platform and an agenda that has been finalised elsewhere. This is hardly either democratic or even political, it may even reek of bureaucratic management of participatory events. It may even render people, consumers of choices made elsewhere. Moreover, international NGOs resist attempts to make their own functioning transparent even as they demand transparency and accountability from international financial organisations. Observers have commented that, since most global NGOs do not issue financial or activity reports or any declaration of objectives, it is difficult to gauge their nature. Even if they do issue such statements, does this make their activities more transparent? And remember that it is precisely these organisations, whose own processes of decision-making are closed to public scrutiny, who happen to be in control of people's lives and destinies.

We also need to wonder how democratic the organisations of global civil society are given the great inequalities of resources between the North and the South. It is more than possible that Third World organisations get sidelined when it comes to the making of global agendas.

For instance, Hart- Landsberg reports that influential groups such as Public Citizen and leaders of labour organisations in the US focused on keeping China out of the WTO at Seattle, citing exploitative working conditions and the unfair trade practices of the Chinese government. However, no independent movement of Chinese workers has called for international support for a campaign to keep China out of the world body. 'In fact, even organizations operating in Hong Kong that seek to promote independent labour organizing in China have refrained from supporting such a campaign'.

To cite another example, environmental NGOs have persistently campaigned for lower emission levels in the atmosphere through control of polluting industries and vehicular traffic. In Delhi, at the beginning of the new millennium, 'polluting industries' were closed down and vehicles that did not meet the standard laid down were abandoned by a decision of the Supreme Court, which was under pressure from the environmental lobby. However, in the process people were condemned to homelessness, massive hardship, and unemployment. The gap between the demands of environment-conscious NGOs and the need of the poorer sections of society was just too starkly visible. We discover dissonance in the way Third World activists envisage crucial matters and the way in which global civil society actors largely based in the West view them.

Certainly we need to acknowledge the outstanding services rendered by some global civil society organisations. We should be grateful that some of these groups have brought issues of crucial importance to the top of political agendas. Nevertheless, the domination of global civil society by organised and well-funded NGOs hailing from the West poses some very vexing questions for issues of political representation, political agency, and politics in general. They may even be a part of the project that seeks to disable activism in civil society and depoliticise it.

Global Civil Society Actors

Civil society is a peculiarly modern phenomenon emerges through the same historical processes that generate both the modern impersonal state and the modern market system. These processes have to do with the separation of the economic and the political, the appropriation of the economy by a private class of proprietors, and the concomitant rise of the institution of private property. They have to do with the emergence of the notion of the autonomous individual and self-directed individualism. They have, further, to do with the dissolution of community as 'face to face' interaction and with the carving out of a space where individuals meet, in the words of Marx, as 'bearers of commodities'.

Classical theory called this space 'civil society' which, peopled by legally autonomous individuals who may well be strangers to each other, was marked by impersonal and contractual relations. All this carried its own problems, as the theorists of early modernity were to tell us in some detail. For instance, Hegel, arguably *the* most distinguished proponent of civil society, in 1821 was to hail the propensity of modern civil society to enhance freedom in contrast to the 'unfreedom' of premodern societies. But at the same time he was profoundly ambivalent about the democratic potential of the sphere or of its capacity to institute ethicality in the Greek sense, or what he called *Sittlichkeit*. For if the material context for the realisation of the self and for the recognition of rights is bourgeois or *bürgerliche* society, this, as he was quick to realise, carried its own momentum.

Because even as modern life witnesses a dramatic expansion of the sphere of social interaction in civil society, this interaction is permeated deeply by the ethos of the capitalist market, that of self-serving and instrumental action. And this can pose a problem for the very reproduction of the sphere; it may well disintegrate under the influence of self-centred reasoning, which is the hallmark of the capitalist market system.

There is another problem that confronts classical political theory: even as the market constitutes transactions in civil society, the market order presupposes a stable and sturdy civil society in order to function efficiently. Market relations simply need to be embedded in nonmarket relations in order to function with some measure of success. Market transactions need disciplined, predictable, and socialised behaviour as a prerequisite for their successful operation. If Adam Smith put forth his theory of 'moral sentiments' in 1759 to accomplish this, a contemporary theorist such as Francis Fukuyama argues that capitalist accumulation needs the presence of trust. And James Coleman and Robert Putnam suggest that 'softer' social norms that guarantee expectation, such as social capital, should buttress economic transactions, *if* we want the domain of these transactions to expand.

Civil society and the market, we realise, are dependent on each other; they need not provide an alternative to each other at all. Therefore, whereas it is perfectly true that global civil society has critiqued the workings of the international economic order, is a critique of corporate managed globalisation, we are compelled to ask, the same as a critique of capital in search of global markets? The problem is that global civil society tends to be broad-based, comprising as it does many groups with divergent purposes and aims. Kaldor, for instance, accepts that only a few of the protestors at Seattle were actually against globalisation; the others wanted to reform international trade and financial institutions as well as make them accountable. And the same theme was echoed at the World Social Forum that met in Porto Alegre in Brazil in February 2002. The meeting, which was attended by 50,000 delegates and which was meant to be a parallel to the meeting of the World Economic Forum in New

York, put forth the idea of an alternative world: 'Another world is possible', went the slogan. However, according to a newspaper report, 'delegates bristle at the WSF being called the "anti-globalisation" meet. They argue that they are not meeting here to register protests but to work out concrete proposals that will be superior to what will be floated at the New York meeting of the WEF'.

Actually, the movement against globalisation can be split into (a) radical individuals and groups who oppose capitalism but are rather clueless as well as powerless when it comes to alternatives and b) established NGOs that work at the margins to reform' the system. The latter would rather that the present system is reformed and made more accountable and humane. They consequently focus on institutional reform rather than on an alternative to the system. And the ones that are anti-capitalist globalisation and dream of a better international order are relegated to the fringes of global civil society, dominated as it is by professional bodies who now are partners in world decision-making forums.

Global civil society, it is evident, by and large prefers to work within the parameters of a system that has been found wanting by many critics both from the Third World and from the advanced capitalist world. Given the plural and somewhat contradictory nature of the protest movements, they can hardly provide us with an alternative system. In tandem with the post-Washington Consensus, some global civil society actors would humanise the capitalist system rather than think of another system that may be able to deliver justice and equity. Therefore, they may reform the neo-liberal platform but they are unable to map a new course. And the anti-capitalist globalisation groups are more romantic than pragmatic when it comes to alternatives.

We seem to live in a world of disenchantment where activists either refuse to dream dreams of an alternative world system or are doubtful about what they want in its stead. For, as Scholte put it in the context of Seattle, 'halting a new round of trade liberalisation is not the same as building a better world order'. In the meantime liberalisation, privatisation, and exploitation of Third World resources continue to coexist with the rhetoric of human rights, environment, democracy, and what the World Bank now calls the Comprehensive Development Framework.

When we come to the state-centric international order, we find that the relationship between states and global civil society is profoundly ambivalent. It is true that global civil society actors have through the techniques of 'naming and shaming' embarrassed individual states and even succeeded in overthrowing individual governments. But it is equally true that states are not at all ceding their power over matters that they consider crucial.

Consider the response of the US to the mobilisation of international public opinion in the wake of the 11 September 2001 attacks on New York and Washington. Political activists were connecting via the Internet, peace marches dotted the landscape from Delhi to Washington to Berlin, and writers were authoring impassioned pieces on why the Bush government should not punish the innocent people of Afghanistan by bombarding the country.

And yet the American government went ahead and declared war on Afghanistan, adding to the already considerable woes of the people of that country. The US, which incidentally claims to speak for the 'free world', refused to heed the voice of global civil society and proceeded to violate the freedom of the people of Afghanistan. The sovereignty of the US remained intact despite considerable criticism by civil society actors.

On the other hand, global civil society actors need states and their institutions to substantiate and codify their demands in law. Transnational organisations may critique the practices of states in, say, the field of human rights, but they also require states to create political and legal frameworks that facilitate setting up of the rule of law, civil and political rights, or environmental protection. Women's groups can hardly demand, say, gender justice without the corresponding demand for state protection and the demand that states set up appropriate institutions for protection of women's rights.

Alternatively, civil society groups fighting, say, violations of civil liberties will need the state to punish offenders. They simply will need human rights commissions, sympathetic judges, and a sensitive police to realise their objectives. Efforts in civil society will come to naught unless states codify these efforts in the form of law or regulations. Civil society actors will draw upon states both to redress violation of human rights and to reform civil society itself through enacting laws restricting sexual harassment in the workplace, for example. This again means—and this is a point that is not generally grasped by many current advocates of civil society—that states constitute the limits of civil society, as well as enabling political initiatives in global civil society.

In effect, the very states that global civil society supposedly opposes *enable* the latter in the sense that only they can provide the conditions within which the civil society agenda is realised. In effect, vibrant civil societies require strong and stable states as a precondition to their very existence. After all, we hardly expect to find a civil society in countries like Afghanistan and Somalia, where the state itself leads a precarious existence as a result of the civil wars that have wrecked the countries and their polities. The shade of Hegel, who suggested that the state is a precondition for the existence of civil society, looms especially large here.

Not only Third World governments but also informed critics belonging to that part of the world argue that the values of global civil society reflect those held by a narrow group of influential states in the international order. Any attempt to institutionalise these values in states of the Third World, is seen as an imposition. This is particularly true of human rights, which are considered to be embedded in a set of norms and historical processes specific to Western Europe and the US and therefore inappropriate for other societies.

Incensed critics regard the imposition of human rights upon societies that may possess other notions of how relationships between individuals and governments should be arranged as an extension of imperialism.Whether these critiques are valid or invalid is not the issue here; the point is that global civil society actors, particularly human rights organisations, are seen as embedded within an ideology that is highly Eurocentric: liberal democracy.

For even though some of these organisations have moved in the recent past to embrace ideas of social and economic rights, which for long have been seen as the preconditions of meaningful civil and political rights, it is the latter, not the former, that inform the consensus on human rights. This really means that global civil society actors reflect the consensus that liberal democracy is the only form of democracy that remains of value in the aftermath of the fall of communism in 1989. Therefore, even as we accept that global civil society actors can launch, and have launched, a critique of the practices of some states, we must ponder upon whether, in doing so, they do not codify values that belong to another set of states.

3

NGOs and Democracy

In a liberal representative democracy a major virtue of government, and the parliament from which it is derived, is the enfranchisement of the unorganised, it gives them a voice and limits the claims that the many organised interests make against the commons. Civil society, whether church, corporations, trade unions or NGOs, provides citizens with vehicles to exercise private initiative. In a liberal democracy they are, thankfully, free to pursue their aims. Indeed, democracy may be enhanced by an energetic civil society.

When civil society organisations, however, organise in pursuit of public purposes they compete with government and the unorganised. If successful in that competition, they become in effect, civil society regulators. There is a new breed of civil society regulators - advocacy NGOs - and their activities have implications for representative democracy. For example, the Australian Conservation Foundation announced in 2001, 'by 2050 Australia will be a civil society. There will be a high level of community engagement in decision-making processes, a higher level of trust with their decision-making institutions.' There is not much wrong with 'community engagement' so long as the form of the engagement is well tested by public opinion. How public opinion is measured is of course, the nub of the matter. Only elected officials put their careers on the line to test that proposition, all the rest just want what they want, they claim to represent public opinion, but the claims are difficult to test. Therein lies the problem of participatory democracy, it is democracy for activists. It prefers to be loosened from the ties of formally tested public opinion. It becomes a means of pursuing minority opinion, its aim is to avoid the trade-offs that are essential to representative democracy.

Civil society is increasingly acting in a new mode. Where, in the past, civil society has acted in *opposition* to government, it has helped to secure guarantees of formal legal, political and civil equality. It has helped to secure the law and institutions that safeguard the liberty to conduct ones business based on 'a kind of trust among non-intimates'.

In other words, it has helped to secure a 'civil' society. Moreover, civil society continues in an *apolitical* mode, when it identifies problems, such as the amelioration of the plight of the sick and the poor, and produces its own solutions. In this mode, it is self-directed and voluntary, and makes few collective moral or resource claims on other citizens. In other words, it exists apart from government and the state.

The dominant mode in which civil society now operates is essentially *communitarian*. The examples above suggest multiple agendas. It appears to want to further democratiseliberal democracy. It seeks a democratic community and collective solutions, it makes increasing claims on the community in an increasing number of guises and ways. For example, it is a vehicle for the idea of citizenship, which becomes the basis and the source of welfare claims. It is used as an ethical or normative idea, a vision and prescription for the good life.It seeks distributive or social justicein an increasing number of areas, including the economy.

Civil society in the communitarian mode has been taken up and pressed into service as a tool to criticise liberal democracy, in particular by those who think that the state has been decimated by 'neo-liberals'. It is used as a political slogan to advance the cause of the democratic community and as a weapon to mediate the effects of the ideology of individualism and self-interest. It may be that liberalism is excessively individualistic and insufficiently democratic.

Whether democratising the community can solve these problems, however, is problematic. Communitarians insist on the need to override the wishes of the individual in the name of the greater good. Democratic communitarians assume or require that participation in politics is the norm, whereas, in fact, it is the exception. The work of democracy always comes down to activists, so the question is—which activists and what recourse to their activity do the citizens have? NGOs expand the range of voices but in doing so, do they expand the participation of the community or the ranks of a political elite?

A cardinal tenet of liberalism is to keep democracy in its place, to regard it as an activity of limited application. By contrast, the democratic way of life encompasses more than the periodic business of government and elections. It is to be applied to most institutions, democracy in the courts (individualised justice, liberal rules of standing) the home (feminism), the workplace (industrial democracy), the corporation (corporate social responsibility), the economy (market socialism). Democracy may work in some of these without destroying the purpose of the institution, but where it does not, there are costs attached. The application of democratic processes to all walks of life should be contingent on its utility, not on its 'morality'.

As for social justice agendas, these attempt to justify the transfer of funds from one group of people to another. 'Justice turns into the problem of how to distribute goods and losses without any very direct relation to law and order or even constitutionality. To mark its new role, the term 'justice' is commonly partnered by 'social', and social justice is what happens when all basic goods, which may notionally include individual talents and skills, are centrally distributed in accordance with a rational scheme.'The welfare state continues to grow, seeking ever justification that is more elaborate. 'The core of the citizenship theory of the welfare state is community membership. From our membership in our community flow the welfare rights we can assert and the *duties we owe* to contribute to the support of our fellows.'Often it is the second part of citizenship that is left out. Moreover, what happens when insufficient people believe in the theory?

Communitarian civil society is growing because liberal democracy's ability to voice citizen disquiet is unprecedented. It makes the present democratic institutions appear inadequate, less trusted. This position is one that cashed-up NGOs and international agencies favour, and business has to live with. The irony is that the critics of liberal democracy - indigenous, feminist, gay, environmentalist, civil libertarian, socialist - have all had their greatest successes in liberal democracies. They are not doing so well in crony capitalist, Islamic or communist states, even less well in tribal polities. In fact, where they threaten to do particularly well is at a supra-national level - EU and UN - where electorates have no direct control over them. Having been granted many of their wishes, these movements challenge the legitimacy of important elements of the system that sustains them - the electorate's veto over policy-makers, the distribution of the economic surplus, the commitment to evidence as the basis for policy, and the rule of law - hallmarks of the liberal democracies. Each of these is being challenged, in part by prominent NGOs, in part by other players within and outside government. The result may herald the rise of a dictatorship of the articulate, the aptly named Culture of Complaint. The work of the state is as much to counter the tyranny of the minorities, including individuals, as well as to counter the tyranny of the majority. The task is to limit the claims on the commons, to depoliticise much of life, to make it less amenable to public dispute.

In the most prosperous of times, in the most prosperous of nations, there is the invention of permanent poverty.In the most benign of modern production regimes, there is the invention of a permanent litany of environmental disaster.In the most egalitarian and peaceful of nations, there is the invention of a permanent litany of human rights abuses.The application of these civil society agendas to the liberal democracies shows a lack of objectivity and loss of sense of perspective and of magnitude on the part of the advocates. Largely, political activism has been contracted out. In the early phase of the establishment of the major political parties there was certainly a strand of, or at least pretensions to mass (class) involvement in politics, although in fact the numbers were never large. At present, the parties are brand names run by professionals, paid for by the state to do the work of politics.This is not a criticism. On the contrary, the criticism is of those who believe that civil society activists are more democratic.

Civil society activists, as represented by NGOs are brand names - WWF, Greenpeace, Amnesty International - run by professionals. They are less constrained by their membership than say business and union interest groups, and totally unconstrained by the need to run candidates for public office. They are good at voicing opinion, not at resolving the myriad claims that present to government. They have a different part to play in the great democratic panoply, but they are no more democratic. Consumer groups, like *Consumers International*, and environmentalists, like *Greenpeace*, and international human rights lawyers, like *Amnesty International* are on a mission to remake the way laws are made. In a representative democracy, laws should be made by consensus, with reference to the people. These groups use participation as a nonconsensual means to regulate the activities of citizens and business. These groups can do good work, but those with an illiberal bent can capture them. Unlike political parties, they do not need to compromise to gain a majority of the public vote.

NGOs, just like any other interest group, are organisations designed to improve their chances of success in public policy. Therefore, there has to be a strategy to combat their influence. That strategy cannot be, in a liberal society, a strategy of control or a strategy to deny them a voice. The best strategy is to have NGOs prove themselves at the bar of public opinion. Governments should test the credentials of NGOs who seek access to government resources or seek to design laws. They should then share with the electorate what they have learned about NGOs. The following enthusiast neatly conveys the rationale for NGO involvement in the international arena, particularly to assist inter-governmental organisations. 'But if it is impossible to abandon the initials 'NGO', perhaps it is possible the reframe their significance in a more positive light. One candidate might be 'Necessary Governance Organizations'. The corresponding reframing of 'IGO' might then be 'Insufficient Governance Organizations'.The sentiment is not entirely misplaced, especially when so many inter-government organisations consist of undemocratic governments.

The intergovernmental organisation with the most intimate connection with NGOs however, is the European Union, which consists entirely of democratic nations. The NGO bid for legitimacy in such circumstances is grossly exaggerated, it exceeds its mandate in fora that consist of democratic governments. The desire to transfer decision-making to forums less in control of the nation state is well progressed in the UN and European contexts. It reaches exquisite heights with those who advocate a single world government.

An example of the desire for a one-world government is the One World Trust of the United Kingdom parliament. Before the 2001, election the group boasted 176 members, making it amongst the largest all-party groups in Parliament. Over 120 of the members are drawn from Westminster, while another 50 members are from the Welsh Assembly and European Parliament. The All-Party Group for World Government to promote a greater sense of world community formed the One World Trust in 1951.

'The Trust believes that sustainable world peace, prosperity and justice will only be achieved when individuals see themselves as world citizens as well as citizens of their own nations.'The Trust supports the work of the Parliamentary Group in its objectives to establish democratic and accountable world governance through reform of the United Nations, global institutions and international law.

A crucial aspect of the Trust's work is to promote stronger more just world law, which will help the nations of the world solve those problems they are unable to solve by themselves. The Trust is a member of the World Federalist Movement and its ultimate objective is a World Government based along federal lines, nations pooling sovereignty. The Trust published a 'Global Accountability Record', claimed to be the first of its kind to compare the accountability of intergovernmental organisations, transnational corporations and international non-government organisations.

Eighteen of the 'world's most powerful organisations' were assessed on membership control of governance structures and access to information.Accountability is a fine thing, and measuring accountability is worthy. But to compare intergovernmental organisations and multinationals and NGOs is a confusion of roles.

The accountability of sovereign governments to their citizens is a complex matter, which involves the entire infrastructure of the state, including the parliament and courts and free press. The accountability of corporations to their owners is essentially a contractual matter, albeit one controlled by not only the markets, but also national legislatures.

As for international NGOs, it is worthwhile pursuing their accountability to their members, but this is a matter of trivial weight compared to the previous two actors. NGOs are free associations governed by an absolute minimum of rules. The members are voluntary, they have a minimal legal presence and no ability to tax. Giving them equal billing with government and multinationals is a problem.

Although accountability by NGOs to their members is of interest, and NGO capture by minority activists is a source of concern, the real accountability of NGOs must be had through governments and corporations. That is, governments must account to their citizens in their dealings with NGOs and corporations.

Corporations must account to their owners and contracted parties within the law, but NGOs need only account to their members. The game of making equivalents of the three pillars of society, state, market and civil society is an overstatement of the importance of the third and misplaces its role, civil society can be its own person, but it cannot substitute for government and it cannot create wealth.

Some very senior international government organisation executives seriously entertain the equivalence game. Mike Moore, former Prime Minister of New Zealand and Director-General of the World Trade Organisation from 1999 to 2002 tells the story, 'All the UN agency heads meet once a year under the chairmanship of Kofi Annan... at one meeting, an agency head shocked me by stating: "We are in a post-parliamentary, post-democratic age; nation states can't function any more, politicians are despised and people can't even be bothered to vote anymore." He went on to assert that the future of governance was with international organizations in partnership with NGOs representing civil society, bypassing politicians. And of course many NGOs subscribe to and push this theory, it gives them power, status and resources.'

Fortunately, some intergovernmental organisations are beginning to reassert themselves. The IMF has observed, 'Many CSOs appear to seek engagement with the Fund as a way to increase their own credibility and standing with member governments. However, CSOs can add real value by building coalitions at the national or local level to support pro-poor reform. Perhaps direct engagement with their own governments would go a long way towards strengthening their own legitimacy and increasing their possibilities to engage more constructively with the IMF in policy constructions.'NGO activism, buttressed by the failures in intellectual public market place is kept within bounds within the nation-state by a regular and responsive forum for all interests. Gregory Jusdanis described it thus, 'The nation is a daily plebiscite.'

Despite the appeals to international citizenship and the wonders of email and the apparent ease of international travel, the daily plebiscite is not available in international forums. Nor is the business of funding the promotion of democracy without its problems. If international democratic practice lacks the legitimacy of an electorate and NGOs lack the legitimacy of a tested representation, so too is their a problem with the west attempting to seed democracy in undemocratic nations.

US and European aid aimed at the development of civil society has grown considerably in the last ten years. It follows on the heels of financial aid, physical infrastructure aid, and governance aid, all attempts to promote development in less developed countries. Civil society aid may be one of the keys to the development of a successful society, but it suffers from so much of the romanticism of the rest of the NGO movement.

It commences with the particulars of electoral systems and government accountability, but soon begins to promote advocacy of interests – environmental, women, indigenous, tenants and so on. NGOs can be attractive to aid donors because they perform some of the same roles as political parties, representing interest, building participation and checking the state – without seeking power. They can appear to make up an 'antipolitical domain'and bypass traditional divisions, beliefs and interests. They do so however, by promoting particular western agendas, which NGOs promote. The danger is that when the donor withdraws, civil society organisations collapse. In other words, aid cannot sustain democracy, it provides an artifice of activism, but not a sustained belief among a populace.

Regulations to Corporations

Business corporations traditionally face two groups, which regulate their behaviour. The marketplace, which includes business competitors, and government. Now there is a new regulator, civil society or more particularly NGOs such as Greenpeace, Amnesty International, Community Aid Abroad, the Councils of Social Service and the like. The tools that NGOs use to regulate business are very different to the market and government; they are, in the first instance, neither price nor law. Often they are just ideas expressed in a new language.

The language of Corporate Social Responsibility (CSR) or its many aliases like Corporate Citizenship, the Triple Bottom Line, the Stakeholder Corporation and so on. This language, these ideas are seductive, they appear benign. Make no mistake - Corporate Social Responsibility is really Civil Society Regulation in disguise.Civil Society Regulation occurs where NGOs set the standards for business behaviour.

Corporations choose to adopt or not to adopt these standards at their risk. While governments have the power of legislation, the ability of civil society organisations to regulate business behaviour through naming and shaming is becoming more powerful.The techniques are many and range from misapplied ethical investment, shoddy reputation indexes, stakeholder dialogue with interlopers, to outright scaremongering aimed to cause maximum damage to corporate brand names.

Some concepts of the corporation are so misguided, they regard the corporation as no more than a process for grievance-settlement in society. For example, One of the most significant things that companies could do to make themselves good 'stakeholder corporations' is to ensure they give ... rights to external review, to stakeholders (and stakeholder groups) with legitimate complaints about the company. The right to access justice—to be able to make claims against individuals and institutions in order to advance *shared ideals of social and political life* [my emphasis] and to rectify relations that have gone wrong— is an essential part of citizenship in a contemporary democracy.Further, We are unnecessarily constrained by the belief that the representative institutions and legal system of the state should be the exclusive or even the primary, home of political deliberation.

These ideas challenge the corporation and the role it has fulfilled in the modern capitalist economy, indeed even in the highly state-regulated modern capitalist economy. Some as 'socialism regards the view that all stakeholders have prima facie an entitlement to a managerial role in a corporation by another name'.Indeed, a problem with CSR, in particular stakeholder theory, is the difficulty of adjudicating between not only the demands of stakeholders who have a contractual relationship with the corporation, but those who do not.

All corporations accept the need to deal with traditional stakeholders, and the law provides the means of settling disputes with each. CSR invites two further impositions. First, it counts as a stakeholder anyone who wants a piece of a corporation. To paraphrase one manager's view, 'a stakeholder is anyone who can do you damage.' Second, it attacks the very purpose of the corporation - its commercial relationship with the market and its owners.

One of the prominent techniques of civil society regulation of corporations is the assault on corporate reputations. Corporate reputations are a serious business, and corporations strive hard to ensure that their reputation is maintained in the best condition. Presumably they do so because it is a component of business success. Which component is difficult to ascertain. Indeed an entire academic journal, the *Corporate Reputation Review*, is devoted to that question. The rationale for the interest in reputation measurement is, it appears, because reputation 'is a growing factor in maintaining corporate competitive advantage'.'

Apparently, because factors such as 'media congestion' and 'fragmentation' and 'the appearance of ever more vocal constituencies'make it so. These factors place pressure on corporations to differentiate themselves from their competitors and to examine their actions and 'stakeholder perceptions' of them. If one accepts such reasons, then it follows that, '[t]o be managed, corporate reputations must be measured'.An example of reputation manipulation is the [Australian] Good Reputation Index, which was published by *The Age* and *The Sydney Morning Herald* newspapers in 2000, 2001 and 2002.

The Index purported to examine, 'through the perceptions of community stakeholders and experts', the ability of the top 100 corporations operating in Australia,to manage those activities 'which directly contribute to their reputations as socially responsible organisations'.In fact, the Index does no such thing. The Index begins with preferred definitions of goodness and expands these, for example by measuring financial performance, to capture the whole reputation of a corporation and labelling the result 'social responsibility'.

In establishing the Index, Reputation Measurement argued that 'there is increasing evidence to suggest that companies seeking to demonstrate their worthiness as *socially responsible* organisations are most successful when they widen their traditional business *stakeholder* base to include community stakeholders.' Further, '[i]nvestors and consumers are increasingly making decisions based on longer-term issues linked to a company's capacity to contribute to a *sustainable* future for all.'In other words, the Reputation Index is an instrument for advancing a number of political agendas: corporate social responsibility, stakeholder capitalism, and sustainability.

The notion of corporate social responsibility suggests a relationship between, for example, a corporation's output and the community's perception of whether a corporation does good work in the community. The suggestion is seductive, it suggests a parallel between corporate reputation and democracy. There are two parts to the seduction.

First, in a democracy the electorate votes on the basis of performance and perception of performance. Perception may belie actual performance. Corporations that cannot rely on actual performance alone to make business gains may have to rely on the perception of performance. Unlike the politician, however, the corporation is selling a more welldefined product than the 'competence to govern'. The political consumer is far less able to make up their mind on whether to purchase, than the corporate consumer who can do so simply on the basis of a product or service. Nor do governments come with a moneyback guarantee! Perceptions no doubt play a role in corporate reputations, but they are hard pressed to overcome the more readily measured commercial performance and compliance with legislative and contractual obligations.

Second, the eligibility to vote for corporate performance is far more restricted than universal adult suffrage. And so it should be. Those with a real interest in a corporation are not the community at large but particular individuals who have a specific relationship with the business. Each of these individuals and groups will make their assessment on whether to purchase from the company, work for it, work with it or invest in it. They will do so less on the basis of a broad 'competence to govern' than on factors such as price, quality, wages, prompt payment and rates of return on investment.

In a democracy, the rules by which corporations carry out their activities are set by consensus. The consensus determines rules across a very wide spectrum of financial and non-financial criteria, but it determines not so much what is good, but what is and what is not, acceptable behaviour. The law also provides penalties for unacceptable behaviour. The Index, on the other hand, is an exercise among civil society activists who wish to appropriate the resources of corporations for their own purposes. It has little to do with corporate goodness, it has a lot to do with increasing the power of NGOs to impose their agendas, which include the appropriation of property (corporate reputation) and the further regulation of corporations.

The Index is extraordinarily arrogant in its assumptions about knowing what is good. It is possible to measure corporate performance so as to enable those interested to assess whether and how they will deal with a corporation. But 'measures' of reputation by groups (some of whom have an adversarial relationship), and others who seek a commercial relationship with the corporations, is at best subjective.

To produce a single figure of which corporation is good and by implication, which corporation is bad, is heroic. Although each research group disclosed its direct relationship to a corporation, it was reported that some of the research groups had touted for work by offering their services to corporations in filling out the questionnaire. These approaches were not disclosed.

Goodness, when not defined in a consensual manner, is an act of rent-seeking. No amount of moralising about goodness has been known to revive a commercially unviable corporation. When a corporation ceases to exist, it does so because it can no longer pursue its intended commercial objectives. Without the commercial objectives

– and these may include profits, growth, and market share—there is no possibility of pursuing good corporate citizenship. Goodness cannot be allowed to threaten the commercial viability of a corporation. On the other hand, 'acceptable behaviour', when based on a widespread political consensus is less likely to interfere with the real contribution that corporations make to society.

Stakeholder theory suggests a model of the corporation in which all interests in an enterprise compete to obtain benefits from the enterprise, but that none has a priority. This simple proposition is very confronting, because it is in effect posing the question, 'in whose interests should the enterprise be run?'It also assumes that society grants an enterprise the right to exist.

Those whose business it is to advise corporations on social responsibility are fond of arguing that corporations have a license to operate in the community. This is accurate at one level only, the community through its law-makers may grant licenses and certain privileges in return for the enterprise complying with the law, and it does not license the activities of stakeholders at large to impose their views on the corporation.

Nor does the theory satisfactorily answer the question of who, or what, produces economic value. Instead 'its focus is on the distribution of outcomes, the harms and benefits, and not on who produced the harms and benefits. It assumes value is produced by the enterprise itself and that stakeholders have a claim on some of this value because the enterprise is a creature of society.'It radically overturns the social contract for business that includes obligations to obey the law, honour contracts and agreements and respect the rights of others. It ignores the fact that economic value is produced by owners who make their savings available to other member of society to put them to use in productive ways. The owners have an exclusive moral claim to the benefits produced by their activities, as others have a moral claim for the benefits produced by their labour or other contracted services.

Those with a contractual relationship with the corporation have rights. The breach of contract with a supplier, the dangerous product sold to the consumer, the accident that befalls the worker, the investor who is misled by a prospectus - each is entitled to pursue the corporation for the recovery of losses. Indeed, the corporation can also pursue any of these individuals for breaches of agreement or misrepresentation and so on.

Ultimately, the managers on behalf the owners are responsible for all of these actions. Poor management may result in losses all around - workers lose jobs, suppliers lose contracts, investors lose money. But only the owners through the managers decide the nature of the enterprise, its purpose and direction. Whom they choose to deal with and how, within the bounds of law and custom, are matters for them. Which is not to say that 'stakeholders' will not have a say, but only in the course of settling matters to the satisfaction of the owners. To assume that everyone starts with an equal say is to assume there is no ownership. There is a suspicion that this is precisely the assumption underlying stakeholder theory, the denial of the rights of ownership.

A second strand of stakeholder theory focuses less on equating the interests of stakeholders with shareholders, and more on their ethical treatment. This means that stakeholders, employees, customers, suppliers, owners, financiers and the community should be treated fairly and justly.This thinking is consistent with those who regard the corporation as no more than a process for grievance-settlement in society.

There is no current case law or provision that requires directors to take into account the interests of stakeholders, or the sometimes touted concept of 'the interests of the corporation as a whole'.While there is no prohibition on directors from considering other interests they can only do so provided there is a prospect of commercial advantage for the company.

One of the principle dangers of stakeholder theory is that managers who can claim to be serving the general interests of society in the name of the public good can invoke it. Such claims are not within the powers of managers. Only those with a mandate from the public – politicians - can make such claims, and they only do so cautiously, in the knowledge that if they do so wrongly, they will be punished.

Sustainability refers to ecological sustainability, and ecological sustainability is premised on the notion of limits to growth, based on limits to resources. It argues that natural resources are becoming scarcer. It ignores the history of technological innovation, often promoted by competition between corporations, and that such innovation has extended physical resources in ways untold. In fact, judged by price, physical resources are becoming more abundant over time. For example, the environment category of the Index contains questions about the level of corporate electricity and water consumption.

It is highly unlikely that conservation and/or recycling will assist in any problems that arise from some future shortage of these resources. Pricing for externalities or to take full account of infrastructure costs is sensible, but pricing for conservation is very unlikely to produce sensible choices among alternatives. The solution to the so-called limits to resources will be found in technological innovation.

One obvious innovation with clear and positive implications for resource use is genetic engineering in food production. Unfortunately, the issue is raised in the questionnaire in such a way that it carries the clear implication that this is environmentally harmful. There are questions as well about greenhouse gas emissions, but elsewhere about nuclear energy production, also with the clear inference that this is forbidden. The environmental agenda is not broadly shared, nor without controversy, it assumes no trade-offs and that abstinence rather than adaptation or innovation is the cure.

The questions in the Index are based on an ahistorical view of sustainability. They represent a very narrow concept of sustainability, an insular and frozen view of human ingenuity. One of the main principles of sustainable development is intergenerational equity, the achievement of which assumes that this generation knows the needs of future generations. Conserving what are considered resources today does not ensure the future is secure, and using them today does not necessarily mean that tomorrow is in jeopardy.

Petroleum was not considered a resource 150 years ago, but today it is vital. Consider the following conundrum, if the choice to draw down resources is held exclusively by future generations, then we, being the future generations of previous generations, have been deprived of that right. Does it make sense for us to condemn our ancestors, who were poorer and much less secure than we are, for using resources to support themselves? Does sustainable development really imply that no generation has the right to use resources, no matter how urgent their needs will be?

Sustainability is just one stream in a more general assault based on public policy advice. For example, the fundamental aim of science and social science has generally been that of explanation. Now, commonly, it is advocacy. Science is too often abused in the public arena, and too many intellectuals in the social sciences and humanities have given up all pretence to rational explanation.

Elizabeth Whelan, President of the American Council on Science and Health remarked last February, 'science – today and every day – is under assault.'The assailants are members of the media, trial lawyers, self-appointed consumer-activists, and environmentalists who constantly promote the fear of health hazards. She concentrates on health topics, but the comments are applicable to whole range of public policy and science.

The example given is the ongoing regulatory dispute over PCBs, synthetic chemicals used, because of their insulating, flame-retardant nature, as coolants and lubricants in transformers and other electrical equipment. Dr Whelan argues that any review of the scientific literature will reveal that PCBs at high dose are toxic and carcinogenic in rodents, and that no human study - including workers who were very heavily exposed, and individuals, including pregnant women, who ate substantial amounts of fish with measurable levels of PCBs - has ever shown any major significant long-term negative health effects.

Regardless, the Environmental Protection Agency is compelling General Electric to spend more than $500 million to remove PCBs from the Hudson River. The EPA states that it wants to prevent cancer. Even the National Cancer Institute concedes it knows of no evidence that eating fish from a PCB-contaminated river contributes to the toll of cancer in the United States.

Scientists find it difficult to counter the anti-scientific policy. Most do not feel comfortable in the public arena and they have no real clue about how to go about challenging what they read and see. In cases where scientists have stepped forward to debunk the "carcinogen scare de jour", they have been subject to ad hominem attacks and labeled "paid liars" for industry.

Science has become so very specialized, that the overwhelming portion of scientists has very narrow areas of expertise. Those with a Ph.D. in entomology, biology, veterinary medicine, or physics might possibly be as duped as the average citizen. The consequences of the silence of the scientific community, which is interpreted as assent, are profound. It distorts health risks, threatens innovation, and jobs.

The abuse and misuse of science is not, of course confined to NGOs, they have some powerful support in the academe. Literary and cultural theorists, poststructuralists, postmodernists, radical feminists, black separatists, Afrocentrists, deep ecologists and animal liberationists are making the assaults on science.These assaults have in some cases gone much further than mere verbiage. They include censorship of books and conference papers, re-writing or banning school textbooks, obstruction of research funding, incessant vexatious lawsuits, sabotage and raids on laboratories, not to mention death threats and assaults on some scientists who have refused to be cowed by their critics.

The origins of much of this extraordinary assault stems from 'science studies', which are inquiries into the nature of science. People in the field have not been scientists per se but sociologists of science, historians of science, philosophers of scientific method and, most recently, people who engage in cultural studies of science. In other words, rather than a province of the physical sciences themselves, science studies are a domain within the humanities and social sciences.The field was designed to impart some understanding of science to students taking arts degrees and to encourage those learning science to reflect on the intellectual and social implications of their field, and the study of the development and social impact of science.

Government-NGOs Co-operation

Each year, Australian NGOs raise approximately $150 million directly from the Australian public. This support is from members of the general community and from Australian corporations. In recognition of the importance of NGOs as development partners, multilateral organisations have increased their support for NGOs. By 1997, NGOs - or community-based organisations - participated in almost half of all World Bank projects.

United Nations organisations also deliver considerable proportions of their programs through NGOs. However, the Government remains the largest single contributor to the Australian development NGO community. In 1999-2000, total Government assistance to Australian NGOs, through NGO-specific mechanisms, is expected to be around $80 million; funding for international NGOs will bring the total to around $105 million.

The objective of the Australian aid program is to advance Australia's national interest by assisting developing countries to reduce poverty and achieve sustainable development. Bilateral partnerships with developing countries are at the core of Australia's aid program. Through consultation, Australia can tailor aid efforts to the needs of the partner country and ensure that Australia's aid meets its objective.

Bilateral programs are able to incorporate a wide range of activities: sector programs, scholarships, technical assistance, supply of equipment and commodities, food aid, and NGO programs. The Australian Government works with both the partner government and with a variety of different groups to implement aid activities. Australian public sector agencies, private companies, educational institutions and NGOs all play an active role in the aid program. Multilateral and regional organisations are also important development partners for Australia.

The Government can broaden the impact of the Australian aid program beyond our region by working with them at the policy level as well as through development projects. By creating stronger partnerships with international organisations, Australia also contributes to donor coordination. The magnitude of development challenges requires an effective Australian aid program to improve the lives of those in greatest need. To meet these challenges, the Government chooses to work with organisations that have most to contribute, discerning between different actors in the development field.

By working with effective NGOs, the Government aims to achieve quality aid outcomes and to extend the reach of the aid program to the communities with which NGOs work. The Government and NGOs share some objectives, including the reduction of poverty and the promotion of sustainable development. While the methods and priorities of NGOs and the Government are not always the same, the common goals of the Government and NGOs mean the relationship can be productive.

There are a number of different dimensions to the Government's relationship with NGOs. The Government is a source of funds for NGOs, contracting them to carry out specific activities. The Government also supports NGOs in aspects of their work that match the objective of the aid program. By engaging in robust dialogue from different perspectives, the Government and NGOs can enhance aid policy. Both the Government and NGOs aim to improve the quality of their aid and to ensure that the Australian community supports Australian aid.

Australian government may decide that bilateral assistance is not appropriate. Before the end of apartheid, as part of a campaign to bring about change in South Africa, the Australian Government restricted much of its relationship with the South African Government. The restrictions included withholding bilateral aid. However, part of the Government's policy to assist South Africa included support for the work of NGOs. Under the Government's South Africa NGO program, priority was given to education and training. A number of NGOs assisted by providing training in areas such as agriculture, health, and education.

A number of AusAID's bilateral programs have funds specifically earmarked for NGOs through country-specific NGO schemes. These funding opportunities recognise the value of NGOs as service deliverers, contracting them to deliver particular aspects of the aid program. Proposals submitted by NGOs are assessed on a competitive basis.

Emergency and Rehabilitation activities: NGOs are able to apply for rehabilitation funding through a series of country- or region-specific rounds. As in Country Programs, only NGOs that submit competitive proposals will be funded. The Government also often funds NGOs to undertake emergency relief activities.

The purpose of the AusAID-NGO Cooperation Program (ANCP) is to support development activities initiated by NGOs that contribute to poverty alleviation. Under this scheme, the Government supplements funds provided by the community, thereby increasing the effectiveness of NGO activities. In 1999-2000 funding under this scheme will increase to $24.2 million. Funding for volunteer sending agencies brings the total to $36.3 million. NGOs can also access commercial funding. To be hired as a contractor NGOs must compete in a tender process and deliver outcomes in accordance with the contract.

Government-accredited NGOs may have expertise and experience in different forms of aid delivery including broad community development, and specific sectoral activities such as maternal and child health. Others have developed the ability to respond rapidly to emergency situations. They also often use their strong links in developing countries to effectively engage local communities in development activities. The Government recognises that in these situations, NGOs can make a practical contribution to quality aid outcomes.

NGOs bring different perspectives to policy dialogue. Where their experience and expertise is relevant, the Government values their input. In addition, the Government acknowledges the important role many NGOs play as channels for expressing community interests in overseas development. Forums for Government-NGO policy dialogue operate at a range of levels. A key mechanism for dialogue is the Committee for Development Cooperation (CDC). Established in 1974, the CDC is a joint consultative body, which draws representatives from NGOs, AusAID and the peak body for NGOs working in overseas aid, the Australian Council for Overseas Aid (ACFOA).

Through the CDC debate is stimulated on policy issues, NGO accreditation and the operation of NGO programs. In addition to regular forums, the Government consults NGOs with specialist expertise in specific countries or sectors. When developing strategies for the aid program in individual countries, the Government may seek the views of NGOs which have well-established links in that country. Similarly, the Government engages in policy discussions with NGOs with specialist knowledge on sectoral issues such as gender, environment, education and human rights.

Furthermore, representatives from the NGO community, in their personal capacity, are represented on the Minister for Foreign Affairs' Aid Advisory Council. The Council discusses key aid policy issues. The Government must ensure that the Australian aid program delivers maximum benefits to the communities it assists in developing countries. Understanding the impact of Australian aid delivered through NGOs enables both the Government and NGOs to determine what works and what doesn't. Aid is delivered in a changing environment, and in a range of different cultures. As a result, the definition of 'quality aid' is constantly evolving.

The Government and NGOs must continually assess their activities in terms of quantity and quality of achievements, then improve their work to ensure that the aid delivered is effective in achieving its objectives. The Government and NGOs need to know more about the performance of activities. The Australian Government has made performance information an integral part of its public sector reform agenda. Performance information is about results. The introduction of accrual-based outcome and output budgeting will also enable a sharper focus on the results achieved through the aid program. These changes will affect all of AusAID's implementing partners, including NGOs. Assessing performance information will help the Government and NGOs to begin to gauge impact and to improve both accountability and quality.

Through its accreditation of NGOs, the Government has worked to ensure effective accounting of inputs. To date, accreditation has assessed NGOs' management systems, but improved performance information will mean outcomes can be included. The next challenge is to broaden the accreditation model to include an assessment of NGO performance in the field.

The Government expects NGOs' systems to give them the ability to measure their own performance. In addition, the Government will expand the number of cluster evaluations of NGO projects to allow NGO self-reported performance to be compared with that of their peers. Quality aid outcomes are also, in part, dependent on the local community's commitment to the development activity. The Government recognises NGOs' ethos of engaging local communities and values the ways they promote participation. Through their strong links with communities in developing countries and partnerships with local organisations, NGOs are well placed to build the capacity of local groups. They thereby strengthen civil society, create a better environment for development activities and increase the potential for longer-term impacts.

In 1995, the Government and NGOs worked together to ensure that NGOs receiving Government funding were both accountable and capable. To access Government funding, NGOs are now rigorously assessed for accreditation. To ensure the quality of Australian aid, the Government must discern among different partners and NGOs. A system of accreditation gives the Government and the Australian public confidence that NGOs receiving funding are professional, accountable for funding, able to manage well, community-based in Australia,work with local partners in-country, and deliver quality development outcomes.

Another way in which the Government discerns between organisations on the basis of quality is through competition. While all accredited NGOs have access to funding through the ANCP, funding through other sources is determined on a competitive basis. NGOs whose projects have the greatest potential to achieve a significant and positive impact are more likely to gain Government support.

The NGO sector also continues to work to ensure quality standards are maintained. A Code of Conduct was developed to address NGOs' governance, integrity, management and communication with the public. A Code of Conduct Committee, comprised of NGO representatives, deals with complaints and compliance issues. All NGOs receiving funding must now sign the Australian Council for Overseas Aid (ACFOA) Code of Conduct. In Stakeholders: Government-NGO partnerships for international development, the Australian NGO Code of Conduct is cited as a model for NGO best practice. In addition, NGOs receiving Australian Government funding for disaster relief must adhere to the Code of Conduct for the International Red Cross and Red Crescent Movement and Non-Governmental Organizations in Disaster Relief.

NGOs are well placed to act as a link between the Australian community and those communities being assisted by Australian aid overseas. NGOs can also give aspects of the Australian aid program a strong Australian identity. The Government recognises the potential for NGOs to engage the community on aid issues and will work with NGOs as part of its aid communications strategy. While the Government already works with NGOs as part of its efforts to increase the awareness of aid issues, it is important that efforts to increase public awareness are strategic, creative, well targeted and coordinated.

To increase support for aid the Government and NGOs must promote a broader and deeper public understanding of the nature and consequences of poverty, by engaging members of the public beyond the traditional supporters of NGOs. A deeper understanding of aid issues, and greater community support can, in turn, improve the effectiveness of Australian aid. As a community-based organisation, an NGO is accountable to its members.

Public accountability is most effective when the public understands development assistance and the context in which NGOs work. Recognising the importance of public accountability, the Government gives priority to funding the work of organisations that demonstrate strong community support for their activities. Currently, the Government measures community support by the amount of funding each NGO raises in donations from the Australian public. However, there are many different ways for individuals, groups and organisations to be involved in overseas aid.

The Government is committed to developing additional measures of community support that recognise effective strategies for promoting greater community involvement. The Government will develop these measures in consultation with the NGO community.

In recent years, private corporations have become increasingly involved in overseas aid. Their roles vary, as they are both providers of goods and services as part of the aid program, and donors to NGOs. The interest of corporations in overseas aid may represent the values of their employees or shareholders, or may be an expression of their interests in developing communities with which they work. Corporations have also begun to work with NGOs.

In some instances NGOs and corporations may have common interests. There is also an increasing recognition of the distinct, often complementary, skills of NGOs and corporations which, when combined, may result in improved development outcomes. For decades, the Government and NGOs have worked together to deliver quality aid. With major reforms to the NGO program in recent years, the Government has aimed to achieve greater transparency and a streamlined program with professional standards.

The Government and NGOs have come a long way toward achieving these aims. Generic guidelines for NGO schemes have ensured greater consistency and fairness. The establishment of an effective accreditation system has increased confidence in NGO accountability. Reforms have enabled both Government and NGOs to increase their professionalism in aid delivery. The challenge now is to ensure that reforms result in the continuous improvement of aid outcomes.

Australian Non Government Organisations (NGOs) as part of AusAID's NGO accreditation risk management cycle and response to the recommendations of the NGO audit reports of the Australian National Audit Office (ANAO). The NGO cluster evaluations serve important accountability and learning functions for both AusAID and the NGOs. The first evaluation was of NGO projects in Vietnam.Africa was chosen as the location for the second evaluation because of the relative size and importance of the NGO program in the overall Africa program and because it offers a representative spread of NGOs involved in development projects both through Country Windows and the ANCP.

All of the Australian NGOs concerned are fully accredited with AusAID. The report includes many generalisations about the performance of Australian funded NGO projects in Africa based on the seven projects. Although the cluster evaluation approach is credible and relatively cost efficient, there are limitations, principally related to the representativeness of the sample in each case and the depth of the analysis. As well, a number of the projects evaluated were designed prior to AusAID introducing enhanced performance, management and operational standards which are now used to assess the performance of bilateral projects and programs.

The NGO community, through the Committee for Development Cooperation (CDC) and other forums, has been informed of the outcomes of the evaluation so that lessons learned can be utilised by both NGOs and AusAID to improve more widely program performance and reporting. The main objectives of NGO cluster evaluations are to provide an independent assessment of NGO project performance in the field and anticipated development impact and to verify the selfassessments provided by

NGOs to AusAID. Thus the NGO cluster evaluations serve important accountability and learning functions for both AusAID and the NGOs.

NGOs in Planning and Development

In India, Non-Governmental Organisations (NGOs) are not formally responsible for implementing plans they are often found to be actively involved in the implementation process. Pune, located near Mumbai is a major software industrial centre of India. The Pune Municipal Corporation (PMC) is the body responsible for implementing the city's plan. While PMC is expected to prepare the plan, it sends the plan for approval to the State Government of Maharashtra. It is only after the latter approves the plan that PMC implements it.

Informants included NGOs, planners, commercial developers, citizens, politicians, bureaucrats, academics, media, architects, engineers, landowners, bank employees, and industrialists. PMC has taken up very few plan proposals for implementation. In order to examine the role of NGOs in the implementation process it is necessary to focus on proposals where at least some action has been taken towards implementation.

The following issues explain why and when NGOs are likely to intervene in the implementation process of the plan. The framework also helps to analyze factors that influence the impact of NGO's intervention in the implementation process.

NGOs may be involved in the implementation of particular proposals and not in others. This may be explained in terms of the mission and concerns of these NGOs. For instance, an organization that is concerned primarily with green belts is likely to be involved in proposals related to them than in proposals related to issues like mass transport.

Resources may include finance, skills, time, information, contacts, and rapport with different sections of the society. It is not uncommon for resources to be inadequate and this limitation may restrain the intervention of NGOs in plan implementation. Not only are resources likely to determine the selection of proposals but also the manner and the duration with which NGOs would participate in the implementation process. After achieving their immediate objective in relation to a proposal, a NGO may turn to other issues. After NGOs withdraw from the scene, events may take a direction very different from that desired by NGOs.

Along with resources, the time span of projects also influence whether NGOs may intervene in implementation. If implementation of a proposal is to take a long time, then it is likely that NGOs might not be keen in getting involved in the proposal.

Moreover, there might be certain proposals that directly affect a NGO or its constituency. A proposal to build a highway running close to the location of a NGO is most likely to evoke an immediate response from the organization.

Implementing a plan is the responsibility of the municipal body. Yet, NGOs might intervene in the implementation process not because they see it as their responsibility but because they disagree with actions of the municipal body. For instance, a municipal body might seek to modify a plan proposal and this may be resented by NGOs. The latter then might try to stop the municipal body from taking the action.

The strength of NGOs lies in its mobilization efforts. This no doubt would depend on the resources available with NGOs but also on how convincing is the argument put forth by NGOs. The argument in turn would depend on the kind and extent of benefits offered by the proposal. If a proposal promises benefits to a large number of people and if this is threatened by change proposed by some actors, then NGOs have a strong argument while mobilizing citizens against the change.

The role of NGOs also depends on relevant planning legislation. If a planning legislation provides for the participation of the public in the preparing and implementation of a plan, then NGOs are likely to take this opportunity. However, much depends on whether a planning legislation is followed in spirit. Moreover, in order that NGOs and individuals participate effectively in the process it is important that they receive the relevant information in time from the political authorities.

Pune is a city where presence of numerous NGOs have been felt, and NGOs here have been active in fields ranging from child care to urban development. These NGOs are Pune based and are concerned primarily with environmental and developmental issues. Convenors of these organizations are highly educated, vocal, and well-known personalities in the city. These NGOs had been earlier involved in similar development issues in Pune.

Several activities took place prior to 28 March 1990, when the proposal was to be voted upon in the General Assembly of the PMC. NGOs that had been active in stopping the deletion of the reservation have moved on to other issues. The number of slums on the site has gone up over the years.

Hills are a central characteristic of Pune, and cover an area of 913.70 hectares of land within the jurisdiction of PMC. Around 41% of these hills are privately owned. Planners have reserved hills for recreation and afforestation and construction is not allowed on them. Hill owners have repeatedly requested PMC and the State Government to get the reservation deleted. In 1993, PMC claimed that it did not have the funds to acquire hills, neither the capacity to prevent slums from encroaching upon them. PMC proposed to the State Government that construction not beyond 4% Floor Space Index be allowed on the hills for recreational purposes like "swimming pools, sports and games centres, health clubs, cafeteria, canteens and amusement parks" on the hills.

The State Government approved the proposal on 5 June 1997 - four years after receiving it. However, the State Government soon revised its decision. Just three weeks after sanctioning PMC's proposal, the State Government directed PMC to permit not 5% but 20% construction upon hills for residential purposes. According to this directive, PMC had to publish the notification within sixty days of the directive being issued. The PMC Commissioner was reported to have opposed the directive of the State Government.

This decision of the State Government to permit 20% residential construction was vehemently opposed by NGOs (ECONET, Parisar, Social Civic & Environmental Forum, Vanarai, etc). While planners had preserved the hills for the benefit of citizens in general, the State Government's proposed change would further the interests of developers and landowners at the cost of the city's environment. Moreover, there were slums on some of the hills.

NGOs also resented the manner in which the State Government had proposed higher construction on the hills. On such a vital issue, the State Government had not thought it necessary to consult citizens. Nor did it think necessary to explain its position by holding a press conference. Instead, the State Government had gone ahead with the procedure of inviting objections from the public without clarifying why it had proposed 20% residential construction.

NGOs mobilised the PMC and citizens against the notification sought by State Government. They wrote articles in the newspapers, held workshops to inform people about the repercussions of permitting construction, and mobilised people to file their objections to the modification of the proposal. The Express Citizens Forum took the State Government to Court in 1998, challenging State Government's notification while the officer concerned was receiving objections and suggestions from the public.

The counsel for this forum argued that the State Government was proceeding towards permitting construction on the hills without telling people why it was needed and what public interest it pursued. In response, the Counsel for the State Government was reported to have stated that it was not required of the Government to make such clarifications while inviting objections and suggestion. The proposal also came under criticism in the Legislative Assembly of Maharashtra. The Chief Minister stated that the State Government would not go ahead with the decision if the citizens of Pune were against it.

On 7 October, 1998 the Chief Minister announced that the proposed modification to allow development on the hills of Pune for residential use had been stalled. The Chief Minister told newspaper reporters that the State

Government had arrived at this decision "after taking serious note of the objections filed by citizens and environmentalists in the city".

NGOs had therefore once more succeeded in stopping changes to proposals. Respondents have mentioned that probably this is more of a temporary gesture on part of the State Government which has come under severe criticism for its actions in the recent past to delete reservations. The Gove rnment probably thought it better to keep a low profile for some time.

Yet, NGOs intervened only after original proposals were threatened by modifications. NGOs had probably thought that it would take them a long time to get PMC initiate implementation on proposals that have been lying on paper for years. By contrast, stopping attempts of 17 the PMC and the State Government to alter proposals was probably thought not to take all that time. The time span of plan proposal may be said to have influenced the response of NGOs.

Moreover, in both the cases involvement of NGOs was largely inspired by action of other actors (developers, landlords, PMC, State Government) - actions that were related to the proposal. These actors were trying to change the proposal and NGOs intervened to stop them.

NGOs had succeeded in their initiative and that was possible on account of its mobilization efforts. They had successfully convinced citizens to participate and oppose the authorities who were trying to change the proposal. The organizations were helped in their endeavour by the type of benefits offered by the proposal viz. collective benefits offered by original proposals. Collective benefits helped NGOs to convincingly argue that modification of proposals would deprive these benefits to the citizens and adversely affect their health, recreation, and environment. This in turn helped NGOs in mobilising support of citizens and seek cooperation of the media.

Media emerged as an important actor. It no doubt provided information to NGOs about attempts at modification, but more than that NGOs emerged as a key partner of these organizations. The Indian Express particularly its development forum, the Express Citizens' Forum had teamed with the NGOs against the attempts to change the proposal. This partnership proved particularly beneficial for NGOs. It is uncommon for 18 newspapers to persistently cover a particular news item for long. However, in this case the Indian Express had covered the two cases on a prolonged basis. This coverage in turn helped NGOs to reach out to the masses.

In its mobilization efforts, NGOs were also helped by the reputation of their respective leadership. Leaders of these organizations are well known names in the city. Moreover, these NGOs have been active in Pune for quite some time and people have seen them perform. The past experience of NGOs helped them in choosing their strategics. Mobilizing the Central Government although city planning is beyond its jurisdiction is a case in point. The past experience of NGOs also seemed to have influenced State Government's decision to withdraw from 20% FSI construction on hills. Leadership and past experience of NGOs that have influenced the response of NGOs need to be incorporated into the framework.

4

NGOs and Global Governance

In view of the adoption of decentralist policies in many developing countries, many development practitioners warned of the possible capture of the local governments by oligarchs and political elite. To minimize such a possibility and its adverse impact on local development, various governance reform measures have been proposed. Some of these measures are intended to upgrade the technical, financial and managerial capacity of local governments to deliver basic services, while other measures facilitate greater democratic participation, through the people's direct involvement in various public project activities.

Increasingly, both types of measures are already directly built into the various local intervention programs of national government agencies, donor organizations and international civil society groups. While the design features of the various governance reform initiatives have been widely analyzed, their implementation schemes however have received lesser attention from development practitioners and policymakers.

One critical aspect of the policy implementation is the choice, inducement and monitoring of the agent of the reform initiative. The engagement or employ of an agent is often necessary for two reasons. First, the principal or proponent of the intervention program – which may be a national government agency, donor agency or another civil society organization – cannot permanently transfer to the area. More importantly, perhaps, the involvement of local agents is meant to develop a sense of local ownership and empowerment, thus ensuring the sustainability and effectiveness of the program.

However, there are many potential agents in a locality, ranging from the local government itself or its sub-units and departments to civil society groups like nongovernment organizations, people's organizations, cooperatives, and business or civic groups. While some of these potential agents conform to certain stereotypes, still, for most of these entities no easy generalizations can be made about their characters and likely performances. Part of the reason is the dearth of comparative analyses of their behaviors, performances or actions.

Civil society permits the elaboration of a legitimate state (or governance) structure by limiting the scope of that structure and by encouraging or facilitating political engagement and mutual solidarity by otherwise alienated individuals. Civil society, then, acts as a mediator between the citizen and the state: it is 'a sphere of dynamic and responsive public discourse between the state, the public sphere consisting of voluntary organizations, and the market sphere concerning private firms and unions'.

The rebirth of interest in civil society in European political and academic life has two main causes. First, the revolutions which swept Central and Eastern Europe in

1989, which at the time were broadly read as the triumph of civil society over oppressive Communist regimes. Second, the twin phenomena in the Western part of the continent of the advent of 'new social movements'(NSMs) devoted to the forging of social change and broader societal solidarity, and the contemporaneous neoliberal project of 'rolling back the state'.

The Europeanisation of civil society - its increased role in governance at the European level, and its adoption of an explicitly European dimension - has risen up the agenda as a potential part of the solution to the notorious 'democratic deficit'. As was the case for EU citizenship, civil society can be represented as part of polity-development in both neoliberal (market-driven) and social democratic terms: as a necessary complement to the internal market and as a means to redress the underdevelopment of social policy at the EU level.

Thus, while they differ about the kind of civil society they wish to see at the European/EU level, most actors appear to agree that a greater role for civil society must be a central feature of European governance in the future. Europeanising civil society potentially offers the means to facilitate greater accountability of, and engagement with, the EU institutions, and encourage at least some sense of solidarity between the nationals of the various member states.

The echoes of the neofunctionalist dilemma when seeking non-institutional cultivators of spillover are obvious. There are limits to what even favourably-disposed national governments can do, because they are formal institutions and, interdependence notwithstanding, territorially defined. The institutions of the EU are similarly incapacitated, mired in the ongoing crisis of the 'democratic deficit' despite what have often been significant reforms, such as the gradual empowerment of the European Parliament.

As preliminary steps, the EU must: repeatedly deliver significant public goods which are valued by the citizen; more closely match its competences with those the public considers appropriate for transnational governance; and offer more frequent, and more useful, opportunities for political participation by the individual. Moreover, to facilitate the Europeanisation of civil society, the EU requires a set of actors from outside official circles to demonstrate the value of engaging with EU decision making processes, and commence, or, more optimistically, to continue, the process of transnational solidarity-generation through the construction of cross-border supporter bases.

In this respect, attention is increasingly being paid to non-governmental organisations (NGOs) such as Greenpeace, BEUC (the European Consumers Union Bureau) and Action Aid as potential catalysts of change. At first sight, this is surprising. In general, interest groups have regarded Europeanisation of their own activities and policy areas instrumentally, mobilising to secure their objectives or in response to enticements by the Commission rather than out of 'European' zeal.

Relations between the NGO community and the Commission are by no means always cordial. By its current practice of providing funding for selected NGOs, the Commission risks undermining their autonomy and their suitability as mechanisms of voice for the otherwise disenfranchised. The Europeanisation of civil society is an enormous task, and one which is clearly beyond the scope of any individual NGO, even should it have such an outcome as its declared objective.

Given that NGOs operating in Brussels are by no means predisposed to collaborate regularly even when they work in the same policy sector, this is a significant problem. Moreover, since NGOs are sectoral in their interests there is a clear limit to their ability to claim general representativity - compared with political parties, for example, their scope is narrower even if their memberships are often far greater.

Additionally, although they can be influential in shaping individual policy outcomes by helping construct the necessary 'policy coalitions', overall the ability of NGOs to influence EU policy output is less than that of commercial lobbyists thanks to their own resource problems and insufficient affirmative action by the EU institutions.

Nonetheless, when seen against the backdrop of the ongoing process of social evolution in the EU, the contribution of NGOs to the Europeanisation of civil society becomes less improbable. In terms of policy influence, given the differentiated nature of the EU's day-to-day functioning - its division into various fairly discrete governance regimes - actors with specialist knowledge and credibility may find their ability to shape policy outcomes is higher than would be the case at the rather more fully elaborated national level.

Beate Kohler-Koch argues that the mobilisation of different groups of actors within society is what will shape the development of the Euro-polity: '(b)y taking part in the common policy process, all kinds of actors help to shape the living constitution of the Union'. NGOs can in principle play their part in such a process just like any other group of actors. Furthermore, in terms of Union legitimacy, it must be remembered that the EU is caught up in an ongoing process of constitutionalisation, in which formal and informal elements of law and policy making combine to produce a shifting, rather than a fixed, outcome.

As an evolving system of 'network governance' shaped by 'various, functionally as well as territorially defined, units with overlapping membership', the EU is in need of actors with narrowly sectoral as well as general concerns.

In the area of development policy, NGOs have been given official recognition as contributors to the entrenchment, and even creation, of civil society. The UN and World Bank explicitly refer to NGOs as key actors in the process of constructing a new civil society in developing countries, and often impose conditionality on their donations of aid to bolster the role and authority of NGOs acting in such territories.

For 6 donor governments, NGOs can be a means of ensuring welfare policies are implemented without having to take an overt stance which could be seen to counter the official neoliberal policy. For the same reason, governments in developing countries can be favourably predisposed to NGOs - in their capacity as implementors of social and welfare policies, the latter ease the cost burden on governments, and also allow them to keep good faith in public with the economic policy requirements imposed on them by donor countries.

NGOs can be highly effective in this role, if they work collaboratively in their own sector and with other official and unofficial agencies. In fact, certain studies reveal that this successful collaboration can, at its best, produce a situation in which governments and NGOs are interdependent, with no evidence of a principal-agent dynamic. This is often the case in Africa, for example, since the cadres in both NGO and government communities often share similar backgrounds and education, as well as values.

NGOs can go further still; they can be responsible for the fostering and safe-keeping of civil society under a dictatorial regime. Looking beyond national borders, there is evidence to support the argument that NGOs could become at least co-shapers of a globalised civil society with the rise of protest at global level. In this analysis, NGOs may (after internal organisational reform) be the harbingers of a worldwide struggle to empower the '4world' (the disenfranchised in any country, developed or otherwise), as the north-south global divide becomes less apparent and the harmful effects of global capitalism become apparent everywhere.

Nonetheless, there are significant corollaries to be borne in mind. According to Covey, NGOs are at an immediate difficulty in comparison with other forms of organisation in that they need to satisfy two sets of accountability criteria: they must not just meet their stated aims but do so in a way which empowers members and clients, thereby reinforcing civil society. Thus, it is not enough for NGOs to be efficient - to justify their claims to difference and the promotion of alternative values, as well as the role in civil-society building which they have been allocated and claim, they must demonstrate quantifiable difference in the politicisation of their client/member group as a result of their work. Thus, the cognitive and affective impact of NGOs' work is at least as important as their practical success rates: existing merely as an efficient service provider is not enough, no matter how worthy the service. In this respect, development

NGOs' contribution to the reinforcement of civil society is rendered problematic since most of them are service providers, an unsurprising fact given the official justification of their role set out above.

The relationship between northern NGOs (NNGOs) and their partners in the South (SNGOs) is also open to question. Several writers have commented on many NNGOs' ability and will to allow SNGOs very little influence in their partnership; indeed, NNGOs often use the alleged failings of their Southern equivalents as an excuse to both ignore their own shortcomings and impose their own agendas on unwilling so-called partners. In addition to this it must be acknowledged that NGOs are often at their most effective when they dissemble, hiding their real motives and strategies under a cloak of adherence to official policy of either an international organisation or the host government.

However, such secrecy rules out internal accountability and also limits the impact of NGO measures upon the local client community, since civil society is unlikely to flourish in conditions of ignorance. Thus, effectiveness as a service provider may mean sacrificing attempts to build civil society and instead concentrating on improving material conditions in hope of an eventual multiplier effect. Such a delayed impact is unlikely: instead, in order to develop civil society in their client countries NGOs must overtly prioritise issues of political citizenship both for and amongst their target groups. Again, however, this is exactly what most development NGOs do not do.

Either through deliberate choice or through lack of viable alternatives, even the most well-intentioned NGOs find that they are merely tools in a project of rolling-back the state whose primary target is to secure economic growth by non-social democratic means. Thus, the very fact which legitimises NGOs' work in the eyes of international organisations and host governments is what makes their contribution to the entrenchment of civil society in those countries highly unlikely. Worse, such governments often use NGOs as part of a strategy to marginalise the sectors of society they most disfavour by promoting a bogus discourse of inclusionvia-NGOs which is in fact deliberately limited to only favoured groups.

Thus, through no fault of their own NGOs often find that they are doing the precise opposite of building civil society: they are reinforcing the power of the state at the expense of the most vulnerable within it, and aiding further social division. Moreover, NGOs can often be too eager to 'gap-fill', rushing to exploit seeming opportunities provided by lack of state provision which in fact stretch their resources and expertise too far: thus, evangelism leads to a no-win situation in which the state refuses to act and NGOs are incapable of doing so.

This lack of critical reflection about their own activities hampers NGOs in other ways, even if we restrict analysis to the issue of civil society formation. The fact that donors insist on conditionality means that NGOs are often compromised by - or complicit in -the promulgation of neoliberal-inspired views of good governance which are often inappropriate for the client communities. Since host governments often refuse to recognise as legitimate NGOs which they do not themselves at least part-fund, this inability to be reflexive is often actually imposed

Thus, NGOs simply fail to live up to the criteria for their effectiveness set out by Covey. Instead of going where they can do most good for the marginalised, they often mimic multi-national corporations by seeking the most beneficial locations in terms of resources. There may be good reasons for this: after all, no organisation can work without funding. However, it is clearly important to remember that this constraint will limit the ability of NGOs to act impartially, for all the reasons set out above.

Studies into the ability of NGOs to foster or construct civil society through work in development policy thus reveal that this is unlikely without a supporting state structure which is both sufficiently strong to provide resources and structures, and sufficiently open to democratisation to allow NGOs a free hand. In addition, they must have a client group which is both willing and able to collaborate in the process of civil society creation. They need, thus, to draw on existing social capital.

Crucially, given that most development NGOs are not set up by client groups or their members, and pay scant regard to internal accountability and transparency, they are unlikely to have this capacity. Thus, it appears that the primary function of development NGOs is to be the providers of welfare services - a worthy and useful task, but not one to be confused with politicisation or the inculcation of participatory political values.

NGOs are certainly able to find suitable partners at EU level. They are entirely capable of finding actors from industry and the EU institutions whose concerns are symmetrical, at least on a given issue, and thereby able to create or at least take part in the 'policy coalitions' which shape EU policy. EU actors can even approach NGO officers in order to secure their support. However, what is less clear is the latter's ability to make strong links with other actors from the NGO community.

Larger NGOs saw this process as one which often allowed them to develop senior roles within issue-specific partnerships, since they had the resources to impose their will on their partners. Smaller NGOs tended to be heavily reliant on umbrella organisations at the EU level, often leaving much of the EU-level campaigning work to them. Nationally-based NGOs tended to focus their campaigning work on national actors instead, hoping thereby to feed their concerns into the EU policy making process.

However, even if only as a result of resource problems, NGOs do not tend to 'gap-fill' at EU level, since they concentrate on dossiers which are crucial to their interests or to which they feel able to make a difference. As a corollary, however, there was no apparent sense that it was always necessary for the NGO community to be represented; if the officers of each NGO in the sample felt that an issue was insufficiently central to their concerns, they would not mobilise even if there would thereby be an absence of NGO voices.

Smaller NGOs in the sample reported increasing difficulty with maintaining their independence. Lack of resources, and low membership levels, were pushing them to undertake more rather than less project work on a contract basis, with funding provided by official sources. Of course, such NGOs retain some ability simply not to bid for projects they dislike - but the need for resources inevitably truncates this, given the widespread imposition of conditionality on project work by funders.

Larger NGOs were less constrained by this problem, since donations from members of the public and such fund-raising activities as operating gift catalogues make up a significant proportion of their income. Even so, officers from such NGOs reported that competition for funding between different kinds of NGO could lead to an insidious extra influence for official funders through an undeclared strategy of divide-and-rule and the privileging of certain kinds of NGO over others.

In the case of one of the umbrella organisations in the sample, it was reported that certain member organisations had affiliated themselves as a conscious strategy for understanding how the EU works and affects their interests. It was possible in some cases for individual supporters with an interest in a particular campaign to work as part of it on a voluntary basis, particularly in smaller NGOs.

However, even in such cases it was reported by NGO officers that such activism was brought to the organisation by the supporter rather than deliberately fostered by the NGO itself. Any input into a specific campaign by supporters tended to be the provision of evidence or expertise in a given policy area, with the primary focus being on securing a solution to a problem, and mobilisation at the EU level seen purely instrumentally if the need for it was understood at all.

Most supporters of the NGOs in the sample were not aware of the organisation's activities at EU level. Their appreciation and understanding of the EU's impact and powers was universally thought to be low. Most NGO officersconsidered that they had no responsibility to explain to supporters why it was necessary for them to engage with the EU, although all NGOs in the sample report their activities at EU level just as they report their work at national level.

In many cases, officers considered that their supporters were largely divorced from the EU policy agenda and unaware of its role in the policy area(s) they prioritised; instead, supporters interested in the non-national arena of decision making tended to be more aware of, and more concerned about, the WTO, IMF and World Bank. Moreover, the fact that certain of the NGOs in the sample had predominantly been active at the European Court of Human Rights and the Council of Europe rather than the EU meant that their supporters thought of these institutions rather than those of the Union when considering the 'European' level of campaigns.

Most NGOs in the sample undertake both campaigning and service delivery work, but in terms of the EU itself only campaigns are pertinent activities: even if the EU funds projects for the sample NGOs they tend to be realised outside the EU, in the former Soviet bloc or developing countries. Nonetheless, the NGOs have not yet placed great emphasis on explicit politicisation of their supporters regarding EU issues, and have not constructed any lasting 'civil society' coalition at EU level, favouring instead issuespecific alliances with any actors possessing symmetrical concerns alongside membership of umbrella organisations devoted to their specific policy areas.

Although issues of accountability and participation were insufficiently entrenched in the culture of NGOs in the sample, the interviews nonetheless revealed evidence of an ability to conduct performance audits and seek solutions to problems. Several of the NGOs studied have undertaken such reviews in recent years, with varying degrees of supporter involvement. There was no uniform trend; the smallest NGO in the sample, European Dialogue, is shifting towards service delivery thanks to resource pressures, yet others were seeking to increase their role in advocacy and campaigning. In all such cases, the decision to shift emphasis came from the officers of the NGO, sometimes under pressure from external funders.

In a very basic sense, this is a key difference between the supporters of NGOs and their target clients in development policy - the former by definition have at least some degree of civic culture and choose to express it through support of selected organisations, whereas client groups may have no, or very different, notions of political participation from those of the NGO officers. Nonetheless, all interviewees admitted that there is a severe dislocation between what their supporters want or are interested in and what the NGO actually does.

Many supporters have no idea about the issues involved in lobbying at national or transnational level; moreover, they may be moved to support an NGO by no more than well-meaning but vague notions about doing 'good works' such as saving the whale or feeding the hungry. This means that NGO officers have to engage with a range of issues about which their supporters usually know little, and in which they may be uninterested. This leads to the conclusion that NGOs often undertake activities which their supporters know and understand very little, and with which they may disagree.

When issues are tackled transnationally, this problem is exacerbated. In one case, it was stated that the NGO had a very active membership drawn predominantly middle class/professional sectors, whose professional and political skills were regularly placed at the NGO's disposal. Smaller NGOs were happy to allow supporters to add their expertise to their teams on specific campaigns on a voluntary basis. However, a key finding of the fieldwork is that most NGO supporters do not seek to play an active role in the governance of the organisation or to influence its policies and campaigns.

Role NGOs in Sustainable Development

Civil society has been characterized as a sphere of social life that is public but excludes government activities. Michael Bratton describes civil society as social interaction between the household and the state characterized by community cooperation, structures of voluntary association, and networks of public communication. The term civil society is generally used to classify persons, institutions, and organizations that have the goal of advancing or expressing a common purpose through ideas, actions, and demands on governments.

The membership of civil society is quite diverse, ranging from individuals to religious and academic institutions to issue-focused groups such as not-for-profit or non-governmental organizations. In the realm of environmental governance, NGOs are the most prominent actors. They are groups of individuals organized for the myriad of reasons that engage human imagination and aspiration. They can be set up to advocate a particular cause, such as human rights, or to carry out programs on the ground, such as disaster relief. They can have memberships ranging from local to global.

NGOs involved in environmental governance are highly diverse, including local, national, regional, and international groups with various missions dedicated to environmental protection, sustainable development, poverty alleviation, animal welfare, and other issues. The diversity of civil society and its value to official intergovernmental processes on the environment are acknowledged in Agenda 21, the comprehensive sustainable development blueprint adopted at the 1992 Rio Earth Summit. The document does not make use of the term civil society, although it expressly recognizes the members of civil society as a major constituency.

The Commission on Sustainable Development (CSD), responsible for implementing Agenda 21, classifies civil society into the following Major Groups:

— Women

— Children and Youth

— Indigenous Peoples and Communities

— Non-governmental Organizations

— Workers and Trade Unions

— The Scientific and Technological Community

— Business and Industry

— Farmers

All of the Major Groups are officially recognized by the United Nations through an accreditation mechanism developed specifically for NGOs. A noteworthy question connected to the definition of civil society is whether business and industry should be included in this social grouping.While Agenda 21 considers business and industry part of civil society, some observers contend that, because they already have considerable influence over international governance processes through informal lobbying opportunities and formal influence channels, business and industry should not be included in civil society.

The participation of civil society in global governance is increasing in significance, but is not unprecedented. NGO involvement is usually considered a late-twentieth-century phenomenon, but in fact it has occurred for over two centuries. The recent rate of proliferation of non-governmental organizations, however, is notable. In 1948, for example, the United Nations listed forty-one consultative groups that were formally accredited to participate in consultative processes; in 1998, there were more than 1,500 organizations with varying degrees of participation and access. Numerous factors, from the development of information technology to the greater awareness of global interdependence to the spread of democracy, explain the rise of NGOs.

The United Nations is the intergovernmental organization that has most openly recognized and endorsed the need to collaborate with the non-governmental sector. Historically, the UN cooperated with NGOs primarily as partners in the implementation of certain programs, particularly in the areas of emergency response, human rights, and election monitoring.

Over the past decade, environmental NGO activity within UN processes has intensified. Prior to the 1990s, while various social movements may have utilized the UN as a global forum to call attention to particular agendas, the focus was not on influencing the offi-cial UN deliberations.

Through the process leading up to the 1992 United Nations Conference on Environment and Development (UNCED), environmental organizations began intense internal capacity building efforts to gain more sophisticated understanding of the international policymaking process. Some of the innovations at the time – most notably, parallel NGO fora held alongside UN conferences – are now a routine element of intergovernmental deliberations.

The UN Conference on Environment and Development was of particular significance to NGOs.

Agenda 21 declared the need for new forms of participation:

> The United Nations system, including international finance and development agencies, and all intergovernmental organizations and forums should, in consultation with non-governmental organizations, take measures to... enhance existing or, where they do not exist, establish mechanisms and procedures within each agency to draw on the expertise and views of nongovernmental organizations in policy and program design, implementation and evaluation. The 1992 Earth Summit thus affirmed that the commitment and genuine involvement of non-state actors are critical to reaching sustainable development goals.

Throughout the 1990s, NGOs continued to focus on official UN deliberations and the international policy arena. A variety of channels have served NGOs in their purpose of participating and influencing international deliberations. NGOs sought accreditation at international intergovernmental conferences where they could lobby government delegates, organize brieflngs, and even offlcially address plenary sessions.

A number of government delegations to international conferences are now formally including NGO representatives. In the preparatory process for the 1996 UN Conference on Human Settlements (Habitat II), for example, NGOs and local authorities participated in the informal drafting groups that drew up the Declaration and Programme of Action.

Within the policymaking circle of the United Nations Economic Commission for Europe (UNECE), NGOs had a say in establishing the agenda and other aspects of the negotiations process for the 1998 Aarhus Convention on Public Access to Information, Participation in

Decisionmaking and Access to Environmental Justice. In both of these cases, a special, semi-offlcial status was accorded to civil society representatives.

New forms of NGO participation have changed the nature of international environmental policymaking. The international community has begun to recognize that effective global action requires meaningful stakeholder involvement in international policymaking and implementation.NGO involvement in global environmental governance can take a variety of forms:

— *Expert advice and analysis.* NGOs can facilitate negotiations by giving politicians access to competing ideas from outside the normal bureaucratic channels;

— *Intellectual competition to governments.* NGOs often have much better analytical and technical skills and capacity to respond more quickly than government officials;

— *Mobilization of public opinion.* NGOs can influence the public through campaigns and broad outreach;

— *Representation of the voiceless.* NGOs can help vocalize the interests of persons not well-represented in policymaking;

— *Service provision.* NGOs can deliver technical expertise on particular topics as needed by government officials as well as participate directly in operational activities;

— *Monitoring and assessment.* NGOs can help strengthen international agreements by monitoring negotiation efforts and governmental compliance;

— *Legitimization of global-scale decisionmaking mechanisms.* NGOs could broaden the base of information for decisionmaking, improving the quality, authoritativeness, and legitimacy of the policy choices of international organizations.

Civil society's involvement in global environmental governance has enriched the process and strengthened outcomes in a number of places and in a number of ways. In fact, it is the participation of nongovernmental groups that makes the process "global" and not simply "international."

While many governments agree that NGO participation is indispensable, many also feel that the drawbacks of civil society participation may outweigh the benefits. Arguments and concerns abound on both sides. Some are fretful that NGOs might constitute special interest groups, and that their participation would invariably result in policy distortions. Others fear that intergovernmental decisionmaking processes would become bogged down by NGOs, which are not necessarily representative of or accountable to their particular constituencies.

Decisionmakers are also anxious that NGOs may seek to usurp the sovereign powers of governments. However, some of these concerns may be overstated, considering the advantages of civil society involvement. Civil society can help build the political will for a new approach to development that integrates environmental and social goals. Non-governmental organizations can serve as alternatives to weak or inadequate democratic institutions, as avenues for more inclusive dialogues, and as conduits for disseminating information on activities and issues within the international system. These and other significant characteristics of civil society participation in governance are explored in the following three case studies.

The Crucible Group: The Crucible Group is a multinational, multidisciplinary gathering of experts that first met officially in 1993 to discuss the control and management of agricultural genetic resources. The initial goal was to identify issues, trends, and use options. While agricultural genetic resources are of crucial importance to biotechnology and genetic engineering, there are serious debates surrounding their ownership and control as well as the equitable sharing of benefits.

The group —twenty-eight individuals from nineteen countries — included grassroots organizers, farmers, trade diplomats, agricultural research scientists, intellectual property specialists, and agricultural policy analysts from both the North and South.

Recognizing the diversity of perspectives and priorities, the group did not seek consensus, but was able to agree on twenty-eight recom-mendations for policymakers. The first summary of the deliberations and the recommendations, People, Plants, and Patents: The Impact of Intellectual Property on Trade, Plant Biodiversity, and Rural Society, was published in 1994. Having now evolved into the Crucible Group II, with more than forty-five participants from twenty-five countries, the group has continued to meet to revisit many unresolved issues and consider a number of new ones.

As a neutral forum, the Crucible Group II has promoted open discussion among participants who might otherwise never have been at the same table. The Group launched a second volume, Seeding Solutions: Policy Options for Genetic Resources, at the April 2002 Conference of Parties to the Convention on Biological Diversity. The report provides valuable input into the debate and development of guidelines on intellectual property issues, rights of farmers,mechanisms for benefit sharing, and appropriate governance structures for conservation of plant genetic resources.

Several conclusions can be drawn from the Crucible Group experience:

— A dialogue does not have to produce consensus to be useful for governance purposes;

— A process designed to include non-state actors will reflect a broader spectrum of views and may generate more creative approaches to solving problems;

— A process where government and non-government participants are equal partners in a project is more likely to generate "buy in" and thus useful results.

Not all governance projects involving civil society, however, have achieved a balance of influence among participants. In fact, multistakeholder dialogues – especially those that are of very short duration – are losing favor with many in civil society. Some feel that the term stakeholder undermines communities and individuals struggling for their rights and that it implies equality among participants, which is not always the case. Clearly, for multi-stakeholder processes to serve as a vehicle for meaningful civil society participation, they must provide mechanisms for open, long-term discussions and deliberations.

Global Environment Outlook and the UN Millennium Ecosystem Assessment : One of the most important roles that NGOs can play in global environmental governance is to provide up-to-date information on critical issues. Governments often turn to NGOs to fill research gaps that stand in the way of effective decisionmaking. Certain NGOs, such as the World Resources Institute (WRI) and

IUCN – The World Conservation Union, have crafted their mandates around the role of information provider. These groups are dedicated to the production of accurate, up-to-date research and data on the most pressing environmental issues.

The Global Environment Outlook (GEO) of UNEP and the recently launched UNMillennium Ecosystem Assessment are good examples of formalized non-governmental assessment processes and inter-organizational networking. At the core of these processes lies a global network of collaborating groups responsible for regional inputs. Global system assessment is integrated with local environmental reporting.

NGOs and other non-state actors such as academic and research institutions are the main contributors, providing reports and data analysis. In the case of the GEO assessment, the final reports are reviewed by government representatives before publication. NGOs have not yet been allowed participation in the verification process. These large-scale assessments require considerable amounts of funding.

The contributions of charitable organizations, such as the United Nations Foundation, for international environmental research are indispensable. Funding matters do raise some concerns in terms of the autonomy of NGO research and analysis. The complicated dependence that NGOs and many academic and research institutions have on governmental and other donor funding concerns some observers in terms of the freedom civil society members have in conducting the research and analysis they contribute to governance processes. The funding situation, however, is not likely to change. Financial relationships and dependencies should therefore be transparent and open to scrutiny.

TRAFFIC: A third example of civil society fulfilling an essential environmental governance role is provided by TRAFFIC, the wildlife monitoring network for the 1975 Convention on International Trade in Endangered Species of Wild Fauna and Flora (CITES).

TRAFFIC is a partnership between WWF – World Wide Fund For Nature and IUCN – The World Conservation Union. It was established in 1976 to assist the CITES Secretariat in implementing the provisions of the Convention. The Convention covers more than 30,000 species of animals and plants and has been endorsed by over 150 countries. The diversity of the traded goods covered under CITES, which range from medicinal herbs to exotic pets, requires a level of international, on-the-ground coordination that would be difficult for a single intergovernmental institution.

TRAFFIC is a key component in the implementation of CITES. The NGOs behind the partnership are able to utilize their resources worldwide to operate twenty-two offices in eight regional programs, making TRAFFIC the world's largest wildlife trade monitoring organization. Its program priorities are threatened species and ecoregions, resource security, and international cooperation. Members lobby decisionmakers to ensure that trade in plant and animal species does not pose a threat to species conservation, and collaborate with governments and the private sector in developing economic incentive programs to encourage sustainable trade.

TRAFFIC has been particularly successful in data collection, on-the-ground inves-tigative tasks, and in-depth research. Through its research and outreach initiatives, TRAFFIC has become a key resource for governments and other NGOs, providing decisionmakers with critical information and analysis and prompting initiatives to ensure sustainable trade.

NGOs in Global Environmental Governance

The NGO community has particular strengths to bring to global environmental governance. The creativity, flexibility, entrepreneurial nature, and capacity for vision and long-term thinking often set NGOs apart from governmental bodies. A revitalized global environmental governance regime would thus benefit from greater participation of NGOs in global policy processes. What follows is a discussion of five key potential roles for civil society organizations in a strengthened global environmental governance system.

Information-Based Duties

As shown by the Global Environment Outlook and Millennium Ecosystem Assessment processes,

NGOs have much to offer in the way of information collection, dissemination, and analysis. Numerous other examples exist in which NGOs serve a key information-based role. One of the most significant relates to the Conferences of Parties and other meetings held in conjunction with multilateral environmental agreements such as the UN Convention on Biological Diversity and the UN Framework Convention on Climate Change. Often, the meetings are distinguished less by what is said in plenary session than by the wealth of research and policy documents produced by NGOs and other civil society constituents and released specifically to coincide with the official events.

Many conference delegates read these opinion papers and other documents, which often shed new light on the costs of inaction and the options for change. Another common opportunity for civil society members to provide input into intergovernmental negotiations comes in the form of a single statement developed by NGOs present and released at the close of the official event. Measures to improve the utility of information exchange could include:

— Wider acceptance and use of the "commission" model. Short-term consultations often yield less valuable information than do multistakeholder commissions provided with sufficient investment of time and resources.

— Assistance in the formation of networks.UN convention secretariats, for example, could facilitate ongoing, high-level multi-stakeholder knowledge networks that make a directed effort to bring expertise to bear on science and policy challenges, including perspectives from marginalized groups.

— Mechanisms to support "give and take."While officials may read the opinion pieces and research documents NGOs release, there is often little feedback and very limited opportunities for back and forth dialogue. The institution of "notice and comment" processes, formal advisory panels, and other informal mechanisms for information exchange between government officials and NGOs could pay real dividends.

— Efforts to agree to disagree. Seeking "consensus" is often a mistake.

Consensus can be difficult to reach, resulting in prolonged discussions of watered-down conclusions, "forced" agreements, and a failure to communicate valid perspectives. An acceptance on the part of intergovernmental decisionmakers of a civil society statement reflecting multiple opinions would often be more useful.

Over the past decades, NGOs have assumed a more active role in the process of agenda-setting and policy development. NGOs have been instrumental in notifying the public, governments, and international organizations of critical new issues for many years.

In 1945, NGOs pushed for inserting human rights language into the UN Charter and have been active in that policy domain since. Global environmental issues gained prominence in the 1970s also as a result of NGO activities. In the 1980s, forestry concerns were included on the agenda of intergovernmental deliberations under the pressure of NGOs. In 1997, six NGOs played a key role, through the International Committee to Ban Landmines, in convincing governments to embrace the successful intergovernmental landmine treaty.

The ability of NGOs to place issues on the global agenda does much to enhance their ability to participate in the later stages of decisionmaking. As pointed out by former Canadian Foreign Minister Lloyd Axworthy, "Clearly, one can no longer relegate NGOs to simple advisory or advocacy roles... They are now part of the way decisions have to be made". The question of what constitutes meaningful civil society participation in decisionmaking, however, is still being explored as NGOs and intergovernmental bodies continue to develop working relationships.

To this end, the development of a structure for civil society participation and engagement in international decisionmaking processes is necessary. Currently, modalities of involvement vary from being a full partner as in the case of the International Labor Organization to denial of access as in the case of the World Trade Organization. While each international agency would need to tailor participation standards to its particular objectives, a minimum set of criteria should be elaborated. The following elements need to be addressed:

— Clear articulation of rules, rights, and commitments to consultation with civil society beyond time-limited NGO fora;

— Clearly delineated selection criteria for NGO participation in consultations and advisory groups, placing an emphasis on diversity;

— Establishment of guidelines for the process of NGO contributions;

— Commitment to respectful treatment of NGO documents;

— Support for publication and dissemination of NGO submissions to delegates at relevant international meetings;

— Formalized submission process for NGO recommendations and comments to intergovernmental bodies;

— Provision for feedback and response to NGO submissions by intergovernmental bodies or national governments;

— Mechanism for monitoring the implementation of these components.

A more formalized structure for NGO participation would be useful in addressing some of the current obstacles to civil society involvement in global environmental governance. The wariness that governments and others have of NGO involvement might be reduced if baseline standards defined the rights and responsibilities of governmental and non-governmental entities in a clear and consistent manner.

The UN system usefully engages civil society entities as operational partners in many circumstances. The role of NGOs in implementation of worldwide policy efforts has greatly increased since the mid-1980s, when NGOs began to fill gaps left in the provision of services by reduced roles for many development agencies.

Non-governmental organizations are particularly useful in an operational context, as they can provide implementation tailored to specific conditions and can "make the impossible possible by doing what governments cannot or will not do". This is especially true with regard to the management of natural resources, which is often best handled by community-based organizations who have a stake in local environmental conditions and are free from many of the conflicting demands experienced by governments. The preamble to Section III of Agenda 21 underscores the need for individuals and groups, especially at the local level, to participate in decisions that may affect the communities in which they live and work.

A significant portion of the world's ecological "hot spots" are located in rural – often very poor – areas of developing countries. As a result, the burdens of ecological damage, as well as the burdens associated with ecological regeneration, are borne primarily by people in these areas. NGOs and other groups in the developing world typically are poorly funded, have little access to information, and often lack a visible presence or audible voice in international governance processes. The activities of Shack/Slum Dwellers International, a network of grassroots development groups in fourteen countries, are illustrative of one way in which Southern groups can build greater presence on the international stage. Through the use of micro-financing and other programs, Shack/Slum Dwellers International leverages the resources of its member groups to provide them with financial support, information, and advice on development strategies and related issues.Using their collective power, the federation has developed a voice on the global policymaking stage.

The operational functions of NGOs within a reformed global environmental governance system could be strengthened by:

— Expanded efforts at inclusion of local, community-based groups with knowledge of the issues at hand;

— Capacity building targeted at enhancing communication between local groups and other governance partners;

— Support for initiatives to measure and monitor service delivery by NGOs — and the use of benchmarking and the identification of "best practices" as a way to improve performance.

Performance assessments and monitoring of environmental conditions undertaken by NGOs may hold decisionmakers in international arenas publicly accountable for decisions in ways that the intergovernmental system itself could never accomplish.

As Thomas Weiss notes, "NGOs are... capable of making sensitive or politically important information public – something that intergovernmental organizations often are reluctant or loathe to do because of their dependence on member states for resources". A number of NGO-led or assisted assessment initiatives are currently under way.

There is an urgent need to account for the needs of developing countries, to acknowledge the limitations they face in conducting monitoring and assessment activities, and to provide support for the enhancement of these functions within governments and civil society alike. Key measures that could facilitate the assessment and monitoring role of NGOs include:

— *Creation of a comprehensive database for information and analysis at different geographic and political levels.* NGOs are key providers of local environmental data and information. A coherent mechanism for data collection and analysis will encourage this function and facilitate a two-way information flow;

— *Involvement of a larger part of the population in assessment and monitoring functions.* The inclusion of civil society groups in data collection would greatly contribute to filling knowledge gaps as well as enhance knowledge development, increase interest, and promote engagement. This will be especially beneficial to developing countries;

— *Support for knowledge-generating institutions in developing countries.* Universities are key generators of knowledge, yet they are among the most under-funded institutions in developing countries. Funding and communication technology transfer will be critical to their ability to perform these functions.

Over the past few decades, NGOs in many countries have been extremely effective in highlighting disparities in who bears environmental burdens and who gets the benefits of environmental investments. Some groups have issued reports. Others have brought public interest litigation to defend environmental rights as well as to clarify and enforce laws.

If a reformed global environmental governance system were to include a dispute settlement mechanism, it is easy to see the potential contributions NGOs and other civil society members could make to such a structure. The submission of "friends of the court" opinions would be well-suited to the skills and interests of NGOs. In fact, the Aarhus Convention envisions a process by which NGOs could seek judicial remedy against other parties, such as national governments or private sector entities, for environmental harms or crimes.

5

Advocacy of NGOs

As non-governmental organisations (NGOs) increasingly move into advocacy and policy work, they are having to respond to a variety of challenges concerning issues of legitimacy and related issues of accountability, governance and effectiveness. Legitimacy questions concern: firstly, the right of the NGO to speak to its target audience, perhaps on behalf of other groups or interests, and; secondly, the wisdom of NGOs moving further towards an advocacy focus.

In the context of the "New Policy Agenda" NGOs have grown in prominence in international development as potentially efficient service and welfare providers, channels of aid and facilitators of democratisation. NGOs have become important actors in the international political economy, a fact borne out by rapid increases in numbers, membership, activities and financial resources.

In the early 1990s policy-makers in leading Northern NGOs became increasingly aware of the limited impact of their development efforts. Despite the fact that more public money than ever before was channelled through

NGOs, their impact on the ground was still temporary and small-scale. Recognising this limitation of traditional development activities, in the early 1990s leading NGOs began to consider a range of strategies of "scaling up" in order to make more of a difference. In the years since the publication of "Making a difference", the focus of NGO thinking, and increasingly practice, has swung behind efforts to develop more effective forms of international lobbying and advocacy.

Although advocacy takes a variety of forms, from careful research and policy advice, to parliamentary lobbying, to public campaigning and development education, the overall goal is "to alter the ways in which power, resources, and ideas are created, consumed and distributed at a global level, so that people and organisations in the South have a more realistic chance of controlling their own development".

National and international lobbying and advocacy has become increasingly important within the NGO world. Some large, mainly Northern-based NGOs have acquired considerable expertise, authority and respect and have gained access to decision-makers in governments and international organisations. By having a foot in the North and a foot in the South, NGOs are in a good position to link the micro and the macro levels, using their experience in the South to inform their advocacy and policy work in the North. In short, NGOs have begun to move from a "development-as-delivery" to a "development-as leverage" approach.

As NGOs have moved further into advocacy and influencing work as part of a development-as-leverage approach they have encountered a variety of related challenges and criticisms. These challenges question the effectiveness of their advocacy work, their legitimacy as advocates for development, their accountability to those they are perceived as representing, and the suitability of their governance structures for a development-asleverage role.

As regards their effectiveness, questions have arisen about whether a shift into advocacy and influencing work will make a difference to the lives of poor and marginalized groups in the South, and additionally whether it is the most cost-effective use of NGO resources. As regards their legitimacy, NGOs have increasingly encountered the criticism that they are not representative organisations in any obvious sense, bringing their credibility as representatives of the poor and marginalized South into question.

In a similar vein, it has been suggested that NGOs are poorly accountable to the people that they sometimes appear, or claim, to represent and that this poor accountability undermines any claim to legitimacy. Finally, encompassing the previous three criticisms, it has been suggested that NGOs' governance structures are poorly suited for a development-as-leverage role. As NGOs move further into advocacy and policy influence these questions are not going to go away.

Questions about legitimacy may seem to be little more than a navel-gazing guilt-trip for Northern NGOs, but legitimacy is central to the effectiveness of NGOs' advocacy work. As regards advocacy, put simply, legitimacy increases the persuasiveness of advocacy, which increases its effectiveness. NGOs have been questioned about their legitimacy from a variety of positions.

Firstly, governments, International Organisations and Multi-national corporations – some of which have been criticized by NGOs for their weak accountabilities – are increasingly asking whether and why they should listen to NGOs. Secondly, institutional funders are asking why they should fund NGOs which are moving further into advocacy work, and why they should fund NGOs rather than other parts of civil society. Thirdly, as they grow in confidence and experience Southern partners and supposed beneficiaries are increasingly questioning the legitimacy of Northern NGOs advocating, supposedly on their behalf. In such a dynamic environment, Northern NGOs are clearly challenged to show that they do have a valid role in processes of international development.

NGO advocacy takes a variety of forms, and relates to a wide range of issues; different types of advocacy about different sorts of issues have different implications for legitimacy. An NGO may be considered a legitimate advocate when it is talking about a "technical" issue which it has a lot of expertise in, such as the latest developments in irrigation technology or family planning, but illegitimate when it expands its focus to reform of the WTO or environmental degradation.

One approach which side-steps the issue of legitimacy is simply to make modest claims which are less open to criticism. Similarly, some NGOs steered clear of the term, and perhaps the practise of, advocacy because they feel that speaking on behalf of others is in itself disempowering for the intended beneficiaries. Their preference was for "influencing"; demanding that institutions consulted the NGOs' client group in formulating their policies.

NGOs claims legitimacy for their advocacy work on a variety of bases: history; organisational structures; principles, rights and values; and Southern roots. However, whilst advocacy is clearly about values, and clarity about the values which underlie an advocacy position is to be welcomed, rather than simply appealing to values NGOs need to explain where their values come from if they are to persuade others to share and enact them.

In many cases the values which NGOs hold and promote, and the advocacy positions that they take, derive from experience in, and links with, the South. For many of the NGOs, it is their experience of working at a grassroots level, implementing projects and programmes in a wide range of contexts that gave them the legitimacy to advocate about development issues.

NGOs which specialise in a particular aspect of development claim that their technical expertise provided them with legitimacy and in some cases took pains to ensure that they did not advocate beyond their experience.

Many NGOs are well aware of the dangers of claiming legitimacy in terms of representation, and cautioned against potentially exploitative attempts to seek out legitimacy through establishing links with Southern NGOs and community organisations. Although many NGOs carefully avoided claiming to speak for the South, or represent the South in any simple way, many struggled to find alternative ways of describing what they are about and, if pushed, would fall back on some sort of representational claim – Southern issues, values, interests or concerns, rather than "the South" - to legitimacy.

Although NGOs make their claims to legitimacy on a variety of bases, a substantial majority of their claims point – directly or indirectly - to their links with and experience in the South. The strength of these legitimacy claims depends upon the ability of the NGO to demonstrate the links, or legitimacy chains, between their operational work and experience in the South and their advocacy work.

Many NGOs are currently thinking about how to develop more synergistic relationships between their operational work and their advocacy, but few have clear systems in place to achieve such a goal. Two potential ways of substantiating legitimacy claims are, firstly in terms of practising accountability, and, secondly, in terms of demonstrating relevance.

For NGOs which make some claim to represent Southern communities, issues, interests, values or concerns – however carefully worded the claim is – there is a need to back up their legitimacy claims with appropriate systems of accountability. As Edwards and Hulme suggested: "NGOs do not have to be member-controlled to be legitimate, but they do have to be accountable for what they do if their claims to legitimacy are to be sustained". As well as being accountable to their supporters and donors for the ways in which resources are spent, one would expect NGOs which make representational claims to try to be accountable for the positions they take.

When advocacy is confined to a specific geographical or thematic issue NGOs may feel confident about whom they should be accountable to. However, if the advocacy aims to change a policy at a more abstract level – reform of the WTO, changes to lending policies of development banks – it can be unclear whom you should be accountable to, and demonstrating the relevance of grassroots work to macrolevel advocacy can be problematic.

Complex legitimacy chains often lead to diffuse accountability and make the demonstration of relevance difficult. Most of the NGOs recognise that demonstrating the relevance of their operational experience to their international advocacy work is far from simple. An approach which sounded both realistic and useful involves trying to understand and illustrate the links in both directions, trying to look outwards and upwards from the Southern grassroots to broader debates, and trying to think downwards from policy issues back towards Southern experience.

There are a lot of layers between the concerns of Southern NGOs and their constituents and Northern advocacy, but explained that his NGO did not confine itself to simply representing the opinions of its partners, but added value in terms of research and analysis. As NGOs recognize the two-way nature of legitimacy chains, from South to North and North to South, and seek to make the links in both directions, Northern NGOs will have to re-define their roles in processes of international development if they are to show themselves as adding value in processes of international development.

Many of the NGOs saw a role for themselves as supporting and facilitating international advocacy, and defended their right to take positions on issues of international development as long as they were developed through "real dialogue" with Southern partners. Partnerships and dialogues have tended to be unequal but NGOs should not give up on the goal of genuine partnerships - characterized by jointly agreed purposes and values, mutual trust, respect and equality, frequent consultation, reciprocal accountability and transparency, sensitivity to political, economic and cultural contexts, and long term commitments. Perhaps the key question which NGOs need to consider in organising their international advocacy is whether organisational structures which developed during a development-asdelivery era are suitable for a development-as-leverage approach. NGOs have been slow to restructure their organisations in order to ensure appropriate downward accountability for advocacy and influencing. Some NGOs have embarked on processes of restructuring, considering decentralization, the setting up of dedicated advocacy offices, and harmonisation across their federations and alliances.

Such efforts seek to move the NGO closer to Southern experience, to give the South a voice in decision-making, and to develop truly international advocacy rather than a Northernimposed agenda. A related and more common approach to re-organising international advocacy is to strengthen the Southern element in a global division of labour through capacity-building. Such an approach takes seriously the joint responsibilities of North and South in advocating for international development. However, before rushing in to decentralisation, membership structures or poorly thought through capacity-building, NGOs must be clear about their reasons for restructuring, avoiding the temptation to follow institutional, at the expense of developmental, imperatives. In re-thinking their roles and seeking to achieve greater accountability, legitimacy and effectiveness for their development work NGOs must start from their core values, being honest and clear about what their values are, and where they come from.

Although often hidden, values are fundamental to the work, not least the advocacy work, of NGOs. Discussions of effectiveness, legitimacy, accountability, governance (and evaluation) ought to take explicit recognition of the values which make an NGO what it is. Effectiveness is relative to the values or objectives of the organisation. Legitimacy comes, or doesn't come, depending upon the processes through which values are arrived at. Multiple accountabilities are balanced on the basis of values. And, governance structures, in effect, institutionalise values.

NGOs Advocates of Good Governance

Related literatures have focused on the organizational issues concerning exclusively local government units (LGUs), business groups, NGOs or other civil society organizations (CSOs), citing, for example, the technical, managerial or organization factors that determine the success of each group. Another strand of the literature looks at the interaction between the members of these groups, such as the relationships between the government and NGOs, business groups and civil society organizations, and donor agencies and NGOs. Taken together, these studies thus provide some insights and useful guides in the selection, motivation and monitoring of local agents.

Towards an agency theory of local program implementation, this section presents the results of a case study of eight different groups engaged in the pilot test of the *Governance for Local Development Index* (GOFORDEV Index). Operating in their respective localities, these eight groups, which include local government units, business/civic organizations, and non-government organizations, are each contracted to generate and disseminate the scores in the GOFORDEV Index, which is a measure of the quality local governance proposed by the Philippine Center for Policy Studies (PCPS) under its Governance Project.

Thus, the pilot test is partly intended to tease out the important behavioral and institutional factors that may impinge on the agent's performance. On the whole, the results indicate that there are no significant differences in the abilities of the different agents in so far as generating the scores in the Index. While local governments with their local development planners are often more technically equipped than NGOs, however, the latter when appropriately trained show no distinct disadvantage than other groups. Further, the usual stereotypes that LGU will necessarily inflate a selfadministered governance rating while NGOs and other groups will tend to deflate it have no basis. The stereotypes, however, are true when they concern the types of participants that attend the public presentations of the Index by the different agents. While the agents do not differ in their compliance with their contractual obligations, nonetheless, they reveal their different levels of commitment to the ideals of good governance with their other activities.

Based on their self-reported activities, the NGOs appear to support or promote the Index more than other groups, although two of the local government partners are pushing for the adoption of the Index as well. In this aspect, business groups do not compare well with the NGOs and local governments. In sum, these findings suggest that different groups with different proclivities nonetheless may all still become effective advocates of good governance when provided the appropriate incentives.

Pilot Test of the GOFORDEV Index

In 1999, the Philippine Center for Policy Studies, a policy research-oriented NGO, initiated a multi-phased research and advocacy project in support of the country's decentralization program outlined in the Local Government Code of 1991. Supported by the Ford Foundation, the Governance Project aims to develop a set of simple, useful and valid indicators of good governance and local development, and to advocate the wider adoption and institutionalization of these locally administered indicator systems. Thus, the idea is to establish a feedback mechanism whereby the citizens' collective assessment of local public service delivery is communicated to concerned officials in a more regular, objective and simpler manner. The establishment of such a mechanism is certainly consistent with, if not a logical implication of, the intent of the Code, which is to make local governments more accountable as they are granted greater fiscal autonomy from the national government.

Developed during the first two phases of the Governance Project, the ten indicators of good local governance are grouped into three sub-indices, namely: the Development Needs Index (DNI), the Development Orientation Index (DOI) and the Participatory Development Index (PDI). Simply put, the DNI gauges the constituency's assessment of public service provision; the DOI reflects the LGU's relative priority for such services; and the PDI suggests the extent of people's participation and consultation of their officials.

The component indicators of these three sub-indices ranging from zero to 100, the three sub-indices together by way of a simple average constitute the *Governance for Local Development* Index (or the GOFORDEV Index). An account of the development of the Index is given in Capuno (2000). The last two phases of the Governance Project involve a two-year pilot test of the Index (2001-02) and a year-and-a-half advocacy program (2002-03).

Essentially, the pilot test is undertaken to validate and to enhance the usefulness of the Index, which once tested and improved shall then be promoted for adoption in and outside the pilot test areas during the advocacy phase. Ultimately, the advocacy program is geared toward convincing the national government, donor agencies or even networks of NGOs to institutionalize the Index as an additional method of monitoring, evaluating or rewarding local government performance.

Broadly, therefore, the GOFORDEV Index is similar in intent, if not in practice, with some international indicator systems such as the Citizen's Report Card Survey adopted in Bangalore, India and the Human Development Index introduced by the UNDP in several developing countries (including the Philippines). Among the similar indices introduced in the Philippines, the GOFORDEV Index is akin to the Minimum Basic Needs Approach (which emphasizes citizen's evaluation), the Local Productivity and Performance Measurement System (which is an LGU selfassessment), the Participatory Strategic Organizational Assessment (which highlights democratic participation), and the Overall Governance Index (which covers citizen's feedback, LGU's internal capabilities and people's participation). The GOFORDEV Index, however, is explicitly designed for cities and municipalities.

To be considered valid and useful, the GOFORDEV Index should lead to desirable changes in local fiscal decisions and processes, and ultimately to local development measured as the enhancement of the constituency's welfare. To tease out these desired results, the Index is pilot tested for two years in twelve areas in the provinces of Bulacan and Davao del Norte. These two provinces were chosen on the basis of their relative levels of socioeconomic development: Bulacan scores higher and Davao del Norte lower than the average province in terms of Human Development Index and fiscal revenues.

Due to its proximity to Manila and its longer history, Bulacan is widely considered as more economically and politically dynamic than Davao del Norte, which is located in the island of Mindanao and is populated mostly by migrants. The introduction of the Index in the two diverse provinces therefore already controls for some socioeconomic, geographical, cultural and historical factors that may bias the results of the pilot test.

Within each province, six cities and municipalities are randomly selected on the basis of their relative levels of socioeconomic development. For each of the two socioeconomic levels (high and low), the pilot areas are further divided into two groups, namely: the experimental group and control group. In the experimental group, the locality's score in the Index is generated and disseminated in the area. In contrast, the score in the Index of those in the control group are simply generated but not disseminated.

Hence, unlike those living in the experimental areas, the residents of the control areas are not aware of the Index at all. Without such awareness, it is hypothesized that the clamor for improved public service delivery and improved quality of local governance would be less than in areas with information campaigns. Hence, the idea here is to isolate the pure contribution of the Index on the changes in the respective scores of the experimental and control areas.

To evaluate the usefulness of the Index, local groups were engaged to undertake the generation and dissemination of the scores. The hypothesis here is that any local group can be induced to use the Index as an advocacy tool for good governance, although local groups respond differently to the same inducement. The variations in the performance of the various groups, therefore, will suggest the types or elements of an incentive scheme appropriate for a given local agent. The recourse to incentives may be desirable in cases where only inconclusive results can be obtained from the preliminary evaluation of potential partners given the time and resources of the program or project.

Partners of the Pilot Test

To come up with a rich set of practical tips for an effective working relationship with a local group, the prospective partners in the pilot test areas are broadly classified into two, namely: the local government unit and civil society organizations. Specifically, formal contracts are entered into with the municipal or city development office (MPDO/CPDO) of the local government unit in certain areas, while, in other places, the business groups, local academic institutions and NGOs are engaged.

The partners were selected using minimal criteria, although they were considered only if they have expressed willingness to participate. Those who expressed interest belong to a pool of various local groups invited during the presentation of the design and implementation of the pilot test, where the terms of the contract with prospective partners were also taken up. In addition to the formal letter of intent, the partners were selected on the basis of their presence in the area (i.e., local office or work in the area), their contact address and their assignment to the project of some of their officers and core staff members. The "residency" requirement is meant to ensure accountability to the local population and, therefore, build the credibility of the Index.

The PCPS formally contracted the chosen partners. The terms of the partnership include the usual delineation of roles and responsibilities and the technical and financial support to the agents. The schedule payment to the agents is based on the accomplishment of certain tasks grouped into generation and dissemination activities.

The major activities involved in the generation of the scores in the Index are training in and the conduct of household survey and the collection of fiscal data, and the encoding and processing of the data. With regard to the information campaign in their respective areas, the agents (in the experimental areas only) were required to attend training in the conduct of public presentations, and the distribution of posters and *komiks* (a short illustrated magazine) about the Index.

Since the payment is based on performance, the agents in the control areas received less than the ones in the experimental areas. In the experimental areas, however, the civil society groups were offered slightly higher financial packages than the partner LGUs, which usually have comparatively greater access to resources.

In addition to the financial package, the agents were provided with the necessary training, materials and other inputs in the conduct of the household surveys and public presentations. It should be noted, however, that beside the "carrots" comprising the financial package, other soft incentives and the possibility of another round of contract, no "sticks" were specified into the contract, although the contract is no less legally binding for the absence of sticks. In addition to the submission of written reports and documentation of their accomplished tasks, the agents were also monitored during the generation and dissemination of the scores in the Index.

The PCPS and an independent contractor made spot checks during field interviews and attended some of the public presentations as participant-observer. More importantly, an independent parallel household survey was conducted in all the areas using similar sampling frame and survey. The results of the parallel survey is used partly to evaluate the results of the agents' own surveys and partly to monitor the welfare impact of the Index.

The Municipal Planning and Development Offices (MPDOs) and the City Planning and Development Planning Offices (CPDOs) are organic departments of municipal governments and city governments, respectively. As their names imply, these offices are chiefly responsible for local development, land use, investment and other plans. They act as the secretariat of the Local Development Council, a mandated local consultative bodies organized to identify projects and programs financed out of the LGU's annual Development Fund.

Although civil service rules simply require a college degree among key government personnel, the head of the MPDO or CPDO is usually a licensed engineer, as in the cases of Panabo and Braulio Dujali, and most of the staff has technical background. Relative to the other local government personnel, therefore, those in the MPDOs and CPDOs are more aptly trained, positioned and empowered to adopt the Index.

Like their counterparts in other parts of the Philippines, the Rotary Club of Angat and the Soroptimist International of Baliuag are associations of civic-minded business people in their communities. Community service through outreach programs, often in tandem with the local government or with other private volunteer orga0nizations, has been the hallmark of these clubs in the country. Many of these programs complement or supplement basic public services (e.g., health, food and nutrition, education); others are directed to help alleviate poverty (livelihood projects); some are for public awareness campaign of certain local ordinances and regulations; and also for sociocultural activities (town *fiestas*, historical heritage).

One common observation about these clubs is their close links with the local and national political elite, which makes them perceived to be more like interest groups than legitimate civil society organizations. Indeed, some members of the Rotary Clubs of Angat and the Soroptimist International of Baliuag are or were elected to local legislative councils, sit or sat as members of local consultative bodies, or are active during elections.

Their political involvement, however, does not necessarily make them interest groups. Of late, these business groups are moving into policy/reform advocacy and even grassroots/community organizing, or taking a generally more activist stance. Before its involvement with the GOFORDEV Index, for example, the Rotary Club of Angat was already a core member of the Angat Parish Pastoral Council, a local multi-sectoral umbrella organization advocating the preservation and development of the Angat River and its protection from illegal quarrying.

Between the two local academic institutions engaged as partners during the first year of the pilot test, the Bulacan State University (BSU) is the bigger one and has a wider experience in field-level research and extension, and particularly in dealing with local governments. In fact, the BSU's Institute of Local Governance and Administration conducted in the 1990s a series of capacity-building training of municipal and *barangay* officials in the province under the USAID's Governance and Local Democracy Project.

For the pilot test, the BSU-Bustos Campus was enlisted as the local agent. While BSU is a province-supported academic institution, the St. Mary's College (SMC) of Tagum City, on the other hand, is a private college run by the Religious of the Virgin Mary. Its Business Resource Center administers the College's research projects and outreach program.

The three other partners – LAWIG Foundation, Davao Provinces Rural Development Institute (DPRDI) and the Rural Development Institute (RDI) – are typical development-oriented NGOs. Operating mostly in the Island Garden City of Samal (IGACOS), the LAWIG Foundation has been involved in environmental protection and eco-tourism development of the island, which used to comprise three municipalities until 1997 when all three were combined to become a chartered city.

Unlike the other partners, the DPRDI and RDI are based outside the pilot test areas. However, both have been working in their covered areas with local farmers' organizations and other marginalized groups on projects like natural resource management, enterprise development, community organizing and capability building of *barangays*. Both the DPRDI and RDI are affiliated with PhilNet, a nationwide network of rural development NGOs.

Research and Practical Issues

One of the research and practical issues addressed in the pilot test is to ensure the validity, credibility and effectiveness of the Index once it is adopted by a local group whose identity, activities and other relevant characteristics are not fully known to the PCPS prior to contracting. PCPS recognized at once that an exhaustive screening is too costly and may not be a totally useful approach since it cannot always be replicated elsewhere. So the decision was made to tap two local area experts, both academics and natives of the pilot provinces, to identify prospective partners from among the local civil society organizations. The PCPS made the final selection of the partner business groups and NGOs based on the aforementioned set of criteria. Note, however, that the PCPS directly contracted the CPDOs and MPDOs in four of the areas following the pilot test design.

The idea behind the selection process is not so much to prove certain stereotypes – that is, the score will be rigged according to the political leanings of the agent – as to determine the critical agent-related factors that may impinge on the validity, credibility and effectiveness of the Index. Knowledge about these factors is necessary if the Index is to be adopted by any local group.

It is useful to frame the operational problem of the PCPS as a *principal-agent* (PA) problem, an analytical framework used by economists to understand the working relationship between lawyers and clients, doctors and patients, parents and teachers, employers and employee, and the like. In this set up, the principal (client, patient, parent, employer) engages the services of the agent (lawyer, doctor, patient, teacher, employee) to do something (cure a disease, defend in court, teach children, operate machine). An agent is employed because of his or her expertise, experience or other personal attributes that enables him or her to accomplish the task more effectively, more appropriately or less costly than the principal.

The essential feature of the P-A problem is that the principal does not know the real objective or the actual effort put in by the agent, possibly because it is very costly to collect and process all the relevant information (some of which may be manipulated by the agent to gain advantage). Without such information, the outcome of the agreement between the two parties may be different from the principal's expectation. When the information problem concerns the agent's real objective (known as the problem of *adverse selection* or *hidden type*), the principal may screen out potential agents by requiring references, work histories, interviews, etc.

Alternatively, the principal may offer a menu of contracts, each of which assures the agents as much as she will get from her next best option and at least one of which best suits her objective. Her choice then would reveal her true objective, innate ability or "type'. For example, a lawyer who opts for a fee contingent on the result of the litigation rather than a flat hourly fee should suggest more about his confidence and ability to win a case. Alternatively, the principal may face a *moral hazard* or *hidden action* problem.

The problem often arises when it is not possible or is costly to fully monitor the agent's efforts, thus leading to substandard results. In this situation, it makes sense for the principal to provide incentives based on performance or outputs. However, because of external or intervening factors, performance or output levels may be poorly correlated with the agent's efforts, work ethics or dedication to her job. Thus, in the contractual bargaining that then ensues, the two parties will agree on the expected levels of performance, activities or outputs with the corresponding compensation (and penalty) and caveats.

Necessarily, the basic agency framework will have to be modified to reflect the fact that in most joint development undertakings the partnership is among equals and the partners usually share the same objectives. Certainly, the relationship between the project proponent (national NGO, international donor or national government agency) and the local implementer (local civil society organization or LGU) is and should be one between equals and not between "superiors and subordinates".

In a partnership among equals, the parties mutually agree on the detailed objectives and activities of the local project. Hence, shared purpose is developed, although the agreement usually does not forbid either party to pursue other activities, provided that these do not undermine the purpose of the partnership.

Conceptually, however, one can think of the bargaining over the terms of the agreement (objectives, activities, deliverables or outputs) as one of solving the adverse selection or moral hazard problem through means other than the use of hard incentives financial package, penalty clauses). The sharing of goals, for example, implies that the agent internalizes the objectives of the principal, who then has less need to monitor the agent. These are some of the arrangements that have evolved in practice that mitigate the screening or monitoring problem faced by the principal.

The P-A framework is adapted here to identity the advantages and disadvantages of having the GOFORDEV Index administered by local groups. To mitigate the adverse selection problem, referrals by a local area expert were considered in the selection of partners. However, since a more thorough screening was at once deemed impracticable and nonreplicable, a minimal set of criteria was additionally employed to chose specific partners. Admittedly, because of the minimal set of criteria, local groups who fit certain stereotypes consequently may be appointed as partners.

For instance, it is often claimed that an LGU-administered index of good governance is likely to be biased, since local officials and their supporters will bloat the rating to win political points. When NGOs or other similar groups instead, administer the same index, concerns about its debasing are raised, especially when the NGOs are perceived to be critical of the local government. Since both LGUs and NGOs are involved in the pilot test of the GOFORDEV Index, it is then possible to verify these stereotypes.

The following criteria are used to evaluate the relative performances of the different local agents of the Index. The idea is to identify the agent-related factors and those outside their control that may impinge on the validity, credibility and effectiveness of the Index as an instrument to enhance the quality of local governance.

1. Compliance with the terms of the contract – Compliance would indicate that the training, financial and other assistance provided to the agent was enough for them to accomplish the assigned tasks. Universal compliance then suggests that the Index can be adopted by anybody given the same set of incentives provided during the pilot test.

2. Differences with the independent estimates of the scores in the GOFORDEV Index – Significant or systematic differences between the agent-generated and independently-generated scores in the Index would help verify whether the commonly held stereotype hold, i.e., the LGU will inflate and the NGO will deflate the true score in the Index. If such

differences exist, then monitoring of the agents becomes very critical.

3. Performance of related but not mandated activities – An incontrovertible proof that the agent shares the objectives of the Governance Project is the use of the Index for their own advocacy and other activities not otherwise required as per contract. It should be noted that the agents are not forbidden to use the Index in their other activities so long as these do not compromise the objectives of the project.

Analysis of Results

The two main tasks of the agents in the eight experimental areas are the generation and dissemination of the scores. In contrast, the agents in the four control areas – Bulacan State University, St. Mary's College and Rural Development Institute, Inc - are limited to the generation of the scores. To generate the scores, each agent was required to attend training for survey enumerators, to conduct household surveys, to collect relevant fiscal and socioeconomic data, and to process the primary and secondary data.

The tasks involved in the information campaign, on the other hand, are the attendance in the training for public presentation, the mobilization and conduct of three public presentations, the distribution of the campaign materials (*komiks* and posters), and the documentation of these activities.

With regard to the activities involved in the generation of the scores, all of the agents attended the training, which was put to use during the conduct of the field interviews. The problems encountered during the field interviews, however, were not agent-specific; misunderstanding in the application of the sampling design, identification of the target respondent, and other survey problems were all encountered with all types of agents. Therefore, these findings indicate that the training was inadequate and that the instructions were not totally clear. In any case, the agents did callbacks or a repeat of the survey and a strict editing of the filled-up questionnaires whenever necessary.

However, the NGOs and the business group partners had difficulty in collecting relevant socioeconomic and fiscal data from the local government offices. The difficulty is partly due to the latter's lack of understanding of the GOFORDEV Index and to the suspected motivation of the agent, especially in the light of the local elections in May 2001. In Samal City, for example, the LAWIG Foundation had a hard time in culling the public documents because the City Administrator suspected that the PCPS and LAWIG would misrepresent the city government.

Furthermore, the CS-partners were not also totally familiar with government accounting and budgeting practices to be able to untangle the reports of public finances and compute the DOI. The CS-partners, however, were resourceful enough to overcome these problems. They were able to secure the help of local government personnel.

While most of the agents were able to complete the collection and processing of the data during the period April-June 2001, the output of the Bulacan State University (BSU) was delayed because of internal problems. Like any government institution, the BSU is subject to rigid accounting rules. This led to delays in the remuneration of the faculty members of the BSU-Bustos Campus who enlisted as field enumerators.

Since the honoraria were deferred, callbacks and the editing of the questionnaires were also delayed. Contractually, each of the agents in the experimental areas was asked to undertake three public presentations of the Index during the period July-September 2001 to coincide with the local budget-preparation and approval period. To comply, the agents were simply advised to invite a minimum of 15 participants, including, whenever possible, local officials and key stakeholders in these activities.

Although not required, however, most of them were able to present the Index formally during meetings of municipal and city officials. In particular, LAWIG Foundation presented the Index during a regular session of the *Sangguniang Bayan* or the city legislative council. Except the Rotary Club of Angat, all the other partners had audience with department heads, members of the local legislative council and mayors or vice mayors.

There were a total of 924 local participants in all these public presentations, with slightly over a half of them (54 percent) are from Davao del Norte. Also, a little less than half of total number of participants (47 percent) are local officials. More interesting, however, is the correlation between types of participants in these gatherings and the type of local agents: LGU-partners drew more local officials than CS-partners, while the latter drew more of the general population than the former.

Although many things could explain this observation, one implication of this finding is that the results of the Index (and similar indicators system) may be more directly and widely communicated to the concerned local officials if generated by a department or unit within the local government itself. Whether or not the scores are internalized within the LGU, however, seems to depend on the support of the local chief executive. For example, the concerned MPDO of Guiguinto was able to use the Index to push for improvements in accounting practices and budgeting procedures because of the backing of the mayor. The accomplishments of the CS-partners, however, are no less significant in so far as raising the level of public awareness concerning local governance issues.

In contrast to the LGU-partners, the CS-partners were able to target more stakeholders, ranging from the youth sector to the senior citizens groups, from the civil society groups to the general public, from the underground sector to the local business groups. Notably, however, only a few local officials attended these activities. Their minimal participation may be attributed to a preconceived notion that the Index is largely a political tool of the CSO-partners.

This is certainly the case in Angat where local officials boycotted the first public presentation of the Rotary Club of Angat. Such preconceptions and biases, especially when the CS agent is associated with the marginalized sector and other political issues, effectively blunt the message of the GOFORDEV Index to the local government.

In addition to the public fora, information materials about the GOFORDEV Index were distributed in the areas. Consisting primarily of *komiks* (short magazine) and posters, these materials were centrally conceptualized and developed; although their distribution was left to the local agents. Enough copies of *komiks* and posters were printed, equivalent, respectively, to 30 percent and three percent of the total number of households per area.

To see how well the agents complied with their instructions, a number of site visits were made. However, the site inspections reveal that the posters were not found in many prominent places. While this could suggest poor compliance, it may also suggest that these materials were posted instead in the rural *barangays* and other less populous areas.

To validate the agent-generated scores in the GOFORDEV Index, an independent survey was undertaken in the areas. This parallel survey followed the same sampling design used by the agents.

Further, the questionnaire used in this survey basically expands the one used by the agents to include questions about the respondent's awareness of the Index, his or her satisfaction with the delivery of basic public services and the performance of local officials, and his or her participation in other public activities.

Two rounds of this particular survey were already undertaken: the first round to provide a baseline result and the other one to assess the impact of the first year of the pilot test. The baseline survey was conducted with the Ateneo de Davao University and Bulacan State University-Malolos Campus, while the second one with the University of Immaculate Conception of Davao City and the University of Regina Carmeli of Malolos. Because of their greater relative experience in surveys and their academic orientation, they are assumed here to be more competent and impartial relative to the contracted agents.

A comparison of the two estimates of the Development Needs Index, the Participatory Development Index and the GOFORDEV Index is shown in Table 1.

Table 1. Comparison Between the Agent-Generated and the Independent Estimates of the GOFORDEV Index

Area	Local Agent	Development Needs Index		Participatory Development Index		GOFORDEV Index	
		Agent	Ind.	Agent	Ind.	Agent	Ind.
BULACAN							
Angat							
Baliuag							
Guiguinto							
San Jose del Monte City							
Bustos							
Plaridel							
DAVAO DEL NORTE							
B. Dujali							
Panabo City							
Samal City							
Sto. Tomas							
Asuncion							
Tagum City							

*There are no independent estimates of the areas' Development Orientation Index (DOI), which is based simply on audited public financial reports. Hence, the independent estimates of the GOFORDEV Index include the agent-estimated score for the DOI. The bold numbers indicate the difference between the two estimates are greater than 10 (in absolute terms).

Note that there are no independent estimates of the Development Orientation Index since the score in this particular sub-index is simply based on fiscal data and other public documents. Although the two estimates generally differ, the critical level of difference is ten points, to account for the ten percent margin of errors obtained for the each of the component indicators because of the small sample size. With this caveat, it can be seen from the table the significant deviations are in the estimates of the DNI and the PDI in four areas in Davao del Norte. The independent estimate for DNI is bigger than the LGUgenerated scores in Panabo City, which suggest therefore that the LGU-agent does not necessarily bloat its scores. In Tagum City, however, the estimate of the St. Mary's College for the same sub-index is 19 points smaller than the independent estimate.

Another evidence that seemingly contradicts the usual suspicion about NGOs is the relatively high estimates of the NGO-generated scores in the PDIs of Samal City and Sto. Tomas. These scores are favorable, rather than disfavorable, to the concerned LGUs. However, these wide discrepancies nonetheless may suggest the need for further training and monitoring of agents.

To further evaluate the relative performance of the agents, some of the results of the impact survey undertaken early in 2002 are tabulated below. Table 2 shows the percentage of household respondents who have received or seen a copy of the *komiks* or posters. The household respondents who gave positive responses are grouped into two, depending on whether the respondent remembered at once the materials without being shown a sample copy.

The showing of a sample copy is meant to verify that the respondent indeed recalls correctly the information material about the Index. Based on the survey results, less than thirty percent of the respondents got a copy of the *komiks*, despite the fact that enough of them were printed so that at least thirty percent of the households per area would get at least one copy. Only less than ten percent of households in Angat, Baliuag, San Jose del Monte City,

Panabo City and Samal City (IGACOS) reported to have received a copy of the *komiks*. Two of the LGU-partners (Guiguinto and Braulio Dujali), however, were able to reach 12 percent of the local population.

*Table 2. Percent of Household Respondents who have received or seen a komiks or posters of the GOFORDEV Index**

Area	Percent of respondents who received acopy of the komiks of the GOFORDEV Index		Percent of respondents who have seen a poster of the GOFORDEV Index	
	Those who remember at once	Those who remember after being shown a sample copy	Those who remember at once	Those who remember after being shown a sample copy
BULACAN				
Angat				
Baliuag				
Guiguinto				
San Jose del Monte City				
DAVAO DEL NORTE				
B. Dujali				
Panabo City				
Samal City				
Sto. Tomas				

The best performer is DPRDI, which was able to cover 21 percent of the household population in Sto. Tomas. The relatively better performance of these three partners at least attests to their deeper commitment, considering that their areas are less densely populated than the other six cities and municipalities. In addition, the DPRDI was able to tap its own network of grassroots organizations and groups of marginalized citizens in the municipality.

While a diligent accomplishment of its contractual obligations alone should merit mark of approval for the local partners, its performance of other complementary, supplementary or supporting activities should reveal more, how much the partner share the objective of the GOFORDEV Index.

The DPRDI and the LAWIG Foundation have used the Index as part of their other advocacy activities, including election-related activities and the solicitation of support services from national government agencies. In addition, DPRDI also modified the public presentation of the Index to include a workshop wherein an action plan was drawn up, thus insuring the deeper appreciation of the Index on the part of the participants.

The Index seems no less useful to some of the LGU-partners, who have seen the value of the Index for budget planning and also in their advocacy activities. For example, the MPDO of Guiguinto used the Index as a basis for improving the classification of budget items, for the development of a systems improvement manual, and for the formulation of the Annual Investment Plan for 2002. The CPDO of Panabo City, on the other hand, gives a regular briefing of the Index to local officials. Further, the Index is an input to the Local Action Plan of Panabo City, one of the city's outputs under the World Bank-sponsored project City Development Strategy.

The partners from the local business groups did not report any activity that directly promote or support the Index. Perhaps this could be explained by the orientation and the usual projects of these organizations, which are mostly direct service delivery.

6

Financing NGOs

A guarantee fund provides a loan or credit guarantee, i.e. it enables a borrower to approach a bank for a loan. Guarantees are particularly useful for borrowers who do not have sufficient collateral, such as land or other assets. Small borrowers almost always lack (sufficient) collateral. Therefore, the purpose of loan guarantee schemes is to share the credit risk with the bank.

Three parties are involved in a loan guarantee scheme: the guarantor and the bank conclude a guarantee agreement. A guarantee agreement provides the lending institution with the right to call on the guarantee to recover loan losses. The bank issues a loan contract with the borrower. The borrower subscribes to a guarantee request to the guarantor.

The individual model: In the individual model borrower and the bank are directly linked. The guarantor and the bank establish a cooperation agreement on the degree of risk sharing. The guarantor may also provide technical support services. The guarantor issues a guarantee certificate or letter of recommendation to the bank. The bank appraises the loan application and, if approved, establishes a loan contract with the client.

The intermediary or "retail" model: In this model, standby letters of guarantee are provided by an international organisation to enable a local organisation to access bank loans or overdrafts for on-lending to their members/clients. There is no loan contract between the bank and the borrower. The guarantor is an international, specialized guarantee institution.

Membership organisations using loans or overdraft facilities obtained through external (stand-by) letters of guarantee finance services to their members, like input supply and marketing services which may lead to substantial cost reductions, while enabling the intermediary to generate revenues to cover interest costs and other bank charges.

Guarantees are backed by a guarantee fund, i.e. money to be used in case a loan is not paid back in time and the guarantee is called. This fund can be deposited in an account with the same bank, or with another bank.

Not all guarantee funds are owned and managed by local, private, not-for-profit organisations such as support NGOs, producer associations, cooperatives or grass root organisations. Other types of guarantee funds are run by local or regional authorities to support micro or small enterprises of a particular region or sector. And not all NGOs own the funds they use for issuing guarantees; the following types can be distinguished:

1) Self-Help Organisations which have created their own guarantee funds on the basis of member contributions with the aim to issue (credit) guarantees only to their members. An example is the mutual guarantee association.

2) Self-Help Organisations and PVOs which have received donor grants to constitute guarantee funds for their members, respectively clients. Here, the ownership is unclear, hence the incentives to use the funds diligently. The NGO acts as a guarantor on behalf of an external guarantee entity, which agrees to issue a standby letter of guarantee to a local bank under risk-sharing conditions.

3) NGOs own the guarantee fund which is topped up by a standby letter of guarantee issued by an external organisation to the local bank. In this set-up, the local organisation operates both guarantees under one single arrangement.

Probably, the accountability of the NGO operating a guarantee programme varies with onwership. Incentives to perform are expected to be higher when a larger proportion of funds are raised by the NGO organisation and its members.

Many guarantee schemes are administered by banks. This reduces costs for the NGO. the NGO is not involved in cash operations. Guarantee fund capital will only be affected in case the bank makes a claim for loan losses. A guarantee fund can be deposited in an interest bearing account, thus generating income. In addition, guarantee funds can be easily protected against the erosive effect of inflation. Cash or current account reserves are not required to the same extent as in direct lending, so - assuming that interest rates received on the guarantee fund will be positive in real terms - inflation affects guarantee funds less dramatically.

In spite of the advantages, local guarantee funds in practice often tend to remain small and relatively ineffective in terms of outreach and graduation; they can easily become a financial burden for their host if costs are not matched by revenues. The management requirements for guarantee funds are often underestimated. The organization's staff does not have enough expertise. This leads often to inadequate planning, unsatisfactory collaboration with a bank and general ineffectiveness. This paper seeks to address these concerns.

It is meant as a guide to NGOs who wish to consider the introduction of a guarantee scheme and to others which operate a guarantee scheme but with mixed results. Some of the questions are: What makes a NGO a suitable host structure for this instrument? What should a NGO expect from a guarantee fund? What are the minimum conditions in the environment to make this a viable instrument? What does collaboration with a bank require from a guarantor?

The factors fostering success include:

1. *External factors:*

   a. *Financial sector development:* The development of the financial sector determines the possibility to find suitable banking partners for a guarantee fund. Financial markets in developing countries are:

      — Often dominated by state banks. The sustainability of such a partnership can be seriously questioned, as financial sector reform may, sooner or later, (have to) take place. Such restructuring is likely to lead to the reorganization, privatization or even liquidation of these banks with dramatic implications for the guarantee funds;

      — in countries emerging out of financial sector reform, it is also difficult to find bank partners for guarantee schemes, since monetary policies and central bank regulations are likely to enhance credit rationing. In these situations, banks are even more hesitant on small scale lending;

— in more developed financial markets, with a wide range of local and foreign banks competing in a limited market and eager to capture new market segments, it should be easier to identify bank partners interested in a guarantee scheme. In practice few developing countries have reached this state and hence downgrading of bank services as a result of increased competition is still rare.

b. *Local banking network:* Some grassroots organisations and support NGOs operate in areas where the closest bank branch may be several hours drive away. Under such circumstances a direct client-bank relationship is difficult. Alternative credit mechanisms may have to be developed. The retail model in which the NGO on-lends through its own loan disbursement system may be an alternative. Such intermediation requires a high degree of professionalism and a certain level of specialization, conditions which are not always met by NGOs.

c. *Inflation and exchange risks:* Inflation is another factor which constrains the implementation of guarantee programmes. Inflation forces banks to raise nominal interest rates, in many cases real interest rates as well. High real interest rates increase the risk of business failures and loan defaults. Repayment difficulties can easily result in a debt trap as a result of rapidly accumulating interest costs and other charges. The lender and, to a certain extent, also the borrower may prefer short maturities and smaller loans. Although this may decrease the default risk, loan losses to be assumed by a guarantor in a period of high inflation will still be considerable. High inflation can also lead to the erosion of fund capital if the fund is placed in an account with a negative real return. Finally, high inflation may rapidly erode the negotiated leverage with the bank, if the guarantee fund is expressed in hard currency, but the credit line obtained under the guarantee arrangement is nominated in local currency. This problem can be countered by periodic renegotiations of the terms of a guarantee agreement.

2. *Internal factors:* Often NGOs engage in the management of credit guarantee programmes without adequate preparation. Many NGOs originally started as welfare-oriented organizations and only at a later stage became involved in financial intermediation. Three of the more critical factors in the preparation and operation of a credit guarantee programme are target group selection, portfolio management and programme sustainability.

   a. *Target group selection*: The guarantor should manage the risk of its portfolio of clients just like a bank, and avoid to concentrate credit guarantees in a single sub-sector. Risk rating of the different target groups and sectors is recommendable. However, it is possible that, for example from a social perspective, the objectives of a guarantee scheme explicitly require targeting of a specific group through support of a single economic activity. The guarantor should realise that, in this case, costs in the form of loan losses are likely to be higher and some kind of risk premium may have to be charged for this purpose.

Some sectors are less risky than others. Trade and marketing activities are generally at the bottom of the risk chart, while agricultural activities have a relatively high risk of default. Similarly, in a single sub-sector risk may vary according to the degree of organisation of the sector and access to (other) support services. For instance, lending to micro entrepreneurs belonging to producer associations is likely to carry a lower risk than lending to non-associated operators in the same trade.

b. *Management capacity*: One of the basic weaknesses of NGOs in micro finance is management. On the basis of several years of observing NGOs manage guarantee funds, the ILO has drafted a checklist to identify strengths and weaknesses in this field. This can help assess the level of institutional adequacy of a local organization and to identify the areas in which strengthening or restructuring may be needed.

c. *Programme sustainability*: Organizations not specialized in financial intermediation tend to make little effort to become sustainable. The availability of donor funding is one of the major reasons for nonfinancial institutions to take the issue of cost control and sustainability less seriously. NGOs should introduce appropriate systems of financial planning and cost control. Detailed figures on costs and revenues allow the organisation to make adequate financial projections for capital needs. If subsidization of some sort is necessary figures on the financial status and projections come in handy to convince donors.

Risks of Bank-NGO Relations

As banks have little information about the financial needs and savings behaviour of small clients, they find it difficult to assess the credit risk. In turn, NGOs and their clients/ members are also generally ill-informed about the way banks operate. NGOs should know what they are looking for in bank with which they wish to enter into a guarantee contract.

This assessment should concern the loan conditions, the physical distance to bank branches, quality and timeliness of services, the autonomy of bank branch managers in the loan approval process and the prospects for a smooth exchange of information on the guaranteed portfolio. These criteria are generally valid. If, in addition, guarantee fund is to be deposited in the bank, it might be advisable to look also at the financial situation of the bank.

Because of their developmental orientation, development banks appear to be most interesting partners, but experience shows that their services are often limited, the branch network is small, and there is always the risk of political interference. Cooperative banks and (municipal) savings banks may be better tuned to provide appropriate small scale financial services.

Guarantee funds operated by NGOs have a number of advantages based on their proximity to the clients and their capacity to offer non-financial services complementary to guarantees, like training, counselling and marketing services. The availability of these services is particularly important for a bank, since they are likely to contribute to the viability of the business of the borrower. These services may also produce extra information on the status of the business and possible problems faced by the borrower. This information would allow the bank to act more rapidly, if required.

A guarantee scheme must effectively allow for a risk-sharing, the precise proportion of which should provide an incentive to the bank to monitor these loans just as normally guarantee loans, i.e. the bank must bear a share of not less than 40% or so; at the same time, the bank's share cannot be too large either, otherwise there would be no point in getting involved with a guarantee scheme.

In many countries specialized public guarantee facilities have emerged which go beyond the mere provision of a guarantee and provide other services to encourage bank lending. For banks unfamiliar with the sector of small borrowers, it is extremely difficult and costly to identify potential borrowers and to collect the required information on their financial needs, their business proposals, their collateral situation and their management capabilities.

Therefore, it is attractive for a bank if the guarantor also appraises clients, screen business proposals and prepare required information for the loan application. The guarantor can also assist the bank in loan supervision and follow-up. A review of the lending costs of different types of financial institutions in the Philippines revealed that lender costs related to loan recovery amount to about half of total lending costs. The effect of the guarantor's intermediation may thus result in a considerable cost reduction for the bank.

NGOs and especially self-help organisations can exert moral pressure on their members, which helps reduce moral hazard.

Leverage of financial resources: Guarantees should induce banks to provide leverage, i.e. multiple proportion loan amount/guarantee. Leverage can be a strong argument for NGOs to enter a guarantee arrangement with a bank. There are cases where banks are prepared to release credit up to ten or more times the amount of the guarantee. The higher the leverage, the more the bank's own resources are exposed to risk. It is a good indicator of the progressive appropriation of a market segment by the bank. The difference with risk-sharing can be seen in the following examples:

Administrative services: Cash operations and loan portfolio administration require a certain degree of specialization and professionalism. Grassroots organisations like MCCH in Ecuador discovered that through telebanking by modem, their house bank could also provide them with accurate and immediate information on the balances of the MCCH accounts in the provinces.

Tasks and responsibilities

From the start there should be absolute clarity about the distribution of tasks and responsibilities between the parties in a guarantee arrangement. Pre-loan orientation for (potential) borrowers is generally assumed by the NGO. However, the bank has a clear interest and expertise to be involved in such orientation to ensure that the right information is given. These orientations can be low cost if done simultaneously with other NGO activities.

Client/member identification and selection is normally assumed by the NGO, in light of proximity to and information about the potential bank clients. Possible assistance in the preparation of a business plan and loan application is more of a responsibility of the NGO. Banks should advise the NGO on the kind of information required for loan applications. Procedures and requirements can be rather formal, particularly when guarantees are issued for longer maturity loans and/or for risky target groups such as start-up businesses.

The information in business plans and loan applications can vary substantially, depending on the situation. Banks tend to emphasize cash flow analysis, market analysis, while NGOs are often inclined to put more emphasis on the profile of the entrepreneur, such as his/her character and capabilities.

Loan appraisal and approval should be undertaken by both the NGO, as guarantor, and the bank, as lender. The NGO presents a complete file on the client to the bank for appraisal and approval after it has internally approved the guarantee application and determined the supplementary services it may possibly provide to the client. In other cases, banks and nonfinancial institutions form joint committees for the appraisal and approval. Loan contracting, loan disbursement and loan recovery is a responsibility of the bank, often in close coordination with the NGO. The NGO should not interfere in loan disbursement and collection, as this will hamper the development of a normal bank-client relationship.

Loan supervision and monitoring are done by the bank and the NGO jointly. Information on loan disbursements and repayments should be provided by the bank to the NGO, at least on a monthly basis. Annex 4 gives an example of how such a monthly report may look like. Arrears and defaults need to be defined clearly as well as the conditions and procedures for loan restructuring and for follow-up problem loans.

Follow-up on problem loans should be left as much as possible to the bank. It should be clear to the borrower that the loan contract is with the bank and not with the NGO. In addition, it will be difficult for an NGO to combine the tasks of business counselling with that of enforcing repayment.

These loans might lead to the realization of securities. Legal action is costly, particularly vis-à-vis small borrowers but may be necessary to maintain the standard of discipline. Again, the higher the risk shared by the bank, the more it will be concerned about timely follow-up on problem loans. Active monitoring and follow-up by the bank is also important from the perspective of eventual client graduation, as this is one of the means through which banks learn about small borrowers.

In the realization or execution of securities, the NGO is usually in a better position to approach the debtor personally and mobilize extra-legal pressure, but it may have limited capacity to take legal action. The bank should have more experience, although it may be reluctant to do so in view of the disproportionately high costs involved.

For very small borrowers/savers the charges for the opening of savings and current accounts as well as other fees often create an unpleasant surprise. Given the small loan size of the target group, these charges may take unrealistic proportions. This could be negotiated.

The NGO will also have to bring forward what it will charge for its services. Certain fees can be directly charged upfront by the NGO. For commissions on the interest rate, it will need the collaboration of the bank. If there are no interest ceilings or other legal restrictions, the bank may be able to charge an additional commission on the interest repayments, which can be subsequently passed on to the NGO. Depending on the bank's involvement and costs related to the scheme, the NGO may try to negotiate a part of the bank's own margin. However, practice shows that this is seldom accepted by banks.

Negotiating risk sharing and leverage requires skills and should be based on an excellent understanding of the mechanisms of a guarantee scheme and a good knowledge of the local financial market. It is important to determine the existing risk exposure of the bank prior to negotiations.

The extent of coverage should also be clarified, whether outstanding loan principal only or also outstanding interest and bank charges. In the latter case, the maximum number of months should be set for which such costs may be charged by the bank. If a bank does not accurately follow up on arrears, such interest and other bank charges can rapidly accumulate. An annual review of the risk sharing agreement is recommendable. It is important to insist on a minimum level of risk sharing by the bank the first year. In addition, the bank should make a commitment to increase risk-sharing, taking into account portfolio performance.

For a bank a guarantee is of high quality if it can be easily called at minimum cost. Banks often claim guarantees for loans in arrears for more than 90 days. The guarantor should negotiate with the bank, to specify clearly what can be claimed: only outstanding principal, or principal plus accumulated interest due or also other charges, such as penalties.

Secondly, a guarantor should satisfy the claim only against evidence of follow-up by the bank between the first date where arrears were registered and the default date. This may entail visits by a loan officer, demand letters to the debtor or co-guarantor or loan restructuring. After the claim has been settled, the bank should continue legal action.

A transparent agreement enhances collaboration and prevents situations which may lead to legal disputes. A written agreement is in the interest of all parties concerned. The agreement should allow for renegotiations.

The bank and guarantor can choose from a variety of risk sharing options: international standby letters of guarantee, local guarantee funds and contingency funds. International standby letters of guarantee: these guarantees, issued by a recognized international bank to the local bank can either take the role of principle guarantee or that of counter-guarantee (a guarantee re-insuring the local guarantees). These international guarantees can be made available by international guarantee institutions, who manage these on behalf of donors or on behalf of non-financial institutions in the South.

Local guarantee funds: guarantee funds placed in the collaborating local bank are another option. One part is put in an interest-bearing deposit account, the other serves as a first-call account for claims. Part or all of the fund may be deposited in hard currency with a view of maintaining the real value of the fund.

Contingency funds: these are reserve funds or provisions for unforeseen costs, which are often demanded by the local bank, when the principal guarantee consists of an international letter of credit. The contingency fund functions as a first-call account in order to avoid that small claims have to be made on the international guarantee. In the context of the ILO-RAFAD project, NGOs have used capital reserves fed by upfront provisions. In Peru this was done by means of a monthly commission, but this can also take the form of a one time levy at the time when a loan is issued. In Sri Lanka a contingency fund was created by the beneficiaries of a prawn farmers' guarantee scheme. The members of the association are the owners of the contingency fund.

Funding NGOs: Role of IMF

The International Monetary Fund (IMF) is one of the most powerful actors in the global economy. As a multilateral institution it lends billions of dollars to countries experiencing extreme economic imbalances and mobilizes billions more from rich creditor nations and other international financial institutions. The richest countries in the world, the Group of Seven (or G-7), have given the IMF the power to bestow a "seal of approval" on borrowers' economic policies. This seal of approval is necessary for poor countries to get debt relief from creditor nations, and it influences the decisions by private investors and aid agencies on whether to lend and invest in those countries. In this way, the IMF has tremendous power over the lives of millions around the world.

The IMF's power is confined mainly to the poorest countries, and, following the most recent global financial crisis, to emerging markets as well. Rich industrialized nations have not borrowed from the IMF in about 20 years, and IMF approval has no impact on these countries' stock markets or bond issues. However, it is the rich countries that dominate decision-making and set policy at the IMF.

With their dominant voting share, the wealthiest countries have been able to use the IMF to further their global economic agenda.

In the United States, this agenda has been dubbed the "Wall Street-Treasury complex," a description of the particularly close-knit relationship that the U.S. Treasury Department has with Wall Street investors and bankers. In making the world safe for investors, the IMF and its ruling shareholders have run roughshod over citizens by excluding them from the decision-making process and keeping important information off limits.

The IMF's ever-expanding mandate, the so-called "mission creep", increases its power as the IMF tackles new issues such as banking and financial systems, good governance, including issues such as judicial reform and land reform, and social sector spending. Unfortunately, the IMF's growing authority and operational secrecy has intimidated and mystified citizens' groups that would like to change the way the IMF operates.

The IMF's primary task was to monitor and manage a system of stable exchange rates in which the value of all the world's currencies were based on gold and the U.S. dollar. In order to provide the stability for this system, the U.S. government guaranteed the value of the dollar in gold at a set rate of $35 per ounce. This system was to be the basis for international trade, which was considered the engine of economic growth and prosperity.

It is worth noting that very few developing countries played any role in the creation of the IMF due to their relatively small economies and the fact that many were not yet independent nations. The IMF's second major function was to provide countries with short-term financing from its vast reserves of foreign currencies and gold to help them overcome temporary balance-of-payments deficits and support their exchange rate values. These reserves came from the contributions by IMF founding members, based on the size of their economy. In the beginning, it was industrialized countries that primarily utilized these funds.

In 1971, the U.S. government abandoned the gold standard due to inflationary pressures and the costs of the Vietnam War. This action undermined the Bretton Woods monetary arrangements by creating a system of "floating" exchange rates in which a currency's value was determined by the market or through government intervention rather than through the IMF and based on gold.

With the abandonment of the fixed rate system, as well as the increasing privatization of balance-of-payments financing, the IMF's original mission became increasingly obsolete. But, rather than closing its doors, the IMF began reshaping its functions and redirecting its activities. It began shifting its activities from determining currency values to monitoring exchange rate policies and increasing its lending to countries with balance-of-payments difficulties.

The oil price shocks in the early 1970s were the saving grace for the IMF. Its financial resources, once again, became desperately needed, this time by non-oil producing developing countries. The oil price hikes in 1973-74 had resulted in large earnings of hard currency for oil producers, and massive deficits for oil importers. To finance these deficits, private banks used the huge deposits of oil-producing nations to extend cheap loans to oil-importers.

The oil price hikes, however, caused prices of many consumer goods to rise in industrial countries, increasing inflation. To curb inflation, industrial countries raised interest rates, which slowed growth significantly and caused an enormous global recession by reducing demand and increasing the cost of borrowing globally. With shrinking demand in the rich countries and higher interest rates on loans, poor countries' economies deteriorated rapidly.

When a second round of oil price increases occurred in 1978-79, the credit-worthiness of deeply indebted countries was so damaged that private commercial banks were reluctant to continue lending to them. This forced many developing countries to turn to the IMF for help in financing their growing balance-of-payments deficits. By mid-1982, the aggregate external debt of non-oil producing developing countries was more than $600 billion, more than half of which was on commercial (higher interest) terms.

As creditors became more nervous about countries' ability to repay, loans became increasingly short term. Low commodity prices, higher import prices and capital flight further weakened these countries' position. The crisis hit its peak when Mexico defaulted on its debt payments in August 1982. The IMF was called on during this time, first with Mexico and then with a long list of other indebted countries, to provide balanceof-payments assistance and orchestrate debt-restructuring negotiations with the international banking community. The objective was to get these countries back on their feet and repay their debts as quickly as possible. The quid pro quo for these IMF-arranged financing packages was that countries had to submit to draconian economic-adjustment conditions.

Beginning in the early 1980s, structural adjustment programs (SAPs) became the cornerstone of the IMF's mission to restructure debt-ridden economies. The IMF designed SAPs to decrease domestic consumption and to generate more exports, more investment, and more domestic savings. Specifically, these policies promoted export-oriented growth, reductions in public spending and the state's role in the economy, and increased taxation.

They also sought to increase countries' trade competitiveness by prescribing currency devaluation. As the IMF has continued promoting SAPs, their scope has broadened into areas such as financial and banking sector policy, wage policy and governance issues.

The financial crises of the 1990s added an even greater dimension to the IMF's power. When the Mexican peso came under assault in 1995, the IMF rushed in with emergency lending to prop up the currency. It did the same in Thailand in 1997 and then in Indonesia, Korea, Russia and Brazil. The IMF has used these opportunities to pursue its economic development agenda. Taking advantage of its leverage over these countries in crisis, the Fund demanded extensive changes across all areas of their economies, including banking laws, labor laws and government spending.

The financial crisis of the 1990s differed from the debt crisis of the 1980s in important ways. The most significant difference is that in the 1990s the crisis involved private actors lending to companies and banks in emerging markets while in the 1980s it was these same banks lending to sovereign countries. So, rather than the threat of countries defaulting on their debts, during the 1990s crisis it was the threat of private firms defaulting on their debts.

Another difference was that during the 1990s, default was easily avoidable as the problem was liquidity shortages. Despite these differences, the IMF employed the same tactics for solving both crises, including high interest ràtes and devaluation. This approach drove up debt and bankruptcy rates, which increased the insolvency of domestic businesses and sparked a recession. The IMF's approach also forced governments to assume the debt that private firms had taken on, thereby socializing private debt.

In addition, foreign lenders were repaid with IMF money, thereby bailing out bankers with public funds. The domestic result is that citizens have been stuck footing the bill for this international bailout. In the wake of this global financial catastrophe, the IMF has tried to shift the blame from its inadequate surveillance and harmful adjustment policies to the borrowers' failure to disclose accurately their financial position. Although the true failure of the IMF's performance remains largely ignored by governments, the issue triggered a worldwide debate among policymakers and economists about the IMF's effectiveness and role in devising economic policies.

Since more than $1.5 trillion crosses international borders every day, many critics are arguing that the IMF is no longer capable of carrying out its core mission to oversee and regulate monetary policy. The power to make or break an economy has, in many ways, shifted to private financial markets and speculative capital. The IMF and its members have acknowledged this fact by adopting policies aimed primarily at keeping the private financial market content, even if it means undermining other economic goals, such as employment creation or the expansion of domestic demand.

The IMF is an intergovernmental monetary and financial organization comprised of 182 member countries.

Membership is restricted to countries that can control their external relations and are willing to implement IMF regulations described in the original Articles of Agreement. The first article of the Articles of Agreement sets out six purposes for the organization:

— To promote international cooperation by members on international monetary issues.

— To facilitate the expansion and balanced growth of international trade and, through this, contribute to high levels of employment and real income and the development of productive capacity.

— To promote exchange stability and orderly exchange arrangements and facilitate the avoidance of competitive currency depreciation.

— To foster a multilateral system of payments and transfers for current transactions and seek elimination of exchange restrictions that hinder the growth of world trade.

— To make financial resources available to members, on a temporary basis and with adequate safeguards, to permit them to correct payments imbalances without resorting to measures destructive of national and international prosperity.

— To seek reduction of both the duration and magnitude of payments imbalances.

Special Drawing Rights (SDRs) are the unit of currency used by the IMF. They act as a reserve asset for IMF members, and serve to denominate IMF transactions and accounts. If the IMF determines that there is a long-term global need to supplement reserves, it has the authority to create additional SDRs, much like a treasury can create more currency. The value of one SDR is determined daily by taking an average of currencies from the United States, Germany, Japan, France, and Great Britain - countries selected because of their large share in the global trading system.

The weights of the currencies comprising the basket are based on the country's exports, as well as the amount of the country's currency that is used as reserves by IMF members. Effective in January 1999, the Euro replaced the deutsche mark and French franc. Periodically, the IMF allocates SDRs to its members based on the size of countries' quotas in the IMF.

Unlike the United Nations, which uses a system of one-countryone-vote, the IMF uses a system of weighted voting power. Each member has a basic allotment of 250 votes. In theory, most decisions made by the Board of Governors or the Executive Board can be adopted by a simple majority of votes. However, in practice the IMF tends to operate by consensus and rarely takes formal recorded votes. For more important decisions, a larger majority is required.

A 70 percent majority is needed to decide upon operational issues such as rates of charges on the use of the Fund's resources and the rates of interest on the holdings of SDRs. An 85 percent majority is required for matters including the structure of the Fund, changes in quotas, the allocation of SDRs, and the use of the Fund's gold reserves. Given the fact that the United States controls about 18 percent of the votes, it has veto power over matters requiring an 85 percent majority.

The borrowing capacity of the IMF is unlimited in the sense that the IMF has full freedom to decide whether to borrow and how much. If a certain currency is needed to replenish IMF holdings or to finance a transaction, it is able to borrow from a member country. Furthermore, the IMF has the authority to borrow from sources in or outside the member's territory, such as private lenders and commercial banks, after seeking concurrence of the member.

Since 1962, the Fund has had a line of credit called the General Arrangements to Borrow (GAB). Under the GAB, the IMF can borrow, at market interest rates, up to SDR 17 billion (about $29 billion) from 11 of its main industrial members (the United States, Germany, Japan, France, United Kingdom, Italy, Canada, the Netherlands, Belgium, Sweden, and since 1984, Switzerland) called, strangely, the Group of Ten. Another SDR 1.5 billion is available under an associated agreement with Saudi Arabia.

The GAB is to be used only in exceptional circumstances, such as when a country's balance-of-payments problems threaten to destabilize the international monetary system. The GAB is reviewed and renewed every five years. In 1983, the review resulted in GAB being enlarged from SDR 6 billion to the current SDR 17 billion. The GAB has been activated 10 times, mostly recently in July 1998 to finance an arrangement with Russia.

During the Mexican financial crisis, policymakers were concerned about the IMF's ability to handle future financial crises with its existing resources. The final communiqué from the G-7 summit in Halifax, Canada in 1995 called on the world's stronger economies to develop financing arrangements to enable the IMF to respond to financial crises. The result was the New Arrangements to Borrow (NAB) which supplements the GAB with an additional SDR 17 billion in credit lines.

The NAB entered into force in November 1998, and was activated for the first time shortly thereafter, in December 1998, to finance an arrangement with Brazil. There are 25 participants to the NAB, with commitments based on these countries' quotas in the IMF. NAB is to be the first and primary recourse when the IMF needs to supplement its ordinary resources. Like the GAB, the NAB is reviewed and renewed every five years. A proposal by the IMF Managing Director to activate the GAB and/or the NAB must be agreed to by the participants in the arrangements, and then must be approved by the Executive Board. During periodic reviews, the NAB may accept new members, but only with the approval of the IMF and of participants representing an 80 percent share of the credit lines. At other times, an 85 percent vote by the IMF Board of Directors can amend the NAB agreement and include additional participants.

Financial and Technical Activities of IMF

According to its Articles of Agreement, the Fund is supposed to oversee the functioning of the international monetary system and exercise tight surveillance over its members' exchange rate policies. Through the Article IV consultations, the Fund assesses each member country's macroeconomic and structural policies that form the basis of a country's exchange rate policy. The IMF may also provide countries that are not drawing on IMF resources with closer monitoring through a shadow program or a precautionary arrangement The Fund's failure to recognize the economic indicators that pointed towards a pending financial crisis in Mexico has been the subject of much discussion and debate.

At the 1995 Economic Summit in Halifax, Canada, the G-7 urged the IMF to improve its surveillance by requiring more timely information on key economic data, establishing standards for timely publication of this data, and engaging in closer and more continuous policy dialogue. The IMF was also told to focus on countries where financial tension is most likely to have spill-over effects and to be more critical and demanding during the policy dialogue. After the Asian financial crisis, the G-7 once again directed the IMF to require more comprehensive and timely reporting of economic and financial statistics. The IMF also commissioned an external review of its surveillance function.

The IMF provides technical assistance to its members in three broad areas: design and implementation of fiscal and monetary policies; institution-building, such as the development of central banks, treasuries, tax and customs departments and statistical services; and drafting and review of economic and financial legislation. The IMF also conducts trainings and seminars through its technical assistance program at the IMF Institute in Washington, DC, at regional institutes in Vienna and Singapore, and through other regional institutions.

The IMF makes its resources available to member countries by selling SDRs which members purchase with their own currency. Members are obligated to repurchase the Fund's holding of their currencies by paying in SDRs (or other currencies as defined by the IMF) within a specified period. The IMF provides assistance through several different facilities depending on a country's specific macroeconomic and structural problems. A member country with balance-of-payments difficulties can immediately withdraw 25 percent of its quota from the Fund.

This generally comprises a country's "reserve tranche," and is not subject to conditionality or charges. If a country needs to borrow more, it then taps into "upper credit tranches," which are subject to conditionality. Conditionality was created to ensure that borrowers will adopt the Fund's policy measures to improve their balance-of-payments positions so that they will be able to repay the IMF in a timely manner. (Timely repayment is essential since IMF resources are supposed to be used temporarily in order to be available to all members).

According to the principles of conditionality, the debtor government must pursue adjustment policies that:

— reduce the basic imbalances in the economy, both in external accounts and in domestic resource use;

— enable the member to avoid or lift existing restrictions on trade and external payments;

— overcome the member's problem within a moderate period of time; and

— augment the member's monetary reserves so that it will be able to repurchase its currency from the Fund.

Typically, IMF stabilization programs are short-term and aim to raise government income and lower government expenditure in order to improve the country's balance-of-payments position and reduce the need to borrow foreign currency. The borrower commits to meeting economic targets which almost always include limits on the expansion of credit and the reduction of public expenditures. Government income is raised largely through value-added taxes (VATs), which are often increased and/or extended to cover more products.

Expenditure-reducing policies are designed to curtail demand and usually include the contraction of money supply and cuts in government spending. These cuts are mainly achieved through reductions in government programs, decreases or freezes in wage levels and civil service retrenchment. In theory, trade balances and reserves should improve as imports are reduced and domestically produced goods are freed for export.

Structural Adjustment Programs (SAPs)

The Fund's medium-term SAPs are based on the belief that the private sector is more effective and dynamic than the public sector and that it responds better in a market economy. Adjustment policies, therefore, have the privatization of public enterprises as a prime objective. This has the additional benefit of generating capital for the elimination of current account deficits. At the same time, a smaller, more effective state can, theoretically, direct its social services in a more targeted fashion.

Deregulation also includes elimination of controls on goods, investments and financial systems. The theory behind financial deregulation is to allow interest rates to rise, thereby encouraging savings and ensuring that money is only borrowed for the most profitable investment projects. To promote greater integration into the world market and to divert productive resources to the export sector, countries are encouraged to:

— lower their exchange rates in order to become more competitive in the market;

— reduce trade barriers to force local industries to become more competitive in order to survive cheap imports;

— provide incentives to increase exports, such as tax relief and financial subsidies; and

— encourage foreign investment by creating free-trade zones or providing tax breaks.

These are a general set of IMF-promoted policies rather than a comprehensive list of measures. It should be noted that in practice there are few clear lines of distinction between stabilization and adjustment programs. The IMF bailouts of Asia, which were short-term stabilization programs, had far-reaching structural reform measures in corporate governance, banking regulation and many other areas that go beyond the traditional fiscal and monetary concerns of stabilization programs.

Lending facility is the principal mechanism for traditional IMF assistance. Stand-by arrangements are typically designed to provide short-term assistance to countries facing a temporary or cyclical balance-of-payments problem. Credit is made available in four tranches, each the equivalent of 25 percent of quota. Stand-by arrangements can be less than a year and up to three years. Countries must meet quarterly performance criteria and pass semi-annual reviews. Repayments are to be made in three to five years.

When balance-of-payments problems arise from structural factors-such as distortions in production, trading patterns and prices-the Extended Fund Facility (EFF) gives countries some more time and resources to address their balance-of-payments problems. The EFF generally runs for three or four years and countries must repurchase their currencies within four to ten years. Under both the stand-by and EFF, members may borrow up to 100 percent of their quota on an annual basis, with a cumulative cap set at 300 percent. The IMF may make exceptions to the access limits.

The new Supplemental Reserve Facility (SRF) was set up in the wake of the Asian financial crisis. It is for countries facing an extreme balance-of-payments problem caused by a sudden loss of market confidence and subsequent capital flight and attacks on its currency reserves. To use the SRF, the country's need is supposed to be very shortterm and able to be reversed rapidly through policy changes. The SRF has no set access limit, but is instead based on a country's need, ability to repay, its previous track record with the IMF and the IMF's own liquidity situation.

The SRF carries a higher interest rate than other IMF facilities-300 basis points higher than the regular rate of charge on lending for the first year, increasing by 50 more basis point each six months after, with a cap of 500 basis points. Countries must repurchase their currencies within two to two-and-a-half years. Emergency financing may also be provided to a country facing a natural disaster or emerging from conflict. A member requesting emergency assistance must describe the economic policies it plans to follow and state its intention to avoid introducing exchange or trade restrictions. In general, assistance is limited to 25 percent of quota, though exceptions can be made. In 1995, the policy on emergency assistance was extended to cover post-conflict situations. In general, the qualifying criteria are the same, though the support must be part of a larger international effort aimed at providing technical assistance and capacity building. The country must also state its economic framework and its intention to move as soon as possible into an upper credit tranche or Enhanced Structural Adjustment Facility program.

The IMF has also established special lending facilities that are designed to respond to specific types of balance-of-payments problems. These include the Compensatory and Contingency Financing Facility (CCFF), the Buffer Stock Financing Facility and the Systemic Transformation Facility. These address problems such as sudden changes in export earnings for reasons beyond a country's control (eg. crop failures and commodity price fluctuations), and the adjustment process of the former communist countries.

The Structural Adjustment Facility (SAF) was established in 1986 as a longer-term, concessional lending facility. One year later the Enhanced Structural Adjustment Facility (ESAF) was established and essentially subsumed the SAF. The function of ESAF is to extend three-year, low-interest loans to low-income countries that belong to the International Development Association. It is designed to service poorer countries that require more extensive adjustment in order to achieve growth and a sustainable balance-of-payments position. As a result, the facility differs from previous IMF operations in both its time frame and the scope of the attached macroeconomic policies. ESAF extends loans based on a comprehensive three-year Policy Framework Paper (PFP) developed by the IMF, World Bank and borrowing government.

The PFP delineates explicitly the macroeconomic and structural policy measures that must be followed to strengthen the country's balance-of-payments position. The programs include quarterly targets to assess performance. Though IMF resources are supposed to be used only temporarily to correct short-term imbalances, many ESAF borrowers have had programs for many years, some even for more than a decade. The conditionality attached to ESAF loans is also extensive, and goes beyond the original trade and monetary) areas of IMF authority. This has made

ESAF a very controversial facility, particularly among citizens' groups. Despite this controversy and a large degree of opposition toward ESAF, the IMF and its members want to make ESAF a permanent, self-financing program.

The ESAF Trust has a total asset base of over SDR 10 billion about $14.5 billion). Access to ESAF is normally topped at 190 percent of a country's quota over a three-year program period, with provisions of up to 255 percent in exceptional circumstances. Repayments are to be made in five to ten years.

The IMF has long been criticized for the high degree of secretiveness surrounding its policies and programs. In recent years, however, the IMF has made some significant strides toward releasing more information such as making loan documents much more available. The IMF appears to be consciously changing its practices and improving its information policy. The IMF has taken important steps to make its web site more useful. However, the IMF should develop more ways to provide information in poorer countries where Internet access is limited. Timely disclosure of information is another major problem that the IMF needs to address.

Currently, loan documents are released after the Board votes to approve the loans. With drafts of loan programs unavailable it is impossible for civil society to have input into their government's agreements with the IMF. Even parliamentarians may not see a draft of the IMF agreement until it is approved even though they will be partly responsible for its implementation. Withholding loan agreement information is a serious deterrent to fostering greater ownership of economic programs and is in many ways a threat to sovereignty and democracy.

Principle of Accountability

The principle of accountability asserts that decision-makers should be held responsible for the consequences of their decisions. Accountability therefore necessarily encompasses the issues of transparency and evaluation. Transparency ensures that interested parties outside an institution have access to information pertaining to what decisions were made, who made them, what factors and options were considered and the criteria on which decisions were based. Evaluation allows the public to ascertain whether or not the decisions made were the right ones. Evaluation also encourages the development of more effective policies and approaches.

The IMF fails to make the grade in terms of its own accountability. A major reason for this is the absence of a systematic, independent evaluation mechanism. Without constant and rigorous independent review, the IMF seems to want to hide its performance and keep its operations from rigorous review. In a direct response to outside criticisms the IMF agreed in 1996 to institute a system of external review on an ad hoc trial basis.

Public Participation

Civil society organizations around the world are becoming increasingly vocal in their demand that the public be involved in the design of economic development programs. As global communications make the world smaller, more citizens are challenging the costs and benefits of economic policies. To date, however, the IMF has largely deflected calls to become more participatory in its economic adjustment programs. While it has made some efforts in recent select cases to reach out to a wider audience, it generally claims that as an institution providing short-term financial assistance and macroeconomic advice, consultation is not feasible or necessarily desirable.

The IMF contends that according to Article V of its Articles of Agreement, which says that finance ministry and central bank officials are the contact points for the IMF, it is precluded from meeting with a wider range of country representatives. This lack of public participation in the design of economic programs means that IMF economic policies are less likely to be endorsed and followed by other government sectors and the public. This is a major reason for countries' terrible record of compliance with SAPs.

An IMF study found that 75 percent of the ESAF programs it evaluated had fallen off-track. It may be true that broad public participation is more difficult in emergency bailout packages, where a rapid infusion of funds is necessary to stave off a run on the currency. However, most of the IMF's staff time is spent on countries with more chronic balance-of-payments difficulties. In these instances, there is more than enough time to have significant public input in program design.

Public participation is critical as macroeconomic policy changes have major social and environmental impacts. What IMF policymakers are ignoring is the fact that the local population is often the best placed to identify shortcomings in these programs. Until citizens feel that their country's interests are being adequately represented in economic reform programs, and until the IMF opens up a process of genuine consultation with affected peoples, IMF economic programs will continue to be plagued by policy failures, avoidable mistakes and program breakdowns.

As structural adjustment loans have become increasingly interventionist, the IMF has played a major role in restructuring the labor market in borrowing countries. Though labor market conditions are not within the IMF's traditional short-term mandate, many of the IMF's current SAPs advocate changes in labor laws and wage policies. The IMF has taken up the mantra of "labor market flexibility"-a polite way of saying deregulation-as the way to encourage foreign investment and make countries more competitive.

The IMF promotes deregulation of labor markets because it contends that labor markets are overburdened with regulations, creating disincentives for employers to hire more workers. While this may be the case for individual sectors of an economy, the reality for the labor force as a whole is different. Deregulation tends to empower employers to fire "surplus" workers and use increased profits to enlarge executive salaries and corporate profits.

According to the 1995 United Nations Trade and Development Report employers are using extra "flexibility" in labor laws to shed labor and downsize, rather than add to productive capacity and create jobs. Deregulation impacts the labor force in a number of ways. One of the most significant impacts is the abolishment of minimum-wage and collective-bargaining laws. In many cases, the IMF encourages countries to keep wages low in order to attract foreign investment.

In Haiti, for example, the government has been pressured to exploit its low-wage labor and institute a freeze on wages. The government was also told to rewrite the labor code to eliminate a statute mandating increases in the minimum wage when annual inflation exceeds 10 percent. By the end of 1997, Haiti's minimum wage was only $2.40 a day, worth just 19.5 percent of the minimum wage in 1971. The deregulation of labor standards in poor countries is especially devastating to workers because they often are not permitted to organize and therefore are unable to bargain for better working conditions.

People end up working longer hours for less pay. Economically, the effect is equally negative: underpaid workers have little purchasing power, and this contributes to more shrinking of the economy and prevents the maintenance or establishment of small- and medium-sized businesses. Workers in industrialized countries suffer as well: not only are they are forced to compete with cheap labor in the developing world, they also face a decline in demand for Northern consumer goods in those same poor countries.

One study found that structural adjustment policies have negatively impacted U.S. exports, and therefore U.S. jobs.8 The deregulation of the economy also results in rapid and substantial job losses as public sectors are quickly privatized. In many developing countries, the public sector has provided a great deal of employment. As the IMF forces countries to downsize government agencies, the ranks of the unemployed grow faster than the private sector can absorb them. Compounding this harsh reality is the lack of existing social safety nets that can support people when they lose their jobs.

Attempts by the World Bank and IMF to construct social safety nets as part of their SAPs have not been nearly comprehensive enough to catch the number of workers who fall through the cracks. In Korea, for example, the financial crisis caused unemployment to rise from a pre-crisis level of 2 percent to almost 9 percent in

February 1999. What's more, unemployment insurance schemes adopted in the adjustment process reached only 10 percent of the unemployed labor force by March 1999.

The IMF's approach to workers is purely market-based: labor flexibility will create the incentives for business and investment, which will inevitably result in higher wages and improved working conditions as a country develops. But in fact, at least one billion adults-more than 30 percent of the global workforce-are unemployed or seriously underemployed. Wages and working conditions have been declining in the United States by 1 percent annually for the past 20 years and in poor countries at a much faster pace. The IMF is not equipped, either in mandate or expertise, to get involved in labor issues, and its insistence on playing a role in these issues is making the situation worse for the world's workers.

While the reduction of world poverty is proclaimed as a major goal of multilateral lenders like the IMF, SAP policies too often hit the poor the hardest and sometimes exacerbate poverty and social inequality. Virtually all developing countries have implemented or are in the process of carrying out SAPs. While SAPs have largely succeeded in shrinking government budget deficits, eliminating hyperinflation, and maintaining debt-payment schedules, SAPs have failed to establish a foundation for environmentally sustainable, locally driven economic development.

For example, IMF programs emphasize the achievement of a balanced budget. In order to balance the budget, the Fund typically pushes governments to rapidly cut spending. Such spending cuts can force governments to shrink or eliminate important social programs, or institute cost-recovery programs for social services that increase prices and often put health care and education out of reach for the poor.

While the IMF has increasingly recognized the importance of social spending and criticizes military spending, tough fiscal targets sometimes make it impossible for the government to invest adequately in social programs, rural development, and other necessary human and physical infrastructure. Revenue-raising adjustment policies can also hurt the poor. Changes in the tax system often emphasize easy-to-collect, regressive sales taxes that disproportionately affect the poor.

Short-run revenue concerns, without consideration of long-run efficiency and equity concerns, often govern privatization. The result in too many cases has been the conversion of government enterprises into private monopolies that are run by elites or foreign interests with few local ties. Tightened credit requirements and higher interest rates meanwhile make it virtually impossible for small farmers and businesses to invest. Although the liberalization of trade does make imported items less expensive, most people in low-income countries consume little besides basic necessities.

The increased affordability and presence of luxury goods is a dubious achievement of SAPs. Layoffs of government workers, wage constraints, higher interest rates, reduced government spending and the closure of domestic industries all contribute to the shrinking of the domestic market. The weak state of the domestic market exacerbates worsening socio-economic conditions. Although there may be a new dynamism in certain elite sectors, social and economic insecurity deepens for most people in countries subjected to SAPs.

The result can be increasing political instability, such as riots over food prices, outbreaks of violence and widespread disaffection with (and non-participation in) electoral political systems. The ways in which structural adjustment hurts the poor undoubtedly are complex. For example, liberalizing the agricultural sector might have the benefit of eliminating corrupt parastatals that pay cheap prices to farmers. However, liberalization can also mean that poor farmers lose access to important price supports, or that the price of inputs like fertilizers might dramatically increase. The IMF, however, has been very simplistic in its assumptions of how SAPs will impact the poor, and there is rarely any explicit analysis of proposed adjustment measures, their impacts on the poor, possible trade-offs or mitigating measures.

The only external review that has been conducted of the IMF's adjustment program, the Enhanced Structural Adjustment Facility (ESAF), called for an explicit assessment of the positive and negative impacts of proposed adjustment measures and an identification of which societal groups would most likely be harmed and hurt by adjustment. It also called for an analysis of the short- and long-run costs and benefits of measures, as well as an explicit assessment of how fast adjustment should be done. These recommendations however have largely been ignored.

The global environment has been another casualty of the way the IMF currently does business. In the push for rapid liberalization and deregulation around the world, IMF loans and bailout packages are paving the way for resource exploitation on a staggering scale due to the failure of the IMF to recognize the economic and social value of natural resources. The IMF has not taken environmental impacts into consideration on lending issues; environmental ministries of borrowing governments are locked out of formal IMF policy discussions; environmental NGOs are not consulted on program conditions and projected impacts; and the IMF's alleged collaboration with the World Bank on identifying environmental hazards of programs is not transparent or even documented.

The IMF's focus on free trade and export-led growth can have significant environmental impacts. To increase exports, countries countries are extracting natural resources at unsustainable rates. Countries that have IMF (and other foreign) loans must also pay back their debts in foreign currency, usually U.S. dollars, which requires that countries accumulate hard currency. One of the quickest ways to get hard currency is to liquidate natural resource stocks. For example, the most heavily indebted and poorest African countries have forest loss 50% greater than forest loss in the other African countries. IMF programs also place a premium on increasing competitiveness and attractiveness to foreign investment, which encourages countries to lower environmental standards.

Government spending cutbacks inevitably target the environmental ministry as one of the first agencies to come under the budget axe. This has happened with many major IMF bailouts, including in Brazil, Russia, and Indonesia-countries that are also renowned for their great biodiversity. The result, according to conservation groups like the World Wildlife Fund (WWF), is a downward spiral of environmental management and protection that primarily benefits transnational corporations. In all but one of WWF's nine country studies on the impacts of structural adjustment, staffs of natural resource departments were reduced, budgets were cut and mandates were scaled back.

Under current SAPs, many of the poor become poorer, and this cycle of poverty places greater threats on the environment. As the poor try to survive, they cut down trees to build makeshift homes and to provide heat for their families. As they are forced off farmland by large landowners, they turn to marginal lands for subsistence, which leads to more deforestation and soil erosion.

The overwhelming debt burdens of poor countries is a major contributor to the crisis that grips the economies of most developing countries today. For the most heavily indebted poor countries, total external debt rose from $55 billion in 1980 to $215 billion by 1995. Debt has continued to climb in most countries. As a result, governments have been forced to divert scarce resources away from spending on health, education, environmental protection and other vital social services and instead dedicate them to pay what are essentially unpayable debts. The origins of the debt crisis are many, from government corruption to misguided aid policies and projects. But the consequence is that people who had no role in contracting the debt in the first place, particularly the poor, are forced to service the debt.

Recognizing that debt threatened the viability of the international economic system, the world's rich governments, the World Bank and the IMF finally agreed in late 1996 to launch the Heavily Indebted Poor Countries Initiative (HIPC). While initially promising because it brought all creditors together for a comprehensive debt agreement. The IMF's (and other creditors') contribution to HIPC is insufficient. Furthermore, instead of using its own resources to provide immediate debt relief the IMF has sought bilateral sources of funding for HIPC. By refusing to use its own funds, the IMF is abdicating its role in the debt crisis.

HIPC's terms and conditions are too stringent. The debt-toexport ratios that determine eligibility for HIPC are too high and are based on export levels and national income rather than human development needs. These levels exclude many debtridden poor countries, and mean that any debt relief granted will be insufficient to deliver a country to economic health. The IMF's Enhanced Structural Adjustment Facility (ESAF) has been directly linked to the HIPC Initiative.

To qualify for HIPC relief, a country must go through at least three years of an ESAF program, which is notoriously difficult to complete because of its unacceptable levels of austerity. The IMF has linked any additional contributions it might make to HIPC to the financing of a permanent ESAF, despite the controversial record of that facility. Some academics and NGOs charge that the IMF and its policies are themselves creating debt, and that attempts to address the debt crisis in the context of IMF adjustment programs are counterproductive.

Adjustment is certainly about integrating countries into the global economy and increasing their trade with the rest of the world. By opening up their economies, countries open themselves up to more foreign investment, which can increase their debt. Trade liberalization means increased imports, as well as exports. If imports increase more than exports, this can also lead to increased debts.

Responding to the pressure of the international NGO movement to cancel the debts of poor countries, the IMF, World Bank, and creditor governments are beginning to revise the HIPC program by lowering eligibility thresholds and increasing financing for debt relief. However, the system still works to protect creditors' interests and ensure a steady flow of repayments, rather than freeing up vast amounts of resources that could be dedicated for health, education, rural development, and environmental protection.

Global Economic Governance

The financial disasters in the emerging markets combined with decades of intractable poverty and elusive development in the poorest countries prove the need for dramatic reform of international economic policy and of the international financial institutions. Proposals vary for reforming global economic institutions like the IMF. Some NGOs and academics call for handcuffing these institutions, which they claim cause more harm than good. Others call for an entirely new set of rules for the global financial system and argue that only totally new institutions with different missions and functions could serve to enforce these rules. Still others believe that the current institutions are here to stay and that the most logical strategy is to reform them through bargaining with policymakers. Whatever the preferred strategy, citizen movements share the same objective: to improve the economic, social, and environmental prospects of all the world's citizens while respecting sovereignty and increasing people's power to determine national policies.

One position that has gained support in recent years is that the IMF is beyond reform. Proponents of this position argue that the root problem is that the IMF has too much power and uses that power destructively. Therefore the most important strategy is to reduce its power and not engage with the IMF in any dialogue that the Fund could use to bolster its public image. Reducing its power is also necessary to level the playing field between citizens' movements and the IMF if real reform is to be achieved. Proponents of this position point out that IMF policies fundamentally reflect the controlling interests of the IMF, banks and multinational corporations, particularly those from the United States.

As long as control of the IMF by these interests is unchallenged, proposed reforms of IMF policies and operations will have little impact in developing countries. Related to this position is a belief that the structure by which the IMF operates, using conditionality as the means to impose reform, is fundamentally undemocratic and disregards national sovereignty and citizens' rights. This position holds that imposing any economic policies on a country-even "good" ones - has harmful long-term effects. Foreign control of national matters, it is argued, emasculates the ability of countries and citizens to make their own decisions, build domestic capacity and learn first-hand what works.

The IMF bailouts in the Asian financial crisis did not stop the financial panic-indeed, the crisis deepened and spread to more countries. What finally stopped the panic were direct negotiations with the banks in East Asia that forced them to roll over their loans. Without the possibility of a major IMF bailout, countries would get better deals from the banks. Proponents of this position generally do not engage in direct dialogue with the IMF, preferring to focus their strategy for change on shrinking the IMF's power by, for example, opposing increases to the IMF's resources or areas of activity.

They would also oppose any attempts by the IMF or its member governments to make promises for long-awaited reforms in return for new funding. The vague hope that sometime in the distant future the IMF will transform itself, these critics charge, is not enough to merit increases in IMF resources today.

The IMF acts too much in the interests of the United States, which exerts a great deal of influence because it holds the largest share of votes. When it comes to formal votes on altering the IMF charter, authorizing the use of IMF resources for special purposes, or other important issues, the United States has effective veto power. Even on issues that only require a simple majority, the United States can, and often does, throw its weight around.

The IMF's decision-making structure is problematic in other ways as well. Most decisions are made by consensus, with few formal recorded votes, and Board discussions are off limits to the public. Recently the IMF pledged to make public more summaries of Board discussions. But given its tendency to release sanitized versions of documents - such as the Public Information Notices (PINs) that summarize Board discussions of Article IV surveillance reviews-this pledge may not amount to much.

The IMF needs to make its decision-making process much more transparent and accountable. The results of Board votes should be recorded and made publicly available. The same should be done for Executive Director statements at Board meetings. The Board should release minutes of its discussions expeditiously after its meetings and in a form considerably more substantive than the PINs. IMF management should also increase its accountability.

But NGOs believe that IMF efforts toward transparency should be deepened in two ways. One is to increase the types of documents, these would include:

1. Article IV Consultations and their supporting documents, such as Staff Reports and Staff Concluding Analysis. These documents provide

important information about the IMF's surveillance activities, particularly in non-borrowing countries. Some IMF members and staff contend that the release of these would "spook" the market and might provoke crises. While the most sensitive information does not need to be made public, providing more accurate information to the markets may actually reassure lenders over time and reduce the size of crises that do arise. Currently, the IMF only releases a four-page summary of its Article IV consultations. Such a short summary does not give much insight into the true economic conditions of IMF member countries. In March 1999 the IMF initiated a pilot project for the voluntary release of Article IV consultations. This is a step forward, but there are still many IMF members, particularly Southern governments, that are resisting full publication of Article IV documents. While still proceeding with the pilot project, the IMF might also consider publishing a document for each country that is more substantial than the PIN.

2. All evaluation and audit documents.

3. The Policy Framework Paper (PFP), Letter of Intent, and Memorandum of Understanding. The IMF should press more countries to release these documents, possibly even making it a condition of an IMF loan. Loan documents should be more standardized in format, with the policy matrix, timeline for policy implementation, performance criteria, structural benchmarks and prior actions all clearly specified in each country's loan agreement. The IMF should also release previous PFPs and Letters of Intent which would increase the

accountability of the IMF and borrowing governments for past loans.

4. Reports by IMF management to the Interim Committee and Development Committee.

5. Detailed summaries of Executive Board meetings.

It is important to recognize, however, that merely releasing documents is not sufficient to become adequately transparent. Therefore the IMF should also make information available to the public in a way that is useful. The improvements in the IMF's web site are useful for many people, but perhaps not for civil society in the poorest countries for whom Internet access is difficult to obtain or prohibitively expensive.

The IMF should make documents available out of its Resident Representative offices. It should also collaborate with the World Bank, UN agencies and the borrowing government to make information available through various outlets. Country program information should also be available in local languages. Prior to Board deliberations the IMF and its member governments should release drafts of Policy Framework Papers, Letters of Intent and policy matrices so that the public and a wider range of government officials have an opportunity to provide comments, raise objections or propose alternatives. Furthermore, the meeting dates and agenda of the Board of Directors should be publicly available so that outside parties have an opportunity for input.

Decentralization

One of the most important ways that a global institution can become more responsive and accountable to civil society is by coming into more direct and routine contact with the public. Decentralization is a trend backed by many international institutions, such as the World Bank and the United Nations, as a way of getting more "in touch" with their clients. The IMF, however, remains a very centralized bureaucracy with most of its staff stationed at its headquarters in Washington, DC. Mission teams travel abroad but generally spend the short time there in the capital meeting with officials. Furthermore, mission teams have little negotiating autonomy-they are sent with a clear agenda and all aspects of the negotiations must be cleared by headquarters.

To become more responsive to the needs of its members and their citizens, the IMF needs to increase its visibility in borrowing countries. One way to do this is by building up its Resident Representative program. The IMF has about 70 field staff or Resident Representatives stationed throughout the world. Usually, there is one representative in each field office which is often minimally staffed and tends to be housed at the central bank of the country. The representative is supposed to meet with government officials and civil society, and monitor program compliance as well as the economic and social conditions. In 1997 the IMF conducted an internal evaluation of the Resident Representative program but has not released it. In general, the IMF has not used the Resident Representative program effectively. The list of representatives is not well publicized and many citizens' organizations are not aware of the program or how to utilize it. The fact that representatives' offices are housed in secluded central bank facilities exacerbates the problem. The external ESAF review proposed several changes to improve the Resident Representative program,, including to: increase the staffing of Resident Representative offices;

station Resident Representatives in each IMF borrowing country; station senior, proven IMF staff in the field; and devolve greater authority to Resident Representatives.

Currently, the program is too dependent on the skills and initiatives of individual representatives. While some representatives make an effort to reach out to more groups and establish better relations, others keep themselves isolated. The IMF should consider establishing "best practices" guidelines that would set the performance standards for all Resident Representatives.

IMF staff also need to spend more time understanding the environment in which they are working. Many have been critical that IMF staff do not read the local newspapers, venture outside of the capital or speak the local language. The IMF should take steps to correct these problems, including conducting greater outreach in the country and making more of an effort to develop a genuine feel for the country.

IMF's Role in Sustainable Development

Though the IMF has no mandate to address such issues, it has involved itself in longer-term restructuring of economies which often has profound social, development and environmental impacts. But even if the IMF returned to its original mandate of economic surveillance and short-term financial assistance it must still address the impacts of its economic stabilization policies on poverty and income distribution, the environment and people's rights. There are constraints to the IMF's capacity to promote poverty alleviation, environmental protection, and human and labor rights.

Other organizations, such as the World Bank, are better equipped in staff expertise and routine activities to pursue many of these issues. The challenge then for the IMF is to explore the niche that it can play in promoting sustainable development.

One of the most important steps the IMF could take to promote sustainable development in poor countries is to help relieve these countries of their overwhelming debt burdens. Debt relief would free up tremendous resources that governments could then dedicate to health care programs, basic education, sanitation and rural development. The people who bear the burden of debt are the poor who are deprived of adequate services because their cash-strapped governments must spend more on debt payments to creditors like the IMF than they spend on social services.

The poorest, most heavily indebted countries owe about $7.8 billion to the IMF. By establishing the HIPC initiative, the IMF has taken the first step toward providing debt relief for these countries. However, the resources committed so far are insignificant compared to the scope of the problem. The IMF has the capacity to tap several sources of funds to dramatically alleviate poor countries' debt burden.

The IMF originally pledged to contribute SDR 180 million for the HIPC initiative, funds that were to come from its ESAF Reserve Account. The ESAF Reserve Account is set up to cover losses that may arise from defaults or arrears on ESAF loans, which are financed partly by contributions from certain IMF members and partly from IMF borrowings from its richer members. To use this money, creditors to this account have to unanimously agree to release the money.

The IMF has gold reserves currently worth about $30 billion. Keeping such vast amounts of gold reserves made sense when countries were following the gold standard and could cash in their currencies for the equivalent amount in gold. The IMF still records in its books the value of the gold when it was purchased. Therefore if the IMF sold or revalued its gold at current world prices, which are much higher, it would actually make a profit on the sale and could use some of those proceeds to finance debt relief.

However, tapping the gold reserves has also been floated as a way of making the IMF's ESAF program self-financing, which would put the IMF permanently in the development business. If NGOs want to mobilize all resources available for debt relief, they must insist that gold reserves not be manipulated as a way to finance ESAF rather than immediate debt relief.

Poverty Reduction Strategies

The external review of the IMF's Enhanced Structural Adjustment Facility (ESAF) criticized the IMF's failure to factor in the potential impact on the poor of its stabilization and adjustment programs. It is this neglect that has earned the IMF the ire of development and social justice groups around the world. The IMF is beginning to acknowledge that its programs can no longer afford to ignore basic human needs if economic and social development goals are to be achieved.

However, the IMF's current strategy to address this issue is focused on increasing funding for social safety nets and better targeting them to vulnerable groups. Increased social spending is an important step. However, it is not enough to ensure that sustainable and equitable development becomes the driving force behind economic policies. One proposal to mitigate the impact of IMF policies on the poor is to force the Fund to stick to its original focus on stabilization. If this were possible, structural issues could be handled by other institutions and agencies more equipped to deal with longer-term growth and development.

In the event the IMF did return to its original mandate of shortterm balance-of-payments stabilization it would still have to work with government officials and institutions like the World Bank to identify how stabilization affects the poor. In other words, as the IMF reduces budget deficits, bolsters central bank reserves, and contains inflation, it would also need to identify how budget cuts are conducted and revenue is increased, and what that means for citizens. However, governments may still have the need for longer-term adjustment, and may still desire financial assistance for doing so.

Whether the IMF succeeds in retaining its adjustment programs, or adjustment is handed off to the World Bank or other institutions, there are still many changes that need to be incorporated into orthodox adjustment programs. The desire to undergo economic adjustment, however, must come from governments and their citizens. The IMF, as well as the World Bank, must become much more tolerant of national priorities and conditions. This could include allowing borrowers to slow the pace of trade liberalization and privatization, pursue their own industrial policy or increasing wages to boost demand.

In areas such as revenue generation, the international financial institutions have traditionally insisted in imposing value-added taxes, with minimal success in generating increased revenues. Therefore, tax policies should have greater flexibility. In Africa, for example, a good deal of revenue has been generated through tariffs, which trade liberalization rapidly removes. Countries should be allowed more leeway in making a smoother transition to new policies. Rather than insist that poor countries export more primary commodities to the rich countries, adjustment policies should promote value-added activities and regional cooperation and integration.

Civil society organizations all over the world are also calling for increased investments in the areas of health, education, infrastructure development, environmental protection, rural development and extension services as these are some of the investments necessary for future growth. To invest in these areas, larger budget deficits may be necessary in the near term. These proposals run counter to nearly everything that the G-7, IMF and World Bank are currently promoting. Yet it must also be pointed out that most of their current programs are astonishingly unsuccessful.

As a macroeconomic institution, the IMF should not play a role in setting labor policy conditions. Rather, the IMF should work with relevant government officials, international institutions like the International Labour Organization (ILO) and labor unions to identify and mitigate any potential negative impacts a loan program could have on labor conditions, wages and employment. The IMF should establish procedures that will enable this consultation to happen. For example, loan programs should involve a dialogue with labor prior to a loan agreement; the ILO should be part of these discussions, and loan documents should reflect and reference this dialogue.

The IMF could also commission studies on the impact of its loans on labor conditions-including on real wages, employment, work hours, jobs created, status of labor rights and unions. These reviews should become part of a feedback loop to inform new economic reform programs. It is also conceivable that the IMF could refuse to lend to countries that systematically violate internationally accepted worker rights, as agreed to under the ILO conventions, to which most nations are signatories.

In fact, some labor unions are calling on the IMF to enforce the core labor standards in the ILO Declaration on Fundamental Principles and Rights at Work, adopted by the International Labour Conference in June 1998.

Environmental Protection

Determining the environmental costs of a particular macroeconomic policy may be more complicated than doing a similar analysis for an individual project. Yet it is still imperative that the IMF incorporate environmental impact assessments (EIAs) into its loans. Only a full assessment of a policy's costs will allow the IMF to pursue policies promoting countries' longterm economic prosperity. While these EIAs should be incorporated into IMF policy and program design, the IMF should work with other institutions like the World Bank, national environmental ministries and credible environmental research organizations.

The IMF should commission such institutions -which have more staff experience and expertise with environmental issues and EIAs-to conduct the studies and incorporate the results into its loan programs. In the past year, the IMF has responded to NGO concerns by increasing transparency in the design of government budgets which it views as a key step toward avoiding unproductive expenditures and curtailing corruption.

Environmental NGOs' major concerns regarding IMF SAPs is the institution's emphasis on creating favorable conditions for private sector development and foreign investment, even if that means weakening environmental laws. The IMF should refrain from discussing laws related to natural resources as it is outside its area of expertise. If, however, any laws have in fact been streamlined, made more flexible, eliminated or strengthened as a result of loan negotiations and economic policy changes, the IMF and government should publicize the changes.

In particular, changes to laws that deal with major extractive industries, such as mining, forestry, and fishing should be disclosed. If an IMF loan program document discusses proposed or revised environmental or resource laws for sectors such as mining or forestry, these laws should be referenced and included as an appendix in the loan document. Again, transparency will pressure governments and the IMF to refrain from touching regulatory standards that protect the needs of communities and their environment.

The lack of broader government participation is a serious impediment to creating programs that promote sustainable development. In countries where natural resources generate a significant portion of national income, it is particularly important for environmental ministries to be represented in loan negotiations so that sustainability and resource management issues enter into the economic discussions. Currently, some IMF loan program documents and staff reports track natural resource exports around and during the loan period, but they contain no mention of what might be the sustainable use of those resources.

In the United States, some of the most important initiatives on IMF reform have occurred when the U.S. Congress was asked to appropriate funds to the IMF. These Congressional appropriations processes have provided citizens' organizations with an opportunity to criticize IMF operations and to demand the taxpayers' right to a certain "quality of performance." In 1989, 1992, and 1998, Congress wrote reform language into the IMF's quota-increase appropriation, calling on the IMF to institute certain changes and calling on the U.S. representative to the IMF to press for these changes.

In 1994, Congress actually withheld a portion of its proposed contribution for the ESAF program, and stipulated that the remaining funds would be available when the IMF released more information to the public. This move has helped persuade the IMF to make greater efforts at transparency. In other IMF member countries, however, funding for the IMF is not approved by parliament and is instead channeled through the finance ministry which is the government agency traditionally most sympathetic to the IMF. This makes it more difficult, though not necessarily impossible, to demand that contributions to the IMF be withheld until reforms are made.

Irish NGOs, for example, successfully pressured Ireland's finance ministry to cease funding ESAF for several years. Even if parliaments do not have authority over contributions to the IMF they are still useful for monitoring IMF performance and present a good target for NGO lobbying. For example, parliaments can hold hearings and inquiries, inviting their representatives at the IMF to testify and answer questions. Parliaments can also order finance ministry officials to file reports on reform efforts that are being pursued. Other parliamentary tools include issuing letters from members of Parliament to the finance ministry or IMF representative advocating a policy position or articulating concerns about programs. All these measures are important methods of generating much wider debate about the IMF, educating more policymakers, raising political awareness and creating media opportunities.

NGOs can also attempt to change their own internal legislative processes to give parliaments a greater say in determining national policy at the IMF. In Brazil, the Senate must approve all loans that Brazil negotiates with International Financial Institutions. Switzerland's lower house of parliament recently passed a bill ordering future quota increases to be approved by parliament. NGOs could replicate this effort elsewhere. Since the IMF is a multilateral institution, international coordination of reform strategies is very important, both for NGOs and for parliamentarians. There have been several international meetings of progressive parliamentarians interested in reforming the institutions of the global economy, including the IMF.

With regard to IMF reform, NGOs have probably had their greatest success in the areas of IMF transparency and accountability and the least success in pushing for changes in the export-led growth model that characterizes IMF programs. In IMF borrowing countries, civil society groups should have regular contact with the IMF's Resident Representative who is supposed to meet with NGOs. NGOs should share their research and analysis, and regularly provide information to the Resident Representative so that NGO viewpoints are constantly being expressed.

NGOs may also want to consider alliances with other segments of civil society - such as labor unions, environmentalists, small business, and women's groups - to increase their bargaining position. Alliances with NGOs in other countries can also be useful, as critiques of IMF prescriptions and NGO alternatives can be shared and pushed with other IMF member governments, whose representatives will eventually have to approve a loan. Another tactic that NGOs can use to influence national economic policy is courtesy of the IMF itself. The IMF is pushing governments to become more open in their budget processes by clearly outlining and publishing government expenditures.

This increases public knowledge about government spending priorities - what funding is being cut to reduce a deficit, and what is being protected. Ultimately, with this knowledge, NGOs will be able to better lobby their governments to protect priority programs and activities and to cut wasteful and unproductive programs. NGOs could use these budget figures in other ways to influence program conditions and gain more autonomy for local people in setting policy.

If state-owned enterprises are considered a major drain on the government budget, or if civil service employment and expenditure is viewed as excessive in a given country, it is likely that the public would demand changes, such as privatization or civil service reform. If state enterprises are profitable and are seen to provide a public good, the IMF should not impose an ideological-based policy. The IMF should concentrate on promoting a transparent budget process, and allow local people to draw their own conclusions and propose home-grown policies.

7

NGOs: Issues and Opportunities

Defining NGOs is not an exercise for the intellectually squeamish. A 1994 United Nations document, for example, describes an NGO as a non-profit entity whose members are citizens or associations of citizens of one or more countries and whose activities are determined by the collective will of its members in response to the needs of the members of one or more communities with which the NGO cooperates.

This formulation embraces just about every kind of group except for private businesses, revolutionary or terrorist groups, and political parties. Other popular substitutes for the term NGO (private voluntary organizations, civil society organizations, and the independent sector) are likewise almost terminally vague. A better approach to understanding NGOs and what they are would focus on their respective goals, membership, funding sources, and other such factors.

Yet although there may be no universal agreement on what NGOs are exactly, there is widespread agreement that their numbers, influence, and reach are at unprecedented levels. In 1948, for example, the UN listed 41 consultative groups that were formally accredited to cooperate and consult with the UN Economic and Social Council (ecosoc); in 1998, there were more than 1,500 with varying degrees of participation and access.

Until recently, NGOs clustered in developed and democratic nations; now groups sprout up from Lima to Beijing. They are changing societal norms, challenging national governments, and linking up with counterparts in powerful transnational alliances. And they are muscling their way into areas of high politics, such as arms control, banking, and trade, that were previously dominated by the state.In general terms, NGOs affect national governments, multilateral institutions, and national and multinational corporations in four ways: setting agendas, negotiating outcomes, conferring legitimacy, and implementing solutions.

NGOs have long played a key role in forcing leaders and policymakers to pay attention. In the early 1800s, U.S. and European bodies such as the British and Foreign Anti-Slavery Society were driving forces behind government action on the slave trade; by the turn of the century, groups such as the Anglo-Oriental Society for the Suppression of the Opium Trade were leading an influential antidrug movement that culminated in the 1912 Hague Opium Convention.

In 1945, NGOs were largely responsible for inserting human-rights language in the UN Charter and have since put almost every major human-rights issue on the international agenda. Likewise, NGO activism since the 1960s and 1970s successfully raised the profile of global environmental and population issues.

Instead of holding marches or hanging banners off buildings, NGO members now use computers and cell phones to launch global public-relations blitzes that can force issues to the top of policymakers' "to do" lists. Consider the 1997 Nobel Prize–winning campaign by NGOs to conclude a treaty banning landmines over the objections of the United States. The self-described "full working partnership" between the Canadian government and a loose coalition of more than 350 humanitarian and arms-control NGOs from 23 countries was key to the negotiations' success.

But what seized the attention of the public and policymakers was the coalition's innovative media campaign using the World Wide Web, faxes, e-mail, newsletters, and even Superman and Batman comic books. Treaty supporters won the signatures of 122 nations in 14 months. When several coalition members announced plans for a follow-on campaign against small arms, the U.S. government sprang into action, meeting with 20 other countries in July 1998 to launch official talks on a possible treaty.

NGOs can be essential in designing multilateral treaties that work. Chemical manufacturing associations from around the world helped set up an effective verification regime for the 1997 Chemical Weapons Convention that could be supported by industries and militaries. Throughout the various sessions of negotiations on climate change, groups such as the Environmental Defense Fund and the World Business Council for Sustainable Development have helped craft compromise proposals that attempt to reconcile environmental and commercial interests; meanwhile, NGOs have been instrumental in helping government negotiators understand the science behind the issues that they seek to address.

NGOs can also build trust and break deadlocks when negotiations have reached an impasse. In 1990, a sole Italian NGO, the Comunità di Sant'Egidio, started the informal meetings between the warring parties in Mozambique that eventually led to a peace settlement. During talks in 1995 to extend the Treaty on the Non-Proliferation of Nuclear Weapons, NGOs from several countries working with the South African government delegation helped forge a compromise that led to the treaty's permanent extension.

NGO judgments can be decisive in promoting or withholding public and political support. The World Bank learned this lesson in the early 1990s, albeit the hard way. After decades of watching the bank do business with only a handful of NGOs and brush off demands for change, more than 150 public-interest NGOs took part in a sustained campaign to spur greater openness and accountability and to encourage debt reduction and development strategies that were more equitable and less destructive to the environment.

Today, partly as a result of this high-profile pressure, about half of the bank's lending projects have provisions for NGO involvement—up from an average of only 6 percent between 1973 and 1988. The bank has even included NGOs such as Oxfam International in once sacrosanct multilateral debt relief discussions—against the wishes of many World Bank and International Monetary Fund (IMF) officials. Even the IMF is beginning to change its tune. In June 1998, the IMF Board of Directors met with several NGO leaders to discuss their proposals to increase the fund's transparency.

NGOs on the ground often make the impossible possible by doing what governments cannot or will not. Some humanitarian and development NGOs have a natural advantage because of their perceived neutrality and experience. The International Committee of the Red Cross, for example, is able to deliver health care to political prisoners in exchange for silence about any human-rights violations that its members witness.

Other groups such as Oxfam International provide rapid relief during and after complex humanitarian disasters—with and without UN partners. Moreover, as governments downsize and new challenges crowd the international agenda, NGOs increasingly fill the breach. Willy nilly, the UN and nation-states are depending more on NGOs to get things done. Total assistance by and through international NGOs to the developing world amounted to about $8 billion in 1992—accounting for 13 percent of all development assistance and more than the entire amount transferred by the UN system.

International NGOs also play critical roles in translating international agreements and norms into domestic realities. Where governments have turned a blind eye, groups such as Amnesty International and the Committee to Protect Journalists call attention to violations of the UN Declaration on Human Rights. Environmental NGOs police agreements such as the Convention on International Trade in Endangered Species, uncovering more accurate data on compliance than that provided by member nations.

Perhaps one of the most vital but overlooked NGO roles is to promote the societal changes needed to make international agreements work. Signatories of the Organization for Economic Cooperation and

Development's 1997 Bribery Convention, for example, are counting on the more than 80 chapters of Transparency International to help change the way their societies view bribery and corruption.

Increasingly, however, NGOs operate outside existing formal frameworks, moving independently to meet their goals and establishing new standards that governments, institutions, and corporations are themselves compelled to follow through force of public opinion. The UN moratorium on driftnet fishing in 1992 and the U.S. International Dolphin Conservation Act of 1994, for example, largely codified changes in fishing practices that NGOs had already succeeded in promoting and then winning from commercial fisheries.

More recently, even as governments and multilateral institutions slowly begin to consider measures to promote the sustainable use of forests, the environmental NGO Greenpeace led a European consumer boycott that persuaded a leading Canadian logging company to announce that it would change the way that it harvests trees.

Despite the demonstrated capacity of NGOs to do good, their growing power on the ground has exposed them to heightened criticism, some of it justified. As salutary as international attention has been to the recent turmoil in Chiapas, Mexico, for example, it is hard to believe that the arrival there of 4,500 foreigners from 276 different organizations necessarily represents an unalloyed good.

One recent study on NGOs and peacebuilding in Bosnia criticized the use of advertising (from signboards to t-shirts) by NGOs to promote their reconstruction programs to potential donors. Such advertising, the study noted, had the effect of denigrating local rebuilding efforts and raising questions about where NGOs were actually putting their money.

In the Sudan and Somalia, NGOs have subsidized warring factions by making direct and indirect payments to gain access to areas needing assistance. In other conflict settings such as Ethiopia and Rwanda, NGO–constructed roads and camps for civilian assistance have instead been used by combatants.

Other longer-term concerns loom for these service-delivery NGOs. The UN High Commissioner for Refugees warned in 1996 that if national governments continue to favor NGOs over multilateral agencies in donor assistance, they may undermine important systems of coordination and cooperation in large-scale emergencies. Intense competition among NGOs in the relief sector has also pushed the sector toward a form of oligopoly that threatens to crowd out smaller players, especially local NGOs in developing countries. Eight major groups now control about 50 percent of the relief market.

But on balance, the record for such NGOs is surely no worse than that of governments. NGOs are increasingly aware of these weaknesses and are moving to address them by adopting codes of conduct and pledging to "do no harm." Moreover, given their origins as grassroots groups, NGOs tend to be wary of organizations that become too big; this innate suspicion can serve as a mechanism for self-regulation.

Yet, the greatest challenges created by the growing influence of NGOs are not in the field but in the arena of public opinion and the corridors of power. Today, in a phenomenon that one environmental activist bemoaned as the "rise of the global idiots," any group with a fax machine and a modem has the potential to distort public debate—witness the demise of not just the biodiversity treaty but the Multilateral Agreement on Investment (mai), which for all its apparent shortcomings still deserved more reasoned consideration than it received.

Even legitimate, well-established groups sometimes seize on issues that seem designed more to promote their own image and fundraising efforts than to advance the public interest: In 1995, for example, Greenpeace continued to attack the Royal Dutch/Shell Group for its plans to sink an oil rig (the Brent Spar) in the North Sea, even after independent scientific analyses showed that the environmental effects of doing so would be inconsequential.

Steeped in a culture that encourages adversarial attitudes to the powers that be, many NGOs seem best suited to confrontation, a characteristic that some U.S. policymakers seized on in noting that the NGO coalition against landmines might have won U.S. support (and hence a stronger treaty) if it had been more patient and willing to compromise.

Governments, multilateral institutions, and corporations face inherent dilemmas in trying to work with NGOs. At their most fundamental level, these dilemmas hinge on two key questions: Who should participate, and how? On the one hand, opening up the floodgates to allow equal access to every group would frustrate decision making. More than 1,500 NGOs were accredited at the 1992 United Nations Conference on the Environment and Development in Rio de Janeiro, for example. Trying to include them all was impossible, so in the final days of the conference, government delegates increasingly retreated behind closed doors. On the other hand, narrowing the field fairly is extraordinarily difficult because no one algorithm or set of criteria can objectively rank the worth of an NGO to a participatory process.

Should the World Trade Organization (WTO) consult and share information with groups that have large memberships but are sworn enemies of the WTO's existence? When seeking to devise a treaty on persistent organic pollutants, should negotiators insist that groups be representative of, and accountable to, large constituencies and thereby exclude reputable, experienced groups that represent future generations or nonhumans (the International Fund for Animal Welfare, for example)?

Some traditional centers for power have done a better job than others at tackling these kinds of questions about participation. Among nation-states, Canada stands out for its role in forging an alliance with NGOs on the landmine ban. Nations such as Norway helped fund the NGO coalition for the ICC. (On the other side of the funding fence, nations such as Sierra Leone and Bosnia received help at the ICC negotiations from legal advisers provided by the NGO No Peace Without Justice.) The U.S. record in working with NGOs is mixed: generally good in areas such as the environment and relatively poor in areas such as arms control and regional issues. China represents another extreme, having chosen to banish NGO delegates at the Fourth International Women's Conference in Beijing in 1995 to a site one hour's drive away from the main negotiations.

Most multinational corporations are still struggling to figure out how to handle NGO participation. One 1996 poll of 51 major European corporations found that although 90 percent of them believed that the impact of "pressure groups" would stay the same or increase over the next five years, only 20 percent had formal procedures in place for dealing with such groups, and only 12 percent for evaluating them. Still, there are grounds for optimism: A 1998 survey of 133 NGOs found that while many rated their current relationships with corporations as "antagonistic" or "nonexistent," most predicted the development of cooperative relationships in the future. The changing attitude toward NGOs of the Royal Dutch/Shell Group may be a case in point.

Stung by fierce NGO campaigns on the Brent Spar episode and its operations in Nigeria, where its ties to the dictatorship of General Sani Abacha made it a target for human-rights groups, Shell has adopted a new Statement of General Business Principles that includes commitments on human rights and the environment; in regions such as Latin America, it now consults with NGOs to ensure that its oil operations take environmental and social factors into account.

The impact of NGOs on multilateral institutions (and national governments) may well be cyclical. As Yale professor Steve Charnovitz has observed, NGO involvement seems to depend on two factors: the needs of government and the capabilities of NGOs. During the nineteenth century, for example, governments had little experience with nonpolitical treaties and therefore needed NGOs; although the young League of Nations later saw NGOs as allies in forming new international organizations, NGO participation diminished in the 1930s as the league's influence declined and governments garnered more practical experience in NGO–oriented issues. The same pattern holds true for the post–World War II years: an early burst of enthusiasm, followed by a gradual decline during the 1950s that reversed itself as issues such as the environment, development, population, and food aid became part of the international agenda.

Today, in the wake of a powerful post–Cold War boost in NGO activity, the receptivity of multilateral institutions to NGO participation varies greatly, from relatively open ECOSOC bodies such as the Commission on Sustainable Development to the more closed UN Security Council and General Assembly, and from an increasingly receptive World Bank to the still recalcitrant IMF and WTO. At bottom, however, the search for a form of perfect democracy that encompasses all NGOs makes about as much sense in the international system as it does in, say, the United States.

Instead, institutions and NGOs should strive to create formal but flexible systems during negotiations to foster dynamism and self-adjustment. ECOSOC is a case in point. It ranks NGOs according to three tiers of status: Category 1, Category 2, and Roster. The small percentage of those with Category 1 status, or top access, have more opportunities to attend meetings, submit written advice, and occasionally speak at conferences. The selection process deliberately favors NGOs operating in more than one country, without barring national NGOs that cannot afford to travel; it also favors groups that are of a representative character but is ambiguous enough to allow in groups that represent perennial values and scientific truths, not members. In 1998, more than 100 NGOs have top status, with nearly 1,500 enjoying some form of consultative status at ECOSOC,versus 978 in 1995, and 41 in 1948. NGOs want more, governments want less, but the system generally works.

Some advocates want to push more UN decision-making forums in the direction of the International Labor Organization (ILO), which gives formal voting rights to business and labor delegates as well as governments. A handful of variations on the ILO model exist that work well, particularly on technical issues and the setting of standards. But trying to win voting rights for NGO representatives in more UN forums is by no means a sure way to improve the representative character of institutions.

The unique ILO system works fairly well because national employer and labor umbrella groups already exist, making the identification of representative employer and labor delegates simpler than in other fields. But it is doubtful in most cases that such systems would actually improve the representative character of institutions; even if NGOs elected their own representatives from among themselves, there would be insufficient guarantees that the pool of electors was truly representative of society or the public interest.

Perhaps most important in the long run are systems to formalize existing means of two-way communication between decision-making institutions and "stakeholders." Although NGOs still see much room for improvement at the World Bank, it has produced better decisions and is rated accountable by more NGOs because it no longer simply provides a sounding board mechanism for selected groups to air their views. The bank now disseminates more detailed information about its decisions and activities so outside groups can weigh in. And it uses a variety of techniques to elicit feedback and track NGO expertise—including surveys, advisory groups, public meetings, and private meetings with staff. Consequently, the bank is more apt to consult and partner with the right groups when designing and implementing specific projects. Because the system is more open, groups that cannot participate directly are more likely to judge the decision-making process as accountable—even if they disagree with the results.

Many governments and institutions—including the WTO, IMF, and several UN bodies—will continue to resist more public participation, arguing that their issues require great secrecy. But history offers a powerful argument that the holdouts suffer from a failure of imagination. Half a century ago, the architects of the postwar international trading system did not contest NGO involvement. The proposed charter for the International Trade Organization (ITO) included the very same language as the WTO charter, providing for "consultation and cooperation" with NGOs.

The ITO framers had a different interpretation than their latter-day successors, however; they envisaged that commercial and public-interest NGOs would maintain regular contact with the ITO Secretariat, receive unrestricted documents, propose agenda items, and participate as observers and occasional speakers at conferences. The spirit of these proposals faded away when the ITO failed in favor of an interim solution, the General Agreement on Tariffs and Trade, or GATT. Ironically, most multilateral institutions today face requests from NGOs that could be met by adopting the standards for participation that the ITO's framers proposed.

The challenge facing NGOs is more subtle but no less important. As these groups acquire the access and influence that they have long sought, they must not lose the qualities that have made them a source of innovation and progress. Some analysts already fear that formerly independent NGOs may become more beholden to national governments as they come to rely more on public-sector funding—which now accounts for around 40 percent of NGO budgets versus only 1.5 percent in 1970.

And many of the schema for increasing NGO involvement may simply foster predictable and bureaucratic behavior among civil society representatives, potentially dulling the passion and richness of views that can emanate from narrowly focused groups. They may also cut off NGOs from the informal channels through which they have traditionally been most influential.

Instead, NGOs, governments, and multilateral institutions need to devise systems of public participation that draw on the expertise and resources of NGOs, their grassroots connections, sense of purpose and commitment, and freedom from bureaucratic constraints. Those NGOs that have seen the most rapid growth in their power will have to contend with inevitable limits on their influence and access. Those governments and institutions that have resisted the advance of these new players will have to permit an unprecedented level of public scrutiny and participation. Over time, this messy process of give-and-take promises to transform the way that international affairs are conducted.

NGOs' Policy Towards International Criminal Court

The establishment of the International Criminal Court (ICC) was a fundamental step towards removing the power to punish from the sole domain of governments. The Rome Statute for the established of ICC was adopted on 17 July 1998. The rapid ratification of the Statute by countries which experienced gross human rights violations very recently, such as Nigeria, Sierra Leone, and Yugoslavia, shows that the present governments of these countries are willing to put their faith in the Court to deal with possible further violence in their own political future. Nevertheless, it would be naïve to believe that the establishment of the Court will prevent gross human rights violations from occurring in the twenty-first century.

The significance of the Court lies in the fact that it is now clear that international law does not only have universal rules to protect human beings in principle, it has an instrument to punish individuals who gravely breach the rules, even if their own government is unwilling or unable to do so.It appears that a majority of states are willing to throw their weight behind the idea of the Court: 120 states voted in favour of the Statute in Rome, and 139 have now signed it. This means that they are prepared to sign away a small but essential part of their sovereign power in order to protect their future citizens against a possible situation where they may become unwilling or unable to prosecute genocide, war crimes, and crimes against humanity committed by their citizens or on their territory.

Unfortunately, a minority of governments, including those of very big and powerful states such as China, India, and the United States, are not prepared to take out this insurance with the international community against their own future. This means that the selectivity that has characterised the enforcement of human rights so far, and the inequality between victims of human rights violations in different parts of the world that follows from it, will not be fully resolved by the establishment of the International Criminal Court—at least not yet. Moreover, it is likely that the fundamental inequalities in resources and power between different parts of the world will also be reflected in the Court: while Northern states will put up most of the resources and play a substantial role in the Court's staffing, the perpetrators brought before the Court are likely to all be from the global South.

The United States has already promised to put up a tremendous fight if any of its citizens is ever brought before the Court, but it may be assumed that the European states who are now such fervent supporters of the Court would also change their stance if the prosecutor ever found it necessary to indict one of their citizens. Whether the Court would be willing to take such a risk is doubtful. The refusal of the prosecutor of the Yugoslavia tribunal, Carla del Ponte, to seriously investigate whether NATO committed war crimes in its Kosovo campaign is not a promising precedent in this respect. On the other hand, it must be acknowledged that, while the hands of Northern governments are not clean, there also have been and will be many, many perpetrators of gross human rights violations in the South. Their victims now have a better chance to see these crimes acknowledged, condemned, and punished.

The legal, political, and symbolic significance of the new Court has been the main focus of attention in the writing of legal scholars, diplomats, activists, and United Nations officials, proponents of the Court, as well as those who think the erosion of state sovereignty has gone too far or has proceeded in the wrong direction.

The first international trial designed to bring someone to justice for what would today be called crimes against humanity may have been that against a certain Peter von Hagenbach in 1474. An ad hoc international criminal tribunal of 28 judges from towns in Alsace, Rhineland, and

Switzerland, with a presiding judge from Austria, tried and convicted him for murder, rape, and perjury, crimes which 'trampled under foot the laws of God and man', during his occupation of the town of Breisach on behalf of Charles, the Duke of Burgundy.

The first proposal for a permanent international criminal court in modern times was made in 1872 by Gustav Moynier of Switzerland, one of the founders of the International Committee of the Red Cross. Horrified by the atrocities committed by both sides in the Franco-Prussian war in 1870, he proposed the establishment of an international criminal court to deter violations of the Geneva Convention of 1864 and to bring to justice anyone responsible for such violations. However, governments showed little interest and many of the leading international experts on humanitarian law criticised the proposal as unrealistic.

After the First World War, the Versailles treaty provided for ad hoc tribunals to try military officials of the Central Powers for breaching the laws of war, but Germany refused to hand anyone over for prosecution, and the Allies soon lost interest after the German Kaiser had been given asylum in the Netherlands. Proposals during the Second World War to set up a permanent international criminal court were rejected in favour of ad hoc international tribunals at Nuremberg and Tokyo, followed by Allied national military tribunals to prosecute nationals of the Axis powers. These were later criticised for imposing 'victor's justice' and for convicting people of crimes not previously formulated in laws.

Immediately after the Second World War, the international community was briefly united in drafting international rules that would help prevent atrocities occurring in the future. The Universal Declaration of Human Rights and the Genocide Convention were adopted in 1948. While there were also plans for an international criminal court, it missed the window of opportunity that closed with the onset of the Cold War.

etween 1949 and 1954, the International Law Commission (ILC), a UN commission of legal experts, actually drafted a statute while also continuing to work on a code of crimes against the peace and security of mankind. The UN General Assembly shelved the idea, however, because of disagreement over the definition of aggression and other crimes.

However, the idea was kept alive in various corners of global civil society. Non-governmental organisations (NGOs) like the International Law Association, which had concluded as early as 1926 that an ICC was 'not only highly expedient, but also practicable', the Association Internationale de Droit Penal, and the World Federalist Movement continued to propagate the court idea as a matter of principle. The independent UN experts of the International Law Commission, led by the Senegalese Doudou Thiam, continued to work on a code of international crimes, and individuals like Benjamin Ferencz, a former prosecutor of the Nuremberg tribunal, and M. Cherif Bassiouni, an Egyptian professor of criminal law, continued to devote academic treatises to the idea of a permanent court.

The watershed In 1989, inspired by its Prime Minister Arthur Robinson, long a supporter of the idea of an international criminal court, Trinidad and Tobago formally proposed to the General Assembly the 'establishment of an international criminal court with jurisdiction to prosecute and punish individuals and entities who engage in, inter alia, the illicit trafficking in narcotic drugs across national borders'.

The International Law Commission was again charged with drafting a statute for such a court. It seized enthusiastically upon this mandate, stretching it from framing the ICC merely as a drugs court to a court with jurisdiction over crimes against the peace and security of mankind. In those years, work on the draft Statute proceeded quietly in the rarefied atmosphere of the International Law Commission, far from the political limelight, where many years were sometimes spent on the definition of a legal clause.

The ethnic cleansing in Yugoslavia and the genocide in Rwanda, and the subsequent Security Council decisions to establish ad hoc tribunals changed all this. The televised evidence of atrocities in Yugoslavia and Rwanda quite literally 'shocked the conscience of mankind'. In the aftermath of the Cold War, and through the activities of human rights organisations, the idea that perpetrators could and should be punished for these atrocities gained a foothold.

In 1993, the International Law Commission invited states to comment on a first draft, and in 1994, at lightning speed by its own standards, it had finished its work. It recommended that states now convene a conference to turn it into a binding treaty. However, while a number of countries, mainly European and Caribbean, supported the idea of holding a conference as soon as possible, other members of the General Assembly demurred.

It was decided that an ad hoc committee of state representatives should study and discuss the ILC draft first. A year later, the ad hoc committee converted itself into a preparatory committee (PrepCom), the difference being that this committee could actually draft text. At the end of the 1996 sessions, a date was set for the conference, a compromise between those states who wanted a conference as soon as possible and those who were in no rush at all: Rome, summer 1998.

While these first three years saw none of the main points of controversy resolved, they did see the emergence of a 'like-minded group' of countries who were in favour of swift establishment of a strong court. This group grew from a handful of state delegates, partly born out of personal friendships, to over 60 states in 1998. The formation, growth, and consolidation of this group was strongly encouraged by NGOs as a counterweight to the permanent members of the Security Council on the one hand and members of the Non-Aligned Movement on the other, both of which were reluctant to establish an independent court with supra-national powers.

The Rome Conference took place between 15 June and 17 July 1998. The draft text that was to be transformed, in Rome, into a definitive treaty contained more than 1,700 sets of brackets, representing competing proposals for the articles. Moreover, about 50 of the state delegations, mainly from developing countries, had not taken part in the preparatory committee meetings at all. The first two weeks in Rome were therefore mainly devoted to letting every state have its say; in the meantime coordinators of thematic working groups were informally trying to forge compromises.

On the basis of these negotiations, the conference Bureau chaired by Canada published a first 'discussion paper' on 6 July, followed by a proposal narrowing down the options a few days later, and a final 'takeit-or-leave it' package deal in the night of 16 July, the day before the conference was to end. The final session on the evening of Friday 17 July was very emotional. Two delegations proposed amendments to the final draft. India sought to include the use of nuclear weapons in the definition of war crimes and to deprive the Security Council of the power to refer cases to the court.

The United States wanted the court to have jurisdiction only with the consent of the country of nationality of the accused. Reopening the debate on either of those issues would have meant missing the deadline for finalising a statute at this conference, and it might be a long, long time before the same momentum could be achieved again. Norway introduced a motion to take no action on these amendments, which was overwhelmingly supported. After each of these votes, the delegates broke into applause, which, on the second occasion, turned into rhythmic clapping that lasted for ten minutes. At the final, formal plenary session, the Statute was adopted by secret vote, with 120 votes in favour, 7 against, and 21 abstentions.

NGOs Working for ICC

Almost half of the 236 organisations represented in Rome were either legal-professional organisations, such as bar associations, or human rights NGOs. Other groups working for the ICC at the domestic level, at the PrepComs, and in Rome included a large number of women's organisations, peace and conflict resolution organisations, groups focused on global governance and strengthening the United Nations, and representatives of churches and religious organisations. Details of the global civil society players working for the international criminal court are describe din the following paragraphs.

Lawyers: The establishment of an International Criminal Court can be considered as a major step towards a more accountable and people-centred international law. At the same time, though, drafting the rules for such a Court was a delicate but fascinating task from a strictly legal point of view: different areas of international law, including human rights law, humanitarian law, and the law of international institutions, and areas of domestic law like criminal law and extradition rules, all converged in a new way in the Statute. It is not surprising then that, from the beginning, the venture attracted a large number of lawyers. While the initial discussions by the ILC were barely noticed or monitored by anyone, the quick transformation of the Yugoslavia tribunal from an idea into a working court excited and mobilised the legal profession.

Human rights groups: Human rights organisations were particularly predominant. After decades of building an international human rights system at the regional and global levels, human rights experts began to realise that, while the body of law on human rights had become substantial, the scale of human rights violations in the world was not actually declining. 'Combating impunity' became a catch-phrase in the human rights idiom, but the experience in many Latin American and other countries even after their transition to demo-cracy was that it was not just legally but also politically, socially, and psychologically very difficult to prosecute perpetrators of human rights violations under previous regimes. Thus, the idea of recourse to an international criminal court came to be embraced by human rights groups.

The Nuremberg and Tokyo tribunals, and the Yugoslavia and Rwanda tribunals, were considered as models to build on, but they were also seen as selective and wanting in impartiality as they had been set up by a few states to prosecute only in a few circumscribed situations. The ICC would be set up by the international community and have a global remit. All the major international human rights organisations, including Amnesty International, Human Rights Watch, the International Commission of Jurists, and the Federation International des Ligues de Droits de l'Homme, were heavily involved in the ICC negotiations, but so were a host of regional and national organisations, including for instance the European Roma Rights Centre, the Arab Commission on Human Rights, the Argentinian Asamblea Permanente de Derechos Humanos, the Ligue Rwandaise pour la Promotion et la Défense des Droits de l'Homme, and the Cambodian Human Rights Task Force, as well as individual human rights professors, lawyers, and activists.

Establishing a criminal court rather than just holding states accountable required some adjustments of thought for human rights advocates. Their focus with respect to criminal trials had always instinctively been on safeguarding the rights of the defendant. Now, the rights of suspects, in effect enemies of human rights, the rights of victims, and the need to create an effective system capable of convicting perpetrators had to be balanced against each other. Amazingly, there was no tradition in human rights law of assigning criminal responsibility to individual perpetrators of violations. Building such rules from existing principles was the intellectual and political challenge of the ICC for human rights groups.

Women's groups: The women's groups were also particularly inspired by the example of the Yugoslavia tribunal in their work for an ICC. While in the past others had pointed out that women were particularly vulnerable to abuse in conflicts, the use of rape as a component of ethnic cleansing in the former Yugoslavia brought the issue to the fore. Although the statute of the Yugoslavia tribunal did not contain any gender-specific mandate, its functionaries recognised that an ostensibly gender-neutral justice system would in fact fail to address gender-specific abuses, and took on board some of the concerns of women's groups. An officer for gender issues was appointed within the prosecutor's office; and it was decided to allow rape victims to give testimony anonymously, and to seriously prosecute rape as a war crime, an issue to which the first prosecutor, Richard Goldstone, was particularly committed. It was in their relations with the tribunal in The Hague that Yugoslav women and their European supporters had their first experience of inscribing women's concerns into humanitarian law, an experience they built on in New York and Rome. Other, more global, experiences included the World Conference on Human Rights in Vienna in 1993 and the Fourth World Conference on Women in Beijing in 1995. These were not treaty-making conferences, however, and the challenge for women's rights groups was to take the progressive texts of these 'aspirational' final declarations into the 'mainstream big-boy venue of hard-core international law' of the ICC negotiations.

While some women's groups, such as Equality Now, had been involved since 1995, most were relative latecomers to the process. The Women's Caucus for Gender Justice was formed on the initiative of a small group of women's rights activists present at the February 1997 PrepCom, who realised that, without a much stronger effort, gender concerns were not going to be adequately represented in the negotiations. It quickly grew to be a coalition within a coalition, with more than 300 member organisations by the time of the Rome conference. Like in Beijing and other fora, the feminist majority of women's groups in New York and Rome focused on women's rights encountered a vocal minority of 'family' groups supported by the Vatican and Arab states, whose preoccupation was to prevent any language that might be interpreted as facilitating abortion from entering the Statute. The clash between these groups and the Women's Caucus will be discussed in more detail below in the case study on gender-specific crimes.

Peace groups: The aims of the smaller peace contingent within the movement for an ICC were less clear. Two kinds of peace groups were represented. The first, typified for instance by the Nuclear Age Peace Foundation and the International Association of Lawyers against Nuclear Arms, were direct descendants of the nuclear disarmament movement of the 1980s, and their primary interest was in having the threat or use of nuclear arms designated as a war crime. They were largely unsuccessful in Rome. The second, characterised by groups like International Alert or the Helsinki Citizens' Assembly, had roots in the same movement but had evolved in a different direction through direct involvement in the non-nuclear conflicts of the 1990s, in which abuse of civilians became a primary method of warfare. They were exploring solutions in the direction of grass-roots conflict resolution on the one hand and a more human rights-based approach on the other. Their interests in the Court were in fact very similar to those of the human rights groups.

Global governance groups: A small but very active contingent of groups could be characterised as 'global governance' organisations, committed generally to promoting a more just and more democratic global order. This included the World Federalists, various United Nations associations who propagate the idea of a strong United Nations while monitoring the organisation itself critically, and three interconnected part-international, part-Italian organisations with strong links to politicians, in all of which Emma Bonino played an important role: Parliamentarians for Global Action, the Transnational Radical Party, and, especially, No Peace Without Justice. These groups were well-placed to make contributions to some of the less contentious issues in the Statute. An early paper by the World Federalist Movement, for instance, summarised state and NGO positions on how the Court might be financed, examined precedents concerning other international courts, and made a concrete proposal stressing that, while it might seem like a minor concern in negotiations, the Court would not be able to function successfully without adequate finance.

Religious groups: A number of churches and religious groups were represented, including many mainstream Christian denominations but also Jewish, Bahai, Muslim, and Buddhist federations. At the end of the twentieth century, 'the century that has seen the killing of more humans by other humans than occurred in all the rest of our history put together', these members of religious groups began to reach a consensus around the need for more earthly justice to set beside eternal, divine justice. Their aim was, however, to go beyond mere punishment, from punitive justice to restorative justice, to help reconcile communities torn by violence and to inject a spiritual dimension into the ICC project. Most of these groups came together in a Faith-based Caucus. They concerned themselves with the less political, more ethically oriented preamble and final clauses of the Statute, the wording of which, they felt, should have a spiritual dimension. According to the Samoan delegation, which coordinated the negotiations, 'Most of the concepts the Faith-Based Caucus espoused can be found in the final product, albeit in different language'.

Regional groups: When the NGO Coalition for an International Criminal Court was founded in 1995, it consisted primarily of international organisations, usually with European or American headquarters, and a permanent representation at the United Nations in New York. However, a strong effort was made to involve national organisations from all regions in the Coalition, and with success.

Latin American organisations had a strong interest in the Court stemming from their own experience of living through dictatorships and the subsequent difficulties in bringing perpetrators of violations to justice. Indeed, most of the Latin-American organisations involved were human rights organisations. African organisations, mainly lawyers' and human rights groups, also apparently believed in the ICC as part of a 'rule of law' solution to the wars and human rights abuses many of their countries had experienced. Their interest may also have been fuelled by the active involvement of African lawyers like the Senegalese Abdul Koroma, one of the most active members of the International Law Commission's subcommission on the ICC, Cherif Bassiouni, and Richard Goldstone, and by the setting up of the Rwanda tribunal.

While a wide range of east and west European and North American organisations were also wellrepresented, there was little interest from organisations in North Africa and the Middle East or from Asia. Indeed, not a single Asian NGO produced a paper during the three years of

PrepCom negotiation. Some groups were represented in Rome, and interest has grown since then, particularly in Bangladesh, the Philippines, and Egypt, but the activities have not been comparable to other regions.

The weakness of global civil society participation from these two regions is in keeping with the figures on membership in international NGOs published in Global Civil Society 2001. It may be related to the corresponding weakness in the development of international law, and in particular human rights law, in the same regions. A glance at the ratification record of existing human rights treaties—for instance, the International Covenant on Civil and Political Rights or the Convention Against Torture—shows that, regardless of their official ideology, states in North Africa and the Middle East and Asia are least likely to become parties.

Many Asian human rights groups have tried unsuccessfully for years to set up an Asian human rights system. It is not surprising, then, that their enthusiasm for setting up an even more forceful human rights implementation mechanism, one that their governments would be even less likely to participate in, was lukewarm. The situation in the Middle East and North Africa is even bleaker. In many of the countries in this region, there is not enough political space for human rights groups to operate freely, let alone to campaign for a Court that might have the authority to bring leaders of their governments to justice for human rights abuses.

Cyprus and Tajikistan have ratified the Statute, while, by contrast, 26 European, 12 sub-Saharan African, and 11 Latin American countries had become parties to the Court.

NGO Coalition for ICC

When the UN General Assembly decided, in December 1994, not to take the ILC's draft Statute straight to a treaty-drafting conference but instead to consider it further in an ad hoc committee, the five or six NGOs following the proceedings were disappointed and shocked, in particular by the excessive willingness of states they considered progressive to compromise.

A phone call between William Pace, Executive Director of the World Federalist Movement, and Christopher Hall, legal adviser of Amnesty International, who had both been observers, resulted in an invitation to a number of groups to discuss the formation of an NGO Coalition. At that meeting, on 10 February 1995, the NGO Coalition for an International Criminal Court (CICC) was founded as 'a broad-based network of NGOs and international law experts'. The Coalition was given a loose structure.

Although there were a coordinating organisation and a coordinator, a steering committee, and ordinary members, no formal decision-making structure was agreed. Moreover, the Coalition chose initially to formulate no common position except 'to advocate for the creation of an effective, just and independent International Criminal Court', and to be no more than a conduit of information between NGOs, state representatives, and the general public, and a resource for coordination between NGOs. On the Sunday before the Rome Conference, the Steering Committee of the Coalition did adopt a list of 'Basic Principles'.

The self-appointed Steering Committee initially consisted almost exclusively of human rights groups, including Amnesty International, the Federation International des Ligues de Droits de l'Homme, Human Rights Watch, the International Commission of Jurists, and the Lawyers' Committee for Human Rights. Coordination, however, was given to the World Federalist Movement.

The legal and human rights groups were already developing strong opinions on specific aspects of the international criminal court, and neither too much agreement nor open competition between them would have been good for the image of the Coalition. The World Federalists merely advocated the idea of an ICC in principle as part of the vision of a 'just world order through a strengthened United Nations' to which they are committed. They were considered neutral enough to be trusted by a whole range of NGOs.

The level of recognition of the Coalition's role by state representatives and United Nations officials was probably unprecedented. The chairman of the PrepComs and many other official delegates took the participation of NGOs in the proceedings for granted, and the Coalition was their first point of contact with them. Before the Rome Conference, the Coalition coordinator was actually asked by the United Nations to organise the accreditation of NGOs to the Conference, a unique form of self-regulation not attempted before at international conferences. By the time of the Rome Conference, the NGO Coalition for an International Criminal Court had grown into a network of over 800 organisations, 236 of which sent one or more representatives to Rome. Thus, the Coalition delegation was far bigger than any state delegation.

Despite the loose formal structure of the Coalition and the wide variety of its members' interests, it was extremely effective in its coordinating role. In order to be as effective as possible, it split into three types of groups: regional caucuses, who lobbied state representatives from their own regions; thematic caucuses on gender justice, victims, children, peace, and a faith-based caucus; and twelve working groups on different parts of the draft Statute. The last of these shadowed the corresponding working groups of state representatives on different sets of articles and made daily reports available to NGOs and state delegates. Through the Latin-American regional caucus, for instance, wavering delegates from Mexico and Peru were pushed toward more progressive positions, partly through debates in their domestic newspapers.

Special themes that cut across various parts of the Statute were tackled by thematic caucuses. Members of the Victims Rights Working Group, the Children's Caucus, and the Women's Caucus all worked together intensively to improve the position of witnesses in the proceedings of the Court. They worked to afford victims better protection, the right to have their own say, rather than being just an instrument of the prosecution, and the right to reparation. According to two state delegates who later wrote on the subject, they played a vital role in the formulation of the relevant articles. The daily reports of the twelve shadow teams on different parts of the Statute allowed all NGOs and the smaller state delegations to keep abreast of all the sub-negotiations even if they could not physically attend. They also maintained close relations with the chairs of the official working groups, most of whom represented states that were strong proponents of the ICC as well as often being personally committed to the Court.

The loose structure and lack of cumbersome procedures of the Coalition undoubtedly contributed to its flexibility and effectiveness. However, this came at the expense of internal democracy. It was not clear how members, other than those represented in the—non-elected— steering committee, could shape or change its policies. As the case study on weapons of mass destruction will show, this lack of internal mechanisms, in combination with the dominating role of human rights groups, made it very difficult for other members to enlist the Coalition in its causes.

Forms of Action

The organisations and individuals involved in the campaign for an international criminal court mainly undertook the following forms of action:

— Lobbying state and intergovernmental representatives

— Writing expert documents, reports, and journal articles

— Convening seminars and conferences

— Disseminating the Court ideal to a wider audience Seeking and giving financial support for Southern NGO and expert participation in the debates Providing experts and interns to smaller and poorer government delegations.

— Street action

Lobbying state and intergovernmental representatives: Lobbying took place at the official PrepComs and in Rome, of course, but also in a wide range of other fora. Organisations sought meetings with officials of their national Justice, Foreign Affairs, and Defence departments, trying to awaken interest in and support for the Court. They were always a presence at intergovernmental conferences, such as the American Heads of State summit in Santiago de Chile in 1998.

Many of these intergovernmental conferences, such as the Southern African Development Cooperation meeting of Justice Ministers in South Africa in 1997, a Caribbean conference in Trinidad and a pan-African conference in Dakar in 1998, were in fact co-organised by governments and NGOs. The informal meetings at Cherif Bassiouni's International Institute for the Higher Criminal Sciences in Sicily provided another very important forum for NGO lobbying. At these meetings, which took place between PrepCom sessions, a select group of NGO representatives as well as mainly 'pro-court' state representatives were invited to discuss and thrash out further details of the future Court.

According to a participating diplomat, these meetings 'were extremely instrumental. No difference was made there between state delegates and NGOs, we were all there as experts. It was very informal, there was lots of sunshine, good food, that had an impact on the negotiations, there was more space, we had fun, it was pleasant, relaxed. It was an instrument for taking further steps'.

Conference lobbying and domestic lobbying were coordinated: 'When national delegations or portions thereof (e.g. specific ministries) needed reinforcement, or when concerns arose that a delegation might be compromising key principles, the Coalition contacted ministers, parliamentarians, and media in the capital through its national networks. This type of conferenceto-capital coordination has been a goal of NGOs at many conferences; for many of us its effective implementation in Rome was a first', writes CICC coordinator William Pace.

Lobbying state representatives was the main purpose of most organisations in coming to Rome, as evidenced by the fact that, very unusually, there was no separate NGO Forum to the Conference. Producing expert documents At the same time, a great deal of specialist documentation was produced by individuals and organisations involved in the ICC process. This took two main forms: journal articles in especially legal journals by individuals, and reports by NGOs. Both had the primary aim of informing and influencing a specialist public of NGOs, academics, and state representatives on specific sub-themes, promoting certain alternatives over others with reference to precedent, legal argument, or political realities.

According to the Dutch delegation leader to Rome: 'The papers of the four or five bigger organisations, Amnesty, Human Rights Watch, International Service for Human Rights, Lawyers Committee for Human Rights, International Commission of Jurists, have been extremely helpful, that was real quality input. They were very good, and they made an impact'.

Convening conferences: One of the most prevalent forms of action in the years leading up to the Rome conference was the organisation of national and international conferences, expert meetings, public debates, seminars, symposia, and workshops. Such meetings were organised all over Europe, in Southern and West Africa, South Asia, North, South, and Central America, and the Caribbean. There was less activity elsewhere in Asia and in North Africa and the Middle East, which is in line with the figures on civil society participation from these regions in Rome. Indeed, in many of these countries there is no tradition of government tolerance for public debates about the country's foreign policy.

The conferences were often either organised by NGOs or academic institutions or co-organised by these and the national governments. They were characterised by an intermingling of officials with the NGO and academic communities and by high-level legal debates rather than political confrontations. Some were regional or international in character, but even the national meetings often boasted one or more international guests, drawn from the ranks of the NGO Coalition, the Yugoslavia and Rwanda tribunals, or the academic community. Thus, a global specialist debate about the ICC, involving academics, NGO advocates, practising lawyers, and state officials, was going on in the years leading up to the Rome conference, through the numerous expert conferences, the Sicilian retreats, and the law journals and NGO publications, as well as in the official PrepCom meetings.

Dissemination to a wider audience: While most of these meetings and the longer NGO reports and law journal articles on the ICC were aimed at an already informed specialist audience, the idea of an international criminal court was also disseminated to a much wider public. A strong effort was made by organisations at the national and sometimes even local level to attract the attention and support of the press for the ICC. The general aims of the court and its consequences for the country in question were explained at press conferences and by putting together media kits.At the same time, 'big name' international lawyers guest-authored articles, even in local newspapers, particularly in the United States but also in Botswana, for instance. Other organisations gathered signatures from celebrities, including the Dalai Lama, Queen Noor of Jordan, Jean-Bertrand Aristide of Haiti, and former US President Jimmy Carter, in favour of the Court, and published these in an appeal in the International

Herald Tribune and Le Monde. Big membership organisations like Amnesty International and the World Federalist Movement, and some of the churches including the Quakers and Mennonites, disseminated the ideas behind the Court to their millions of members.

A hybrid between the mass media and the specialist publications were dedicated newsletters, as came out in Australia and Peru, as, on the international level, was the Coalition's own ICC Monitor, which kept interested audiences abreast of the developments in articles that avoided or explained specialist legal jargon. At the Rome conference, no fewer than three daily news teams set up camp. The Coalition transformed its two-monthly Monitor into a daily newsletter, the InterPress Service published a series of its Terra Viva newspaper, as it does at all major UN conferences, and the Advocacy Project, an NGO that specialises in activist newsletters, produced On The Record, which was also e-mailed to about 4,000 subscribers. According to one participant, 'numerous delegations awaited with interest and enthusiasm the "new highlights" from these news sources'.

Seeking and use of funding: The Coalition and its constituent organisations needed, of course, to raise funds for their activities to support the establishment of the Court. Initially, the World Federalist Movement went tens of thousands of dollars into debt, and relied largely on volunteer labour by graduate students, in setting up the Coalition. Later, the Ford Foundation, the MacArthur Foundation, and the European Union, as well as some governments, made grants both to the Coalition and to some of its constituent organisations. The money thus raised was used especially to take more Southern NGOs and academics to New York and Rome, and to a lesser extent to prepare and disseminate campaign material. The participation of other relevant experts was made possible by funding channelled through civil society: thus, the presence of high-level officials from the Yugoslavia and Rwanda tribunals was made possible by an external grant applied for by the Coalition.

The coordination, research, and lobbying efforts of the Coalition and its members were mainly selffunded, however, by member donations, by the use of volunteers including many students and academics, and by finding ways of allocating staff and resources from other departments and projects to the ICC. Provision of experts and interns Another type of activity that supported the process of negotiations, and particularly the fuller participation of Southern governments in the process, was the provision of legal experts and interns from civil society to the state delegations. This allowed them to be present at more parallel meetings as well as helping to develop their legal arguments.

Some governments, such as those of Canada and Costa Rica, included NGO representatives in their delegations as a gesture of goodwill. Others, including those of Bosnia, Trinidad and Tobago, Sierra Leone, Senegal, Burundi, and Congo, relied on a technical assistance programme by the NGO No Peace Without Justice to augment the size and expertise of their delegations. Other countries engaged the services of domestic—Germany, the Netherlands, and the US—or foreign—Samoa, the Solomon Islands—professors of law as delegation members. Needless to say, this kind of expertise would not be as neutral and malleable to government positions as the contributions of professional diplomats. These 'experts on loan' came with independent views, which influenced the delegations from within. Andrew Clapham, the lawyer engaged by the Solomon

Islands, for instance, sought, ultimately without success, to make it possible to indict not just individuals before the Court but also companies. It seems most likely that he acted on his own judgement, not on government instructions, in this respect.

Street action: Some more direct actions were organised in relation to the ICC. Amnesty International and No Peace Without Justice were two organisations that took on many of these actions aimed at attracting the attention of the general public. Amnesty's Croatian section organised a demonstration in 1996, and its Ukrainian section collected signatures in Kiev's main square. In Rome, Amnesty International organised an open-air manifestation, a 'human carpet' to represent the victims of genocide, war crimes, and crimes against humanity on 4 July, and No Peace Without Justice undertook a 24-hour vigil outside the conference building on 16 July, waiting to celebrate or mourn the final outcome of the meeting. Such actions were few and far between, however: for every demonstration, there were dozens of conferences on the ICC.

In terms of militancy and visibility, the ICC campaign formed a sharp contrast to other recent global civil society manifestations, such as the demonstrations in Seattle, Genoa, and Porto Alegre. As Benedetti and Washburn write, 'NGOs . . . had learned to accept a great deal in the institutional culture and style of international treaty conferences, which many of them had previously inclined to ignore. This included matters of procedure, timing, access to documents, decorum, and even dress'. If these people were representing the 'wretched of the earth', they certainly did so in less dramatic fashion than those bashing at the gates in Seattle and Genoa. However, the fact that they had adopted the style, procedures, and clothing of state delegates does not mean that they were being co-opted on substance.

The methods of most members of global civil society involved in the ICC campaign, and their interaction with state representatives, are characteristic of what Peter Haas and others have termed an epistemic community': 'The epistemic community members' professional training, prestige, and reputation for expertise in an area highly valued by society or elite decision makers accord them access to the political system and legitimise or authorize their activities'. An epistemic community consists of more than technocrats, however: 'Unlike members of a profession or discipline, who seldom limit themselves to work that is closely congruent with their principled values, members of an epistemic community tend to pursue activities that closely reflect the community's principled beliefs and tend to affiliate and identify themselves with groups that likewise reflect or seek to promote these beliefs'.

The match between the ICC actors and what Haas et al. have called epistemic communities is not perfect. These authors describe groups of 'typically under thirty-five people' with highly homogeneous beliefs. The ICC groups consisted of hundreds, perhaps thousands, of people, and fell into different sub-groups according to their profession, their moral and technical priorities, and their preferred methods. While they placed much emphasis on informing and persuading state representatives, they devoted attention to informing wider public as well, and, while their relations with state delegates were mostly cordial, they did not hesitate to expose and condemn official behaviour they did not like. Nevertheless, seeing the global civil society activities with regard to the Court as those of an epistemic community, credited with expertise and imbued with moral values, helps to understand them and their influence.

Influence of Global Civil Society on the Rome Statute

Global civil society attempted to influence almost all aspects of the Statute, ranging from its general principles and its relations with states to its composition to jurisdiction rules, definition of crimes, rules relating to prosecution and trial, and financing.

The 1994 draft of the International Law Commission listed only two ways in which an investigation could be initiated (or 'triggered', as it came to be called). States parties could lodge a complaint, alleging that a crime had been committed, or the UN Security Council could refer matter to the Court. Unlike in domestic criminal law systems, the Court's prosecutor could not institute any investigations him- or herself.

The NGOs and individuals constituting the NGO Coalition were united in insisting on a third 'trigger': the prosecutor should be able to institute his or her own proceedings. In fact, this independence of the prosecutor was the single biggest issue on the agenda of the Coalition and many of its constituent organisations. An Amnesty International representative called it a 'collective bottom line'. According to the Argentine state delegate Silvia Fernàndez de Gurmendi, an early and active member of the like-minded group who chaired the negotiations on this issue and had frequent contact with NGOs, 'Non-governmental organizations led a strong campaign in favor of conferring such power as an essential feature of an independent, credible Court. The issue became a central point in the discussions'.

As an alternative to the prosecutor's own initiative, it was suggested that individuals, and perhaps also NGOs, might lodge complaints, as they do under various human rights treaties. NGOs also pointed to the practice of the European Court of Human Rights, the Inter-American Court of Human Rights, and domestic courts in this respect.

One of the main reasons why NGOs insisted on extending the prosecutor's powers was that they feared very few cases would come to the Court if only the Security Council and states could trigger proceedings. They pointed out that, in existing human rights treaties, states very rarely lodge complaints against each other because it strains relations, and they would not be likely to do so under the Statute either. The Security Council has likewise been selective in using its powers in response to grave crimes. When a state or the Security Council does act, it is likely to be wholly or partially politically motivated. NGOs argued that limiting prosecutions in this manner would compromise the perceived impartiality and legitimacy of the Court as well as its effectiveness.

In August 1995, a few states, including Austria, Greece, the Netherlands, Norway, and Switzerland, began to voice the idea of a prosecutor initiating proceedings on his or her own behalf. They did so in very cautious terms, saying for instance that the prosecutor's role was 'too narrow' and needed to be more active' and that 'possible enhancement of the prosecutor's role needed further examination'. An even smaller number of states, including Chile and the Czech Republic, made the further-reaching suggestion that individuals, victims, and/or NGOs should be able to trigger a procedure. In April 1996 the support for such views was still so weak that a UN Press Release stated: 'Speakers were almost unanimous in opposing the granting of powers to the prosecutor of the court to initiate an investigation on his own, based on information received, without the consent of the States concerned.'

In August 1997, in order to overcome some objections, Argentina informally proposed that the Prosecutor might be allowed to pursue his own investigations subject to the permission of a pre-trial chamber of judges. This became a formal Argentine-German proposal in April 1998, and remained in the draft that went to the Rome conference. However, the entire article was in square brackets, which meant some states objected, and the whole text might yet be struck.

Although there was significant opposition, it was becoming increasingly clear in Rome that the majority of states favoured some form of own initiative. Despite the majority view in favour, rumours abounded in the last day or two of the conference that the independent prosecutor might yet be sacrificed to placate US opposition. However, the final Draft Statute of 17 July essentially incorporated the Argentine-German proposal, giving the Prosecutor the right to investigate cases on his own initiative, subject to the permission of a pre-trial chamber. This was accepted by the Conference.

Civil society strategies and influence is impossible to say for certain that it was the civil society campaign which tipped the balance in favour of the independent prosecutor. This is the strong belief of many activists, however, and it appears to be shared by state delegates who were closely involved in the negotiations, like Silvia Fernandez de Gurmendi of Argentina and Theo Van Boven of the Netherlands. The latter called this 'the most important point on which the NGOs booked success'.

The NGOs in the Coalition contributed to the adoption of the prosecutor's power to investigate on his own initiative in various ways. First, they proposed the even more radical idea: that victims and/or NGOs might institute proceedings by lodging a complaint. This proposal moved the previously most radical proposal of having an independent prosecutor closer to the middle of the spectrum of opinion.

According to a member of the NGO Coalition, 'it was clearly understood by the majority of the Coalition that it was unlikely for States to agree to individuals having the capacity to initiate proceedings. However, such a "radical" suggestion made the prospect of an independent Prosecutor appear more acceptable and less threatening than that of individual citizens "triggering" the Court. An independent Prosecutor was thus seen as a less extreme option'. The credibility of this tactic was strengthened by the fact that a few states also referred to this option, so threatening to others, early on in the negotiations.

NGOs also made a contribution, before and during Rome, to the substance of the debate by combating the arguments of opponents of an independent prosecutor. In particular, they constantly rebutted the arguments of the most prolific opponent of the prosecutor's initiative, the United States. On 22 June, for instance, the United States submitted a position paper about the prosecutor. On 24 June, the US-based Lawyers Committee for Human Rights hit back with a document rebutting the arguments as well as drawing attention to inaccuracies in the US paper.

All through 1997, the Coalition pressed the like-minded group of states to assert itself and show its hand by formulating its guiding principles. In December 1997 it finally did so, and the prosecutor's initiative was one of those principles. A related activity of the Coalition was not so much to convince state delegates that an independent prosecutor was desirable as to make those who already thought so believe that it was also politically possible. This was done by demonstrating the existing support for the position and, consequently, continuing to build on it. Despite the fact that they had a stake in a certain outcome, this 'barometer' function of the Coalition was apparently credible in the eyes of state delegates. On 23 June, for instance, NGO representatives reported for the first time that a majority now favoured the prosecutor's initiative, with Brazil, Mexico, Venezuela, France, and Syria having recently shifted into that direction. They also candidly reported that Kenya had moved in the opposite direction.

A particular form this took was to transpose the statements made by delegates into virtual votes on different positions towards the end of the Rome Conference. This showed that 61 states explicitly expressed their approval of the prosecutor's initiative in the opening statement to the conference. On 10 July, 76 per cent of the 80 states speaking were in favour of the prosecutor's initiative, and four days later 83 per cent of 76 states took this position. According to Richard Dicker of Human Rights Watch, 'that bit of work, of accurately recording and putting together immediately where each state stood on the major issues, was the single greatest contribution of the NGOs.

Each state might have done it, except they didn't really have the capacity. We spent late nights . . . getting it out into the newsletter, getting it to the delegates, and they faxed it to their capitals, that was crucial, stiffening the resolve by accentuating the number of states that wanted an effective independent court'. Finally, in response to rumours in the final days of the conference that the independent prosecutorial powers might be dropped, 'the major international human rights groups then formed mixed swatteams, Human Rights Watch, Amnesty, the ICJ, Lawyers Committee, to approach specific delegations with this message, so it didn't come from one particular group by itself, it was a very important theme for all of us'.

Gender-specific Crimes

The original ILC draft paid no explicit attention to the gender dimensions of any of the areas of law it covered. This reflected the existing state of humanitarian law and international criminal law, as codified in the The Hague and Geneva Conventions and the statutes of the ad hoc tribunals for Yugoslavia and Rwanda. The practices and jurisprudence of these tribunals between 1995 and 1998 were beginning to change this situation, however, and provided inspiration for the demands of the women's rights groups united in the Women's Caucus for Gender Justice.

Gender concerns related to many parts of the Statute. 'Forced pregnancy' is the term used for a practice, within the context of war or crimes against humanity, of raping a woman and then keeping her confined so she is forced to carry the baby to full term. This practice occurred as part of a programme of ethnic cleansing in the war in Bosnia. Other concerns of the women's groups, including a reference to gender in a general non-discrimination clause, the definition of gender, a gender dimension to the definition of slavery, the inclusion of persecution on the basis of gender as a component of crimes against humanity, and protection for and gender-sensitive treatment of victims and witnesses, will not be dealt with here. All of these concerns, however, came to be reflected in the final Statute in a way that either completely or partially satisfied the Women's Caucus.

In a paper for the December 1997 PrepCom, the Women's Caucus first proposed a separate sub-paragraph on sexual and gender crimes in the definition of war crimes, which was to include 'rape, sexual slavery, forced prostitution, forced pregnancy, forced sterilization and other sexual or gender violence or abuse'. It recommended this extra paragraph, partially based on the prosecutorial practices of the Yugoslavia and Rwanda tribunals, because 'sexual and gender violence are severe and particular and their particularities should not be lost by mainstreaming. Where not explicit, they are too often ignored, even today'.

Anti-abortion groups like REAL Women of Canada voiced objections to the inclusion of forced pregnancy as a war crime, arguing that the term had been used by the American Civil Liberties Union in a US lawsuit as meaning 'forcing women to continue pregnancy against their will for the purpose of serving the state's declared interest in preserving unborn human life', i.e. to describe an anti-abortion law or policy. They also generally opposed the use of the term 'gender' in the Statute, predicated on the idea that it might 'provide protection for "other genders" including homosexuals, lesbians, bisexuals, transgendered, etc.'

Early proposals relating to the definition of crimes made scant reference to rape as an 'outrage on personal dignity' and none to other gender-related crimes. This changed with a joint proposal in February 1997 by New

Zealand and Switzerland to include rape directly as a war crime. The United States, however, favoured a much more restrictive definition of war crimes, and the whole text remained bracketed. At the same time, 'rape, other sexual abuse and enforced prostitution' were included, unbracketed, as a crime against humanity. In December 1997, a special sub-paragraph on 'rape, sexual slavery, enforced prostitution, enforced pregnancy, enforced sterilisation, and any other form of sexual violence' was included in the draft text on war crimes for Rome, without brackets, that is, reflecting widespread consensus among states, despite an objection from the Vatican to 'enforced pregnancy'.

This became the most contentious gender issue at Rome, with opponents, including the Vatican and some Catholic and Arab states, arguing that making enforced pregnancy a crime implied a state obligation to permit abortion. Proponents of the clause, including many Western states but also conflict states like Bosnia and Rwanda and Muslim states such as Azerbaijan and Turkey, argued that it was meant to codify a terrible crime, such as witnessed in Bosnia, and had nothing to do with viewpoints on abortion. Bosnia issued a paper documenting the practice and calling for the retention of enforced pregnancy as a separate crime in the Statute, and lobbied other Muslim countries on the issue.

After three weeks in Rome, an informal working group was formed, chaired by an Australian delegate, to bring the two sides closer together and to try to define forced pregnancy in a mutually satisfactory way. The definition that came out of these negotiations in the final week of the conference was as follows: 'The unlawful confinement of a woman forcibly made pregnant, with the intent of affecting the ethnic composition of any population or carrying out other grave violations of international law. This definition shall not in any way be interpreted as affecting national laws relating to pregnancy.' The second sentence was clearly inserted to protect the anti-abortion laws of the objecting countries. The sub-paragraph was then included in the definitions both of war crimes and of crimes against humanity.

The first proposal to make rape and other sexual and gender crimes punishable as war crimes, made in February 1997 by Switzerland and New Zealand, was taken over almost verbatim from a paper by the International Committee of the Red Cross, reflecting developments in the Yugoslavia tribunal in particular. The Women's Caucus was just beginning to be formed at that time, and probably did not play a significant role. By the time these proposals were being refined and finalised in the December 1997 PrepCom, the Women's Caucus was fully operational, and it made inclusion of sexual and gender crimes one of its five lobbying issues for this PrepCom. The sub-paragraph adopted then, which was substantially more comprehensive than the earlier proposals, mirrors exactly the wording proposed by the Women's Caucus in its preparatory paper, and it can safely be assumed to have been proposed at its instigation. The preservation of this clause, however, over strong opposition to forced pregnancy in particular, probably owed more to the strong advocacy of Bosnia, which had the moral high ground on this issue, and the patient but tough negotiating by Australia than to the Women's Caucus, although its statement in Rome that 'this will not affect national abortion laws', may have been helpful.

The Women's Caucus was highly visible in Rome. One of the main reasons for its success was probably its sheer numbers: it had between 12 and 15 people at Rome at all times and, with more than 300 member organisations, it could legitimately claim to be representing a global women's movement. The delegation, moreover, included both women from conflict areas and experts on the 'hardcore legal stuff'. While the former could speak with moral authority about violations of women's rights, the latter could invoke emerging precedents in national and international law. Finally, the Women's Caucus was able, due to its large numbers and energy but also its natural advantage in often—but by no means inevitably!—finding allies in female state delegates, to get many states on its side. One member of the Caucus mentions Australia, Bosnia, Canada, Costa Rica, Mexico, the Netherlands, European countries generally, South Africa for ten Southern African countries, and Sweden among the countries the Caucus had very good relations with: a formidable list. The right-to-life groups arrived on the scene even later than the Women's Caucus. They came not just with an anti-abortion agenda but more generally with anti-feminist and anti-homosexual concerns.

They lobbied and worked together with the Vatican and Catholic and Arab countries. Their links with the Vatican gave them a privileged position: they were given their own office in the conference building in Rome, while all other NGOs had to share one room and very few state delegations had offices. According to one source, moreover, it was rumoured that the Pope personally placed phone calls to leaders of Latin American countries on the issue of forced pregnancy. Their main tactics were to equate use of the term 'gender' with endorsement of homosexuality—an argument strengthened by the fact that 'gender' is difficult to translate into other languages, including Arabic—and use of 'enforced pregnancy' with support for the right to abortion. This probably had some impact in the last PrepCom and early in Rome, but it was countered by the tactic of states sympathetic to the gender clauses negotiating an agreed definition to both terms to allay fears of such interpretations. Once such definitions had been agreed, their role was pretty much played out and, although the Women's Caucus might have preferred slightly different definitions, it cannot be said that 'profamily' groups had a noticeable influence on the wording of the Statute.

Indiscriminate Weapons

In 1997, a number of groups involved in the ICC process formed the Weapons Systems Caucus, later renamed 'Peace Caucus', which aimed to 'make the Statute as restrictive as possible in regard to nuclear weapons, landmines, and other weapons inflicting indiscriminate harm and unnecessary suffering, including blinding laser weapons'. It was a small caucus, consisting of about ten groups, many of which were also members of the anti-nuclear Abolition 2000 Network.

The ideal outcome the Peace Caucus aimed for, as elaborated in a proposal for the December 1997 PrepCom, was to have both a general prohibition of weapons that caused 'superfluous injury or unnecessary suffering' or were 'inherently indiscriminate' and a specific list of prohibited weapons, including expanding bullets, chemical and biological weapons, landmines, and the threat or use of nuclear weapons. Its fall-back position was to have only a general prohibition of weapons that cause unnecessary suffering or are inherently indiscriminate, as also proposed by the Red Cross. Its third choice was to have at least an incomplete list of prohibited weapons, with a reference to future expansion.

The 'superfluous injury or unnecessary suffering' phrase was based on language in the Hague Conventions and Protocol I to the Geneva Conventions, the 'inherently indiscriminate' phrase on the humanitarian law principle that a distinction must be made between the treatment of combatants and that of civilians. For the prohibition of the threat or use of nuclear arms, the Caucus referred to the 1996 Advisory Opinion by the International Court of Justice, and for landmines to the Landmines Ban Treaty. It did not explicitly defend the need for other weapons to be on the list, reflecting the fact that, while there was some interest in landmines and other weapons, the activism of the Peace Caucus was primarily anti-nuclear.

Inclusion of the use of certain weapons as a war crime was first seriously discussed in February 1997. The United States proposed listing biological and chemical weapons and expanding bullets. Syria proposed the threat or use of nuclear weapons. New Zealand and Switzerland put forward a proposal, once again based on the ICRC paper, that no specific weapons be listed but that the use of weapons 'of such a nature as to cause superfluous injury or unnecessary suffering or being inherently indiscriminate' be prohibited.

In December 1997, the US and New Zealand-Switzerland options were maintained. Canada suggested a compromise option including the weapons listed by the US plus 'such other weapons or weapons systems as become the subject of a comprehensive prohibition pursuant to customary or conventional international law'. The Philippines proposed a fourth option with both a general prohibition and a longer list of weapons, including nuclear weapons and landmines. This whole text, with all the options in brackets, went to Rome.

The Non-Aligned Movement (NAM) adopted a position a month before Rome that made explicit prohibition of nuclear weapons one of its key objectives for the ICC. However, while India continued to pursue this objective, the unity of the NAM was much weakened at the Rome Conference by the defection of many states to the like-minded group. Like-minded leaders like the Scandinavian countries and Canada were timid, not only on nuclear arms but even on landmines. The credibility of India's antinuclear stance was, moreover, much weakened by the fact that it had carried out its own nuclear tests only a month earlier. Many NGOs and state delegates believed that India's real objective was to wreck the Statute rather than to insert anti-nuclear language.

When the first Bureau proposal was presented on 6 July, it still included the short US list of weapons, the longer list including nuclear weapons and landmines and, as a third option, the general prohibition. It was becoming clear that a majority of countries were prepared to sacrifice nuclear weapons, with 57 states in favour of option 1, 25 for option 2, and 6 for option 3. The next Bureau proposal included only this option, i.e. prohibition of biological and chemical weapons and expanding bullets, with a reference to future expansion to other weapons that 'become subject of a comprehensive prohibition'.

However, worse was to come. Some states argued that, if nuclear weapons were not expressly included, then biological and chemical weapons, 'poor man's weapons', ought not to be included either. In the last week of the conference, in closed negotiations the Dutch chair of the working group on nuclear weapons succumbed to this line of argument, reportedly pursued by the Arab states, and, in what he refers to as a 'Solomonesque' solution, deleted the explicit reference to biological and chemical weapons, leaving only expanding bullets, poison weapons, and poisonous gases and analogous materials, relegating all other weapons which might be subject to prohibition to a future annex, yet to be negotiated. This is the formulation used in the final Statute. The poisonous weapons phrase, based on an old treaty, can be read as meaning 'chemical weapons', but it is harder to read biological weapons into it as well. On the evening of 17 July, India proposed an amendment to the Statute to reinstate biological, chemical, and nuclear weapons. However, reopening the negotiations at this point was seen as ruining the prospects for a Statute, and a no-action motion by Norway, opening the way to adoption of the Statute, was overwhelmingly supported.

The Rome Statute does not advance the state of international law on weapons of mass destruction; indeed, it might be argued that the exclusion of biological weapons sets it back. There are, however, many provisions in the Statute which may be used indirectly to prosecute the use of such weapons, such as those prohibiting attacks on civilians, and military attacks that have 'clearly excessive' effects on civilians in relation to the military goal. Nevertheless, the efforts of the Peace Caucus must be considered almost entirely unsuccessful.

The Peace Caucus had a difficult mission because its main objective, the explicit criminalisation of nuclear weapons, was 'at odds with the aim of obtaining support or at least tolerance of the Statute from the nuclear weapons states'. The introduction of an option including landmines and nuclear weapons by the Philippines in

December 1997 may have been orchestrated by the Caucus, but, as one of its members put it, he went to Rome knowing 'there was just no way nuclear arms were going to be explicitly made a crime'. According to the NGO Coalition's coordinator, 'peace groups understood that a hard push for nuclear weapons would undermine the overall cause, so they backed off'.

The Peace Caucus's second option, a general clause prohibiting weapons that are 'inherently indiscriminate' or cause 'unnecessary suffering', was not realised either. This was partly because it was only a small Caucus. The Coalition and most of its participants avoided the topic of weapons of mass destruction because they were more interested in human rights issues and because it was seen as a potential conference wrecker.

In fact, the Coalition's 'Basic Principles'incorporate concerns on gender, children's rights, and victims, but nothing on weapons of mass destruction. The groups in the Peace Caucus might have done better to abandon their ideal of explicit nuclear weapons language, instead pushing hard for a general prohibition clause and attempting to make this a Coalition principle.

However, it might have been difficult to push this through within a Coalition that was generally more interested in human rights issues and disinclined to jeopardise the Statute for other reasons. Another problem for the Peace Caucus was that, in these negotiations, it had few allies among states.

Unlike in the case of the independent prosecutor, the 'barometer' function of the Coalition actually worked against it by showing that a strong majority of states was prepared to accept the short weapons list of the US.

Moreover, it strongest ally, India, was not perceived by other states as a bona fide negotiating partner and, in particular, it lacked credibility with respect to its stance on nuclear weapons.

The groups in the Peace Caucus do, however, bear some responsibility for not jealously guarding the draft language on biological and chemical weapons. It is true that this was lost in closed negotiations, but they never made much of a case for these weapons either. In fact, they may even have made things worse by arguing that including these weapons, but not nuclear ones, amounted to 'criminalizing the poor man's weapons of mass destruction', an argument also put forward by states.

Civil Society's Contribution to Law-making

The intense involvement of global civil society in the negotiations for an international criminal court was viewed as very positive by those individuals who played a role in it, as well as by many state delegates. The virtue of such involvement is not self-evident, however. It is clear that global civil society was influential in these negotiations, but was it legitimate? This section will consider this legitimacy along two dimensions: global civil society's contribution to democracy and to ethical principles.

Contribution to Democracy

Although international law-making has never been a democratic process, there is an increasing sense among national and international diplomats that, as more decisions have moved up to the international level, international decision-making and international law-making in particular ought to be democratic. This idea is related to a more general recognition by political thinkers that, while more states have been converted to parliamentary democracy, the onset of globalisation has eroded the substance of democratic participation and choice. The view, widely echoed among state delegates as well as activists involved in the ICC process, that civil society involvement somehow made the ICC process 'more democratic' than pure state deliberations would have been, should probably be seen in this context.

However, at first sight, this is a peculiar notion: the activities of NGOs, students, academics, and journalists cannot be said to have much to do with democracy in the traditional, literal sense of 'rule by the people' or 'majority rule'. In that sense, state delegates might actually come closer to being 'democratic' now that most states have multi-party elections, even though diplomats are not elected and international issues such as the ICC are not exactly electoral themes in most countries. It is on this basis that some dismiss the claim that global civil society brings democracy to international decision-making processes.

Kenneth Anderson, for instance, under the trenchant headline 'But who elected the international NGOs?', criticises both the Landmines Ban Coalition and the ICC Coalition on this basis. He correctly points out that the present enthusiasm of officials from governmental and intergovernmental institutions is partly based on their own crisis of legitimacy and the hope that global civil society can provide it for them. He also points out, again correctly, that most NGOs are 'not very often connected, in any direct way, to masses of "people"' and that in domestic contexts they are not usually seen as a 'substitute for democratic processes'. However, such critics cannot move beyond lamenting the perceived loss of democracy—the loss really is just perceived here, as international law-making was never democratic—because they cannot conceive of democracy in any other than representative and territorial terms. Democracy on a planetary scale is literally unimaginable to them. Therefore, the only recipe they have is to return decision-making power to the level of the nation-state.

More imaginative responses are possible, and necessary, to give the global demos a more substantive sense of participation in the development of decisions that affect it. Global civil society has been conceptualised as a 'functional equivalent' or 'alternative mechanism' for democratising global governance. Such conceptions suggest that global civil society can make the following contributions to enhancing democracy:

— fostering deliberation;

— developing alternative proposals;

— promoting access/giving voice to unheard groups;

— improving transparency for and accountability to a wider public; and

— diminishing power distortions among states.

Deliberation: First of all, did global civil society contribute to the airing and deliberation of different viewpoints in relation to the Court? The idea of deliberative democracy is that proposals can be debated on their merits through rational arguments rather than on the basis of representation of interests. This aspect of democracy is therefore related to the ethical contribution discussed below. There are two components to this question: whether global civil society made the official state debates more deliberative and less focused on narrow interests, and whether there was a form of deliberative decision-making going on within global civil society. On the first count, the answer is clearly 'yes'.

There is no doubt that the numerous conferences and seminars, the Sicilian retreats, academic articles, and NGO position papers contributed to a global, albeit specialist, debate on the merits of the international criminal court, which informed and influenced the ultimate decision-making by state delegates.

On the second count, of internal deliberation, there is rather more doubt. The NGO Coalition for an ICC was inclusive and tolerant in principle and in practice. A very wide range of groups who supported the broad goal of a 'just, effective and independent court' joined the Coalition. This included even the small minority of 'family-oriented' groups who were opposed to the aims of the Women's Caucus, unless it became clear that they were generally hostile to the idea of a strong Court. They were met with irritation by most NGOs and many state delegates, but tolerated, accredited, and given access to the same facilities as others.

Some of these groups themselves on the other hand 'did not play by the rules' according to one activist, for instance circulating lobbying materials without institutional affiliation and dumping Women's Caucus documents in the waste-paper basket. However, it must also be said that the Coalition did not favour extensive internal deliberation.

As Burroughs and Cabasso write, 'there was no thorough debate, still less any formal collective decision-making, among all participating NGOs. Partly this was for practical reasons, because of the number of NGOs, the cumbersome internal decision-making procedures of some NGOs, and the onslaught of events, and partly because it was deemed too divisive to get into controversial matters. Partly, too, the NGO Coalition lacked the kind of culture of consensus reflecting commitments to social transformation, non-violence, and representation of popular demands.'

The Coalition emphasised pluralism rather than internal democracy and chose to take few common positions. Admittedly, the Steering Committee, and the Coordinator in particular, had good reasons for such an approach, having 'experienced the breakdowns and break-ups of NGO steering committees' all too often, and it was a matter of 'amazing grace' that this Coalition survived such pressures. However, the few common positions taken, and even informal understandings about the priorities, were crucial, as leading state delegates often channelled their consultation with NGOs through the Coalition.

These decisions did not come about through genuine deliberation among all or most members of the Coalition, and it must be said that, in terms of internal deliberative democracy, the Coalition was wanting. While in the case of the ICC this does not seem to have detracted at all from its effectiveness, such lack of space and time for open and free deliberation can have consequences for the legitimacy as well as the creativity of global civil society, and hence for its influence, in the long term.

Alternative proposals: Global civil society produced thousands of pages of text developing different proposals in relation to the ICC. It is clear that these academic submissions and NGO position papers had an impact on the negotiations. However, they had no official status. Therefore, states often copied these papers, or passages from them, and introduced them as their own.

In this respect, it would be desirable if civil society involvement could be taken one step further in future negotiations, allowing NGOs and individuals to introduce proposals in their own name: not only does their work deserve to be credited, it may also be assumed that the actual authors of certain positions can be expected to be their most effective defenders. A limit might be imposed on such powers by requiring that at least one state co-sponsor the proposal so as to prevent the flooding of negotiations with proposals which do not stand a chance among states.

Access and voice: The ICC Coalition met the challenge of including representation from the global South at least as well as their more colourful global civil society counterparts on the streets of Seattle and Genoa, and perhaps better. It also represented the interests of the under-represented, including victims of war crimes and human rights violations, and women and children in particular, securing better protection for these groups than they might otherwise have had. It must be said, however, that this representation was often rather abstract.

Many of the civil society representatives were well-heeled, university-educated cosmopolitans with little direct experience of violence. There were also more grass-roots representatives, including for instance women from Afghanistan and the grandmothers of the Plaza de Mayo, Argentina, but it appears that their presence served a symbolic purpose rather than actually involving them in the negotiations. This emphasis on expertise rather than experience was perhaps inevitable in this law-making process, but it is to be hoped that, when the Court is up and running and dealing with actual rather than abstract violations, the direct representation of victims will become more of a reality.

Transparency and accountability: While the internal transparency of decision-making within the Coalition left something to be desired, civil society involvement certainly did succeed in making the official decisionmaking process more transparent: for its members, for journalists, and, through them, for a wider interested audience and even for delegates of smaller states. Funnily enough, the fact that the final conference took place at a UN building in Rome with which most delegates were unfamiliar, contributed to this transparency, making it very difficult for them to slink off into remote rooms for secret meetings. It is unlikely that international negotiations will ever be entirely open, just as at the domestic level, for instance, Cabinet meetings remain confidential.

The working method of the Coalition—forming teams to monitor negotiations on different parts of the Statute, debriefing friendly state delegates after informal meetings, and keeping 'virtual vote' tallies on crucial issues—was very effective, however. It took the potential for making international negotiations transparent to its limits, and it is an example worth following in other fora.

Redressing inter-state power imbalances: Many of the ways in which global civil society contributed to the ICC process also served, deliberately or accidentally, to empower smaller and poorer states in the process and to give them a more equal footing with traditionally powerful states. The documents produced by individuals and NGOs helped to educate them with respect to the issues involved.

The provision of interns and legal experts swelled their delegations in quality and quantity. The monitoring, by the NGOs, of both public and, as far as possible, secret negotiations, in terms of both the substance of the debate and the numbers in favour of certain positions, made the process more transparent and easier to follow for such states.

Global civil society did well on injecting deliberation and transparency into the negotiations, but not quite so well on fostering internal democracy and transparency. Its alternative proposals were taken seriously and contributed to the process. The Coalition was wide-ranging and inclusive in nature, and succeeded well in representing the interests of the oppressed, although there was little direct representation of victims. Monitoring and education activities made the process much more transparent, which also had a positive effect on the position of smaller and poorer states.

Contribution to Ethical Principles

The most valuable contribution of global civil society to the international criminal court, however, was not the dimension of increased democracy but the dimension of morality and idealism. It furthered the goal of achieving a particular type of court, a Court that takes, 'a fundamental step towards removing the power to punish from the sole domain of governments'. This is not universally considered as progress. Unilateralists fundamentally object to it. Kenneth Anderson calls it 'international legal imperialism' and accuses international lawyers in general, and those involved in the landmines and ICC campaigns in particular, of an unreasoned 'fundamentally religious and mystical' belief in the supremacy of international law. While he attacks these beliefs from the left, his position, and that of most opponents of the Court, belongs to the larger category that Global Civil Society 2001 termed the 'rejectionist' or 'sovereignist' position towards globalisation held by traditional leftists, right-wing unilateralists, and nationalists alike.

The ethical project of global civil society embraces the supportive and reformist position, focusing on a globalisation of the rule of law. It is undoubtedly based on a belief, but not an unreasoned belief. It is predicated on the twentiethcentury experience with powerful states unaccountable to any higher powers.

The genocides, war crimes, and crimes against humanity that states have committed over the past century far outstrip any misdeeds that global institutions, fallible though they be, have ever performed. While only one of many avenues, drafting international human rights and humanitarian law and, even more importantly, creating institutions that can help implement such law is seen by lawyers and activists in this field as their contribution to preventing such crimes in future.

Olivier de Frouville has described the essence of the 'ethical project' of the ICC campaign in terms of George Scelle's doctrine, which holds that, in international law-making, each state has a double function: to defend its own national interests but also the global public interest, or interest of humanity. It was the continual strengthening and encouragement of states, and tendencies within states, towards the latter interest that was the contribution of global civil society. According to Adriaan Bos, the Dutch chair of the negotiations up until Rome, 'the aims of the

NGOs and the like-minded group werecompletely parallel'.

William Pace, the NGO Coalition coordinator, agrees with this assessment, 'with the caveat that some like-minded group delegates were willing to achieve much less, NGOs pressed for greater specificity and strength . . . The official line is often quite good, but in personal negotiations in many instances they go in with a Realpolitik idea, and they would have allowed a very weak, US-controlled ICC. Richard Dicker of Human Rights Watch also stresses that, while expertise was very important, the 'strategic vision' civil society brought to the negotiations, stiffening the resolve by accentuating the number of states that wanted an effective independent court', was crucial.

It was through this contribution that what Canadian Foreign Minister Lloyd Axworthy has termed 'the New Diplomacy' could prevail, rather than the traditional lowest common denominator approach to treaty-making. The alliance of civil society and progressive states enjoyed a double advantage over the opponents of the Court by having an informal but robust agreement both on the goal—a just, independent, and effective Court—and on the means—forming a common front between NGOs and states in favour of such a Court, which simultaneously boosted the status of civil society and strengthened the resolve of states in the negotiations.

Bibliography

Anderson, Mary "Humanitarian NGOs in Conflict Intervention" in: Chester Crocker and Fen Osler Hampson with Pamela Aall eds. Managing Global Chaos: Sources of and Responses to International Conflict Washington, DC: United States Institute of Peace Press, 1996

Arruda, Marcos, "NGOs and the World Bank: Is It Possible to Collaborate Critically?" Rio de Janeiro: PACS, 1995

Biekart, Kees, "The Politics of Civil Society Building: European Private Aid Agencies and Democratic Transitions in Central America" Utrecht: International Books, 1999

Boli, John and George Thomas, "Constructing World Culture: International Nongovernmental Organizations Since 1875", Stanford: Stanford University Press, 1999

Carroll, Thomas, "Intermediary NGOs: the supporting link in grassroots development" West Hartford, CT: Kumarian Press, 1992

Chiang, Pei-heng, "Non-governmental Organizations at the United Nations: Identity, Role and Function", New York: Praeger, 1981

Clark, Ann Marie, "Non-Governmental Organizations and their Influence on International Society" *Journal of International Affairs*, Winter 1995

Esty, Daniel, "Non-governmental Organizations at the World Trade Organization: Co-operation, Competition, or Exclusion" Journal of International Economic Law, vol.1, March 1998

John Boli and George Thomas, "World Culture in the World Polity: a century of international non-governmental organizations" American Sociological Review, 62, no. 2 : 171-190, 1997.

Nelson, Paul J., "The World Bank and NGOs: The Limits of Apolitical Development" New York: St. Martin's Press, 1995

Paul, James A., "NGO Access at the UN: A Narrative Account" New York: Global Policy Forum, 1998

Pentikaiinen, Antti, "Creating Global Governance - The Role of Non-Governmental Organizations in the United Nations" Helsinki: Finnish UN Association 2000.

Schulze, Peter M., "NGOs - Non-Governmental Organizations, in: Helmut Volger (ed.): A Concise Encyclopedia of the United Nations", The Hague/London/New York: Kluwer Law International 2002, pp.378-387.

Yolanda N., Kakabadse and Sarah Burns, "Movers and Shapers: NGOs in International Affairs", Washington DC: World Resources Institute, 1994

Index